# Bean Blossom

MUSIC IN AMERICAN LIFE

*A list of books in the series appears
at the end of this book.*

# BEAN BLOSSOM

## The Brown County Jamboree and Bill Monroe's Bluegrass Festivals

THOMAS A. ADLER

UNIVERSITY OF
ILLINOIS PRESS
Urbana, Chicago,
and Springfield

© 2011 by the Board of Trustees
of the University of Illinois
All rights reserved
Manufactured in the United States of America
1 2 3 4 5 C P 5 4 3 2 1
∞ This book is printed on acid-free paper.

Library of Congress Cataloging-in-Publication Data
Adler, Thomas A.
Bean Blossom : the Brown County Jamboree and
Bill Monroe's bluegrass festivals / Thomas A. Adler.
p. cm. — (Music in American life)
Includes bibliographical references and index.
ISBN 978-0-252-03615-6 — ISBN 978-0-252-07810-1
1. Brown County Jamboree—History.
2. Bill Monroe Memorial Music Park & Campground—History.
3. Bluegrass music—Indiana—Beanblossom—History and criticism.
4. Monroe, Bill, 1911–1996. I. Title.
ML37.B38B74      2010
781.642079'772253—dc22      2010051968

For
Betsy Adler—my darling
Archie Green—my mentor
and
Neil V. Rosenberg—my inspiration

# Contents

# Preface

My first trip to Bean Blossom and the Brown County Jamboree came on a pleasant Sunday in September 1968, when I rode there with Neil V. Rosenberg and several others who had been visiting that weekend at Indiana University. I was twenty-one years old, raised in Chicago's South Shore, and had been a bluegrass fan and banjo player for a decade. Yet I was still a relative newcomer and cultural outsider to bluegrass music, being part of that rising wave of urban fans captured by the driving, plaintive sounds of recorded bluegrass music in the late 1950s. As the middle son of two Chicago physicians, both Viennese refugees, I was completely engrossed by the Brown County Jamboree show, where Bill Monroe and His Blue Grass Boys were the featured act. That day I paid scant attention to the town and surrounding region. But my interest in bluegrass music turned out to be a long-standing one, and a growing awareness of the musical traditions underlying bluegrass helped put me on a path leading to this history of a musical place.

Beginning in June 1969, I annually attended Monroe's Bean Blossom bluegrass festivals, becoming ever more familiar with the town, as well as the Brown County Jamboree festival grounds and its main features: the old barn, the outdoor stage, the parking lots, the campgrounds, the rustic concession stands. Slowly, too, I met people who regularly returned to take part in the temporary festival, making it an annual homecoming to a familiar community of campers, pickers, and singers. Over time I encountered many new fans there as they made their own first life-altering trips to one of bluegrass music's magnetic hubs.

My unbroken string of attendance ended after a 1979 move to Lexington, Kentucky, but I've returned to the site of the Bean Blossom festivals and their temporary community as often as possible since. Many annual June festival attendees have become genuine friends, and this music-park history was written for those Bean Blossom regulars. The place that drew us all together seems exceptional, and its story turns out to be a colorful one that demands telling not only for our experiential interest, but also to highlight the poorly documented history and value of other similar places, twentieth-century rural music parks, in American social and musical history. My aim is to describe what happened at Bean Blossom from the pre–World War II inception of musical events there through a sequence of owners and events to the present. I also want to explain what this musical site has meant to those who were involved, both directly and more distantly and abstractly.

Although I sought documentation in the usual historian's range of contemporary sources—newspapers, legal documents, deeds, and collections of surviving ephemeral promotional materials—most of this story lives in people's reminiscences. Other participants' memories, however evocative and important in shaping my understanding, are, like my own, incomplete. The real historical record of a shared musical site is infinite, though a written history never can be. Knowing that thousands of individuals took part in events at Bean Blossom in the long period covered by this book is inspiring, but it can also be nearly overwhelming. Many helpful souls consented to add their stories to this book, and their words vividly recall events that happened at this special place. Each fan has his own memories of hearing music played at the Brown County Jamboree and at the Monroe bluegrass festivals, or her own sense of why it was important in her life, and I am grateful that so many were willing to share their experiences with me. This story embraces a sequence of different eras at Bean Blossom, and although the cast of characters—movers, shakers, and hangers-on—inevitably changed through the years, their intertwined chronicles can also be seen as suggestions of an incremental and continuous one, a story of the *place*.

Telling the story also poses questions: To what extent has the musical history of the park at Bean Blossom and the Brown County Jamboree influenced the rest of bluegrass, as both a musical style and an evolving genre of musical performance? To what extent does this story of musical creativity and expression reflect a local or regional indigenous product? What have been the unique contributions of the site's various owners, particularly the well-known "Father of Bluegrass Music," Bill Monroe? How does the history of this one small place serve as a microcosmic link to the larger world of American music and culture?

For me, the tale of Bean Blossom can never be truly complete. I'll always be learning about Bean Blossom and will relish not only the new facts and stories I acquire, but also the rewarding interest and generosity of those who aid in the discoveries. For many of us in the Bean Blossom family who've known one another through and because of Bean Blossom, and shared time there together, it is one of our most treasured places.

# Acknowledgments

In recognizing the deep debt I owe all those listed in the interview section, I must also single out a few more who helped me in key ways: Guylia Bunge Smith kept alive the history of the earliest phase of the Brown County Jamboree through her mother's scrapbook and her own warm memories of her father. In their own ways, Archie Green, Jack McDonald, Jim Peva, and Neil Rosenberg each set me on the pathway of discovery that led to this work.

Many more deserve special or additional thanks as well, including Betsy Adler; Richard Blaustein; Dana Cupp; David DeJean; Bill Evans; Sue Galbraith; Frank and Marty Godbey; Doug Hutchens; Tom Isenhour; Jack Lawrence; Bernard and Genevieve Lee; David and Janice McLaughlin; Jack Morrow, Fred Heckman, and Jon Quick of radio station WIBC; Bobby and Sonny Osborne; Frank Overstreet; Gary Reid; Andrea Roberts; Sandy Rund; Dave Samuelson; Brian Sawyer; Sam Shehan; Chris and Tom Skinker; David Toomey; Bill Weaver; Charles K. Wolfe; and Darryl Wolfe.

# Rural Country Music Parks

This book is a history of one small special cultural scene devoted to vernacular music. Although its story is unique, it exemplifies a type of live music scene that arose in the United States in the first half of the twentieth century: a *rural country music park*. Hundreds of these parks were established from the 1930s on, but for the most part, they have appeared and disappeared without much written notice, remaining stubbornly below the level of historical scrutiny.[1]

In *Bluegrass: A History*, Neil V. Rosenberg describes the older country music parks of the 1950s and before, emphasizing their simplicity, rural settings, accessibility from urban centers, and presentation of Sunday-afternoon shows and music contests to family audiences. Bill Monroe biographer Richard Smith also describes these parks, noting features including picnic grounds where families and friends would enjoy "dinner on the ground," a phrase evoking the historical context of church-based all-day singing events. Smith observes the parks' roofed-over stages, benches, and unsophisticated sound systems and highlights their value in bluegrass music history as an informal network of family performance venues. Finally, he points out their significance to a "growing subculture of northern enthusiasts," like Mike Seeger and Ralph Rinzler, whose subsequent careers repeatedly acknowledged initial encounters with Bill Monroe and other seminal artists at the country music parks of southeastern Pennsylvania.[2] All the early rural country music parks presented outdoor performances of country music, but some other common factors enriched the idea: weekly Sunday-afternoon shows, family orientation, limited use of advertising, picnic facilities, private ownership, the rural location, and the possibility of camping on the grounds.

Other sorts of venues functioned similarly in presenting country, bluegrass, and related music yet differed in critical ways. For instance, historical fiddlers' conventions and radio barn dances, though grounded in the same social matrix noted by Ralph Rinzler to be characteristic of the country music parks, typically took place in major cities like Atlanta or Detroit or regional centers like Bristol, Tennessee, or Galax, Virginia. Public parks in or near major cities have also hosted bluegrass or country music shows, but public parks are neither focused on that function nor owned by an individual or family who promotes a particular kind of music. Some private music parks concentrate on other styles of music, offering only seasonal events like festivals. Many "little Oprys" offer weekly country music and bluegrass music shows, but (in an obvious parallel to Nashville's Ryman Auditorium) are usually set in indoor facilities like converted small-town theaters.

Cultural scenes are tied to the physical settings of each music park. Old music parks that survived the longest often underwent major alterations at the hands of their owners and managers. The most successful parks often added new features like a second stage, better concessions, or an improved campground. The evolution of each park informs both the fact of the park's survival and new commercial directions for the park's owner.

There was a rapid early development of modern outdoor music festivals in the mid-1960s, and then an amazing explosion of them after about 1970. As the bluegrass festival movement spread, some older Sunday-show country music parks, like Virginia's Watermelon Park, lost their weekly show focus and became *festival parks,* known nationally for presenting annual music festivals. The transformation could be sudden or drawn out over years. From the seventies onward, builders of new festival parks re-created many functional elements familiar to them from the older parks.[3] Later, campgrounds and recreational vehicle parks and other theme parks added music-show facilities, further muddling the paradigm.

No rural country music parks existed before there was something identifiable as "country music," which effectively began as an industry in the late 1920s. But the small parks did not become truly viable until after the Great Depression's hard times subsided. For most, a sense of returning prosperity did not arrive until the late 1930s, even later in some areas. Sometime in this period, a revived degree of personal wealth and automotive mobility brought rural sites within the ready reach of audiences. By the mid- to late 1930s, the earliest country music parks were founded.

The conceptual origins of rural country music parks are elusive. Few historical overviews of music parks exist, and even the best examples, like the story of southeastern Pennsylvania's Sunset Park, were usually written after the parks' demise.[4] The histories of most ephemeral country music parks, even clues to their very existence, are now hidden away in yellowing scrapbooks kept by former owners or performers, or in their evanescent memories, or those of aging attendees. Even when such resources are tapped for historiographic value, they usually do not point at antecedents for the concept.

But parks have a long lineage. More than a thousand years ago the word *park* meant a privately (or royally) owned enclosed outdoor hunting area.[5] By the twelfth century, "deer parks" had been built by those at the top of the feudal system for their own use, the word *deer* then meaning game animals in general. The family name *Parker* identified the keepers of a deer park.

Public municipal parks arose in the mid–seventeenth century. In 1632 England's king Charles I opened London's Hyde Park to the general public, and throughout the seventeenth century, especially after the huge London fire of 1666, many old royal parks opened to the public, as planners added new recreational green spaces, public gardens, and zoos. By the eighteenth century, wealthy patrons commissioned new generations of private parks, zoos, grottoes, and gardens, perfecting and controlling nature in ever more culturalized ways. For example, Marie Antoinette's *petit hameau* was a fake peasant farm built for her amusement around one of the landscaped lakes at Versailles.[6]

The modern era of amusement parks opened with the Chicago Columbian Exposition of 1893, the last of the nineteenth-century World's Fairs, which inaugurated the Ferris wheel and other rides and presented them to an eager public in conjunction with the carnival-like Midway.[7] In the aftermath of the Columbian Exposition, private developers created the first modern ride-centered amusement parks. All used music to some degree, but a few made popular and classical musical performances a key part of the draw for their urban audiences.

Transportation to rural parks was always an issue. The first wave of modern amusement parks followed the upsurge of urban light electric railway construction from 1890 to 1905. "Trolley parks" were built by the trolley or light-rail companies on cheap land at the end of the line.[8] The initial suburban amusement parks consisted mainly of picnic facilities, often on the shores of a lake or river, and dance halls, restaurants, and games. Later, new trolley parks added roller coasters, Ferris wheels, and other rides.

Early-twentieth-century Philadelphia had four such trolley parks. The most important was Willow Grove Park, constructed on a hundred acres and featuring three picnic grounds, a four-acre lake with a spectacular electric lighted fountain, numerous restaurants and concessions, fifty thousand electric lights to allow evening use of the park, a "mountain railroad" (roller coaster), and a special focus on musical amusements. The Willow Grove music pavilion had a grand band shell that repeatedly attracted leading band and orchestra artists like Victor Herbert and John Philip Sousa.[9]

Suburban North Chicago's Ravinia Park, which bills itself as "North America's oldest music festival," was the Chicago and Northwestern Railway's "trolley park." The thirty-six-acre suburban site acted from its inception as a summer venue for classical music and opera. The Ravinia concept of music "festival" is unique in popular entertainments for embracing each entire summer season of musical events. Today that means jazz and popular music appear alongside the classical orchestra and opera concert repertoire that originally dominated.

As a promotional idea, privately developed rural music parks may have evolved in part from the early success of large well-publicized amusement parks or musically specialized theme parks like Ravinia and Willow Grove. As a cultural idea, the rural music parks also echo earlier American social institutions, including the religious camp meeting, the Chautauqua movement, and regional fiddlers' conventions. All these historical institutions contributed to the development of the rural country music park *idea*.

Religious camp meetings date to the dawn of the nineteenth century, with deeper roots in the "Great Awakening" of evangelistic fervor that swept through Europe and America prior to that time. The "Second Great Awakening" brought the new institution of the religious camp meeting to the Kentucky frontier. Camp meetings, created by early American Methodist, Presbyterian, Pentecostal, Baptist, and other Protestant churches, pulled together dispersed rural congregations for "revivals" of worship and fellowship.[10] Held annually in wooded areas or attractive groves, camp meetings brought together like-minded families who lived in tents or covered wagons and constructed makeshift shelters, "brush arbors," for worship, singing, and communion. In places where an annual camp meeting succeeded and flourished, the original brush arbor was eventually succeeded by an open-sided "tabernacle" or pavilion, under which participants met for singing, worshiping, and socializing.

Outdoor stages are central in depictions and photos of nineteenth-century camp-meeting sites, and their simple designs directly foreshadow the stages of many music parks. The camp meetings also prefigured the music parks' social settings, which arose predictably wherever southern visitors literally camped on the grounds for the duration of an extended multiday event.

Another source for the idea of music parks was the Chautauqua movement, which President Theodore Roosevelt famously characterized as "the most American thing in America."[11] This late-nineteenth- and early-twentieth-century movement, rooted in the older Lyceum concept of adult education, used natural or park environments for fresh, informal presentations of music and art intended to ennoble and uplift audiences. The original Chautauqua Lake Sunday School Assembly was created at a rural western New York site in 1874 as an educational experiment in out-of-school vacation learning. That first Chautauqua's "auditorium" was an open-sided pavilion, shading and protecting both the musicians or lecturers and their audiences. Chautauqua quickly succeeded and broadened almost immediately beyond courses for Sunday-school teachers to include academic subjects, music, art, and physical education. "Daughter-" and tent-based circuit Chautauquas soon followed, diffusing across the nation, bringing summertime outdoor lectures, dramatizations, and performances—particularly musical performances—to large numbers of rural Americans. In many states, both public and private parks were built in attractive natural settings for the use of daughter Chautauquas. Virtually all the original "Chautauqua Parks" surviving in Ohio, Iowa, Nebraska, Colorado, and beyond have in common their regular use for public musical performances.

Characteristically, Chautauqua parks had one or more focal points for performance. Amphitheaters, open-sided pavilions, and outdoor stages were planned, built, improved, altered, and maintained as permanent park facilities. From early times, too, those attending special annual summertime Chautauqua events camped on or near the grounds, generating the feeling of a camp-meeting community and heightening the emotional impact of all that was presented.

Another precursor of the rural country music parks was the desire to compete at music making. Fiddlers' contests or conventions have been held in America since the early 1700s.[12] A fiddle-contest boom occurred in the mid-1920s with the advent of radio, when many large, nationally promoted fiddling championships were broadcast. Henry Ford sponsored many such competitions to help promote his conservative vision for the American lifestyle.

In addition to the actual competition or contest, the cultural scene at most southern fiddle contests included much more. Neil Rosenberg describes it: "Acquaintances were renewed, tunes swapped, drinks taken (often clandestinely), and new musicians (often youngsters) initiated. Meals were shared, news exchanged, instruments swapped or sold, late hours kept; all were part of the offstage aspects of these events."[13]

Beginning in the mid-1930s, entrepreneurs and fans first began to create simple parks dedicated to presenting country music. They were located in fields and groves and on former farmsteads at the edges of small towns. Plotted on a national map, the locations of current or former rural music parks show concentrations

Rural Country Music Parks. A: Prior to 1942, parks only in
Kentucky, Indiana, Pennsylvania, New Hampshire, and Maine.
B: Distribution of known country music parks and festival
parks, 1938–2005.

in the mid-Atlantic and upland South regions. Country music parks were also created in the Midwest, the Near West, the Deep South, and even the Northeast. Many of the earliest parks—those established before 1941—paradoxically seem to lie on the outermost fringes of the "core" country music heartland. The oldest rural country music parks documented to date are in Maine, New Hampshire, Indiana, Kentucky, and Pennsylvania. Perhaps that pattern reflects the needs of isolated minorities of early country and western music fans in the outermost "sphere" of that music's influence.[14] Most parks created between 1935 and 1955 emphasized "cowboy" and western themes that were then pervasive nationally in country music, and many even incorporated the word *ranch* in their names.

Each rural country music park had as its focal point a formal performance structure: a stage or amphitheater. A few were elaborate, but most outdoor stages followed camp-meeting precedents, featuring modest structures with a deliberately rusticated style or intentionally old-fashioned design. Such venues in formative stages were often cobbled together by rural property owners to provide a place for free music shows with and for family, neighbors, and musicians in a local network. But most named music parks were unabashedly commercial ventures as well right from their beginnings. The range of musical styles presented at such parks as "country music" was wide, encompassing western-swing, cowboy, old-time, "Opry," "folk," string-band, and bluegrass music. The range of instrumental music encompassed an expansive heritage of dance-related forms, with jigs and reels and breakdowns for clogging, step dancing, and square dances or play parties and "round-dance" music like waltzes, polkas, and two-steps.

Superficially similar music-hall stages were sometimes created in fully enclosed urban buildings. Such schoolhouse auditoriums and repurposed movie houses in towns and small cities across the South and West are often found today but are called "Oprys" or "little Oprys" as opposed to ranches and parks.[15] Few early rural country music parks used enclosed performance venues; when they did, they called them "barns," emphasizing the rural roots of music played inside such structures. Most country music parks emphasized simple outdoor platforms or stages as their central performance feature. Around stages, pavilions, or buildings were parking lots for automobiles; by the mid-1950s, some rural music parks also offered campgrounds for those who wished to stay overnight or permitted overnight camping in the parking lots. Depending on the types of music brought in by the park's owners, there might also be dance floors or covered dance pavilions.

Rural music park entertainment was almost always seasonal, offered spring, summer, or fall. Few music parks had fully enclosed buildings suitable for shows in winter or during spells of truly inclement weather. Most park owners put on shows according to whatever schedule they preferred. Most put on regular week-end shows, adding special shows if a major headline act could be booked.

In its locale, each park was an important cultural scene, a place where the worlds of music-as-work and music-as-play intersected. This book is the story of one such place, a uniquely important Indiana rural country music park, and the cultural scenes centered there.

Bean Blossom

# 1

# Brown County
# History and Roots

About thirty-five miles south of Indianapolis on State Highway 135 lies a tiny Indiana town with the quaintly improbable name of Bean Blossom. A visitor to the southern Indiana hill country might zip through Bean Blossom while traveling to the busy county seat, Nashville, or to lovely Brown County State Park, a few miles farther south. For most of the town's modern history, automobile passage through Bean Blossom didn't take very long, and to most travelers, the small town's sights probably seemed unworthy of notice or memory: a few houses, a couple of churches, some boarded-up storefronts, a gas station, a restaurant or two, and at the center of Bean Blossom, the intersection with Indiana Highway 45, a blinking yellow light and a thriving corner supermarket. In summer, the front porches of several houses sported faded hand-painted signs offering quilts or "country crafts" for sale, and a tent-covered flea market mushroomed into life on a sporadic weekend basis near the town's crossroad focal point. It was easy, too, before the 1970s, to overlook the little rural music park as you zoomed through.

Apart from its especially old-fashioned-sounding name, Bean Blossom seemed to be just another fading hamlet, too far away from the state capital in Indianapolis or the university town of Bloomington to be a convenient bedroom community, too ordinary a rural place to have any redeeming value to most city dwellers, too obviously a place unimportant to the world at large. Yet after the 1960s, Bean Blossom, Indiana, became an increasingly famous place. Pictured often since the 1970s in public media, it is now constantly recalled and celebrated by a multitude of musicians from across the United States, Canada, Europe, and Japan. Some know it as the long-standing site of the country music park called the "Brown

County Jamboree" that Kentuckian Bill Monroe, the "Father of Bluegrass Music," owned and ran from the early 1950s until his death in 1996. Since the late 1970s, most of those who have learned about Bean Blossom think of it chiefly as the location of a famous bluegrass music festival. Although Bean Blossom was not the site of the *first* bluegrass festival, it now features the oldest continuous annual bluegrass festival anywhere, and its fame and notoriety are legendary in bluegrass circles.[1] Fans who never attended the Brown County Jamboree or the Bean Blossom festivals while Bill Monroe was alive often lament their lost opportunity. It is a place that has touched the hearts of generations of fans—not only fans of Monroe's bluegrass music but also fans of many other kinds of entertainment showcased there through the years.

The history of the Brown County Jamboree intertwines with the particulars of its unique geographical site.[2] In 1836, the Indiana legislature created Brown County from hilly sections of three older Indiana counties: Monroe, Bartholomew, and Jackson. The new, sparsely inhabited county was named for the War of 1812's Hoosier veteran and hero, Maj. Gen. Jacob Jennings Brown. A twenty-mile-by-sixteen-mile north-south rectangle with a stubby panhandle in its northwest corner, Brown County today consists of four townships: Hamblen, Jackson, Van Buren, and Washington. It straddles the geographic divide between the southern Indiana hills and the flat plains of central and northern Indiana. Brown County also lies right on the fuzzy line where the cultural "North" and "South" meet.

A strong case can be made for the impact of environment on the course of history there. Brown County's hills and plains resulted from the Illinoisan and Wisconsin glaciations, which molded regional topography beginning more than 140,000 years ago. During final serial glaciations some 11,000 years ago, the glacier furrowed the earth into the countless hills and valleys of the southern limestone country making up the southern two-thirds of the county. Three major creek systems drain the lands of Brown County, generally from northeast to southwest: Bean Blossom Creek to the north, the north fork of Salt Creek in the center, and the middle fork of Salt Creek in the southern part of the county. All eventually drain into the White River's tributaries, and thence into the Ohio River.

Elementary school students in northwestern Brown County's Jackson Township, which includes Bean Blossom, have been taught for years that the long, high ridge just to the south of Bean Blossom marks the precise final extent of the last great prehistoric glaciation, a conclusion well supported by aerial photographs and satellite imaging.[3] The entrance to the Brown County Jamboree Park site lies just six-tenths of a mile north of the spot where a traveler going north on Highway 135 descends from the hills of Brown County onto the southern edge of the

Tipton Till Plain, where central Indiana's landscape was flattened beneath the weight of the glaciers.[4]

Because of these prehistoric glaciations, Brown County's terrain and local geology differ from those of the rest of the state. Topography and natural landscape shaped the history of "the hills of Brown County," affecting agriculture, economic development, and folklife patterns. Bean Blossom, like the rest of Brown County, developed as it did because of its geography, which was a root cause of the area's relative isolation and late commercial development.

Rocky land and poor soil at the glacier's end made the subsequent agricultural economics of Brown County, in the words of folklorist Dillon Bustin, a "dubious proposition."[5] The area's blend of soil types includes more than twenty-five named subtypes, three identified by soil scientists as unique to Brown County. Most of it is disappointing soil for a farmer. Thin and clayey, it defies the easy agricultural practices of the flat alluvial lands to the north and west. Exposed patches of soil in Brown County turn into a deep, sticky mud every spring and dry to a hard, dusty light-brown powder in the summer heat. The hilly land in Brown County is excellent for apple orchards, stands of nut trees, and berry farms and patches. It is not favorable for corn, wheat, or most large livestock. By the mid–nineteenth century, the original native forests of hickory, oak, beech, tulip poplar, and yellowwood were mature woods, with a rich deciduous overlay of shaded moist soil, perfect for generating the morels that draw ardent southern Indiana mushroom hunters into the woods every spring.

The human history of Brown County is similarly tied to the land. Native Americans in Indiana at the time of the earliest contact with French fur traders included members of several Great Lakes Woodland tribes: Illini to the north and west, Potawatomis to the north, and Miamis to the northeast and in the rich hunting lands of central Indiana. There were also displaced Shawnee people, who had moved from their original central Ohio lands, and Delawares, who had moved west from the Chesapeake Bay area. From the early 1700s onward, the initial gentle invasion of European traders quickly gave way to a much more forceful takeover of land, punctuated by many treaties and ordinances. Following the defeat and expulsion of the French after 1763, British and then American demands became ever more forceful. At the end of the eighteenth century, new treaties demanded increasing cession of Indian lands, increasing tensions between Native Americans and Euro-American newcomers. The conflicts that resulted reached a peak with the rise of the "Shawnee Prophet" and the crushing defeat of his brother, the war leader Tecumseh, by William Henry Harrison in 1811 at Tippecanoe, near present-day Lafayette. More treaties and land cessions followed, always to the detriment of the Indians, and by 1840 the new state was virtually emptied of both its original and its transitional Native populations.[6]

The first permanent generations of Euro-American settlers, who came from the South and East, generally followed pathways of settlement from the German-dominated cultural hearth of the mid-Atlantic and from the Anglo-American South.[7] Some of the first residents who arrived in the two decades before the Civil War were foreign-born immigrants, then about a tenth of the total population. Half the immigrants were from Germany, the remainder mostly from Ireland, England, and France.[8] The Germans tended to settle in towns, providing a population of businessmen and merchants, particularly grocers. English, Irish, and their Anglo-American descendants settled in outlying areas to farm and hunt. In Brown County, settlement began on the agriculturally superior bottomlands in the Salt Creek and Bean Blossom Creek valleys.

Bean Blossom was originally named George's Town, later amended to George-town, commemorating the town's founder, George Grove. Before 1875, to comply with emergent postal regulations requiring that each post office be uniquely named, the town's residents changed the name to "Bean Blossom" (frequently spelled as a single word, "Beanblossom").

The new town name reflected an older feature, Bean Blossom Creek. Miami Indians had called the stream *Ko-chio-ah-se-pe,* or "Bean River," so the stream's name seems a simple translation.[9] However, a local oral tradition refers to a soldier named Jack Beanblosom who tried to swim the creek and nearly drowned. Gen. John Tipton, U.S. senator from 1832 to 1839, then named the creek in Beanblosom's honor—or so it is said. Another tale fragment recounted later by Bill Monroe cites a legendary incident in which a wagonload of beans was tipped into the creek. When the beans sprouted and flowered on the site, local residents named the creek for the blossoms they saw there.[10]

The people of Brown County, as journalist Ernie Pyle described them in a 1940 essay, were "hill people":

> In this hill country of Indiana more than 100 years ago came immigrants from the east—English people from Virginia and Tennessee and Kentucky—pushing on into their new frontiers, but never out of the hills, for they were hill people.
>
> Because of a certain necessary resourcefulness which makes hill people proud and somehow self-sufficient, the natives of Brown County for a long time lived their own lives in the woods and the tobacco patches and the little settlements, asking nothing of any man, and eventually they came to be known to the rest of Indiana as "quaint." That is what first attracted the artists to Brown County 40 years ago—the log cabins, the lounging squirrel hunter, the leaning sheds, the

flowers and the autumn leaves and the brooks and hillsides. That, too, is what eventually attracted the sightseers.

The typical Brown County man plays a guitar in the woods, and raises a little tobacco, and goes to church, and drinks whisky, and is a dead shot with a squirrel gun.[11]

Historian Howard Lee Nicholson characterizes the resulting settlement of Brown County as, essentially, that of an "Appalachian" community.[12] For most of the nineteenth century, Brown County agriculture and animal husbandry were based on swine, which were left loose to forage for mast in the expansive forests, and then caught and butchered by the farmer for his own sustenance and for profit.

After the Civil War, new state fencing laws made owners of swine confine their animals, while higher prices for corn, wheat, oats, and especially timber led most farmers to change their crops. The value of the native Brown County hardwood trees quickly appreciated, and serious commercial logging began. By 1900, tree cutting on the ridges produced deforestation and erosion, which in turn ended the swine culture's dominance for good and led to significant population losses. Brown County's population declined by one-quarter between 1890 and 1910, and by one-half over the longer period from 1880 to 1930. Since there were no significant mineral or petroleum-based resources, and because the hand-labor cultivation of the hill farms could not compete with the successful farming being mechanized and expanded in the flatter land to the north, Brown County suffered financially. As Dillon Bustin puts it, "Brown County was suddenly poor. As it could not afford prestigious improvements it came to be considered a backward place, the home of coarse, shiftless simpletons. According to Social Darwinism, a dominant ideology of the time, hard luck was easily interpreted as laziness, and Brown County was used as a negative example by the business and political elite in Indianapolis, inspiring countless jokes, sermons, and editorials."[13]

At the turn of the twentieth century, progressive local forces vigorously pursued a railroad connection for the county, which slowed and eventually stemmed the loss of population. At the same time, the outside world began to find new value in Brown County's remote and—from the urban perspective—unspoiled rural landscapes and vistas. Brown County attracted urban visitors seeking a respite from city life. By 1900, newspapers in Chicago praised the southern Indiana hill country for its scenic beauty, noting that pioneer-stock families lived there in log houses nestled in quaint valleys. That rose-colored view of the Indiana hill country, and especially of "the Hills o' Brown," would be echoed repeatedly down through the years.[14] Indeed, it constitutes a central theme in efforts to promote cultural tourism in Brown County to this day. The arrival of the new Indianapolis Southern

Railroad at Helmsburg in 1902 brought greatly improved access to the northeastern part of the county. Nashville, the county seat, had labored for two decades to lure a railroad company to the area to create a connection to Indianapolis and the northern rail hubs, but at first Nashville was embarrassed and dismayed when it was ignored by the railroad. Eventually, however, Nashville and the county as a whole benefited from its image as an isolated place, "lost in the past."[15]

With physical access to the area finally enabled, poets, newspapermen, social observers, and artists soon fixed on Brown County. Their attraction to the area was uniformly rooted in their vision of an unspoiled natural and historical place. In those days, the touring visitors, many of whom came from Chicago (home city of the Illinois Central Railroad), would alight from the train in Helmsburg and ride a "hack" buggy to the small, scenic, and deliberately rusticated crossroads community of Nashville. The first outsiders to make a permanent impact were the artists. Nashville's reputation lured a few artists into the area even before 1900, and in the first twenty years of the twentieth century, the county began to develop its prevalent reputation as an "artist colony." An impressively large number of northern painters moved to the county, temporarily or permanently, to practice their forms of impressionist art. Many artists painted the county's only covered bridge, built in 1880 across Bean Blossom Creek. Among the earliest and most significant of the artists was T. C. Steele. The fame of the "Brown County Art Colony" spread far and wide from the 1920s on, abetted by the creation in 1926 of the Brown County Art Guild.

In addition to the art colony, a second key part of the national image of Brown County early in the new century was its perception as a rural backwater. In fact, social change, though inevitable, was sometimes inhibited in nineteenth-century Brown County by self-styled "Regulators," who monitored the actions and morals of their neighbors. During the Civil War, local Southern sympathizers formed a vigilante group called the Knights of the Golden Circle, who, along with some draft dodgers and deserters, holed up not far from Bean Blossom. They eventually became known as "Whitecappers," named for the pillowcase hoods they wore. Whitecappers were ideologically allied with the Ku Klux Klan in their avowed regard for law and tradition, justifying their anti-Semitic and anti-Negro stances. The Ku Klux Klan maintained a strong presence throughout Indiana, and Brown County was hardly unique in hosting such vigilantes.[16] But their effect was widely felt: an old road leading out of Bean Blossom was once known as "Whitecap Road" after the group left their signs, a bundle of switches on the front step, to warn antisocial residents. When northern artists began to infiltrate Brown County from Chicago after the railroad line was built, some were warned to reconsider their destination because rural Brown County was "such a primitive region of moonshiners, rough hill folks, and much rougher White Caps."[17] As late as 1907, the *Brown County Democrat* reported that a strong contingent of "Regulators" was still at work in the remote and underdeveloped county.

Brown County also remained truly rural because it was isolated by poor roads. Even State Highway 135, the main road leading through Bean Blossom, south into the hills toward the county seat and north toward Indianapolis, was poorly graded and unpaved until the mid-1930s. Electric light and power service, available much earlier in Indianapolis, was not inaugurated at Bean Blossom until 1936.

Given the county's early settlement but relative isolation, urban visitors might easily have imagined typical Brown County farmers to be "hillbillies." The image of local Brown County culture as a relic of simpler times was based not only on a foundation of reality but also on a memorable cartoon image. Early in the century, a fictive hillbilly named Abe Martin (generally presented in a more flattering light than the later "Li'l Abner" hillbillies of cartoonist Al Capp) began to make his national reputation. Brown County's emblematic character was created by *Indianapolis News* journalist and political caricaturist Frank McKinney "Kin" Hubbard (1868–1930). Hubbard promoted the area's reputation beginning in 1905, when his humorous political-commentary character, the sparsely whiskered Abe Martin, announced that he was moving to Brown County. In the next day's cartoon, Abe Martin sat in a wagon full of household goods and commented on the relative inaccessibility of the place with a long-remembered quip: "By cracky, it's sum travelin' ter git ter Brown County." For the next twenty-five years, Abe Martin's bewhiskered visage and eye-dialect quips and observations (for example, "Now an' then an innocent man is sent t' th' legislature") were a daily mainstay of low-key political commentary in Indiana. Eventually, the single-panel cartoon featuring Abe Martin was syndicated nationally in about two hundred newspapers. Collections of Hubbard's sketches were released as independent books during his lifetime, and Martin's image has been revived periodically through ensuing decades by Brown Countians.

Hubbard called Brown County "a rugged, almost mountainous, wooded section of Indiana without telegraphic or railroad connections—a county whose natives for the most part subsist by blackberrying, sassafras-mining and basket making." Abe Martin and a variety of other fictitious characters with colorful names (gleaned in part from Kentucky jury lists) helped fix the image of Brown County as a remote, backward area populated by canny and perceptive hillbillies.[18]

The popular image of Brown County, based on topography, isolation, and poverty and exacerbated by the Abe Martin caricature, had growing consequences for the region in the twentieth century. The popular image was reinforced by a key state decision in 1929, when the Indiana Department of Natural Resources created Brown County State Park, the state's largest, just to the south of Nashville. Three years later, when the DNR built the sixteen thousand–acre park's first major visitor feature—a rustic hotel-lodge and group of tourist cottages—it bet on the fame of the Abe Martin character as the best-known symbol of the region's positive rural character. The Abe Martin Lodge sits on Kin Hubbard Ridge, and Hubbard's colorful cast of characters—like Tell Binkley, Fawn Lippincutt, and Cale Fluhart—was used to identify individual rental cottages. This marketing decision by the state, along with the park's natural scenic beauty and recreational facilities, drew thousands of visitors each year from all over the greater Midwest and beyond.[19]

Despite some early resentment within the county, Abe Martin came eventually to be a locally beloved figure, as well as a durable one. In the late 1950s a Brown County resident named "Vene" Schrock posed around Nashville as the "original Abe Martin." Dressed in overalls or a vest, and sporting a felt hat, he would kid the "furriners" visiting Brown County, bragging that he was the inspiration for Kin Hubbard's cartoon.[20] In the 1970s and '80s, another local man, David Hawes, revived the memory of Abe Martin with his occasional one-man shows. Hawes eventually produced a book and a play recalling the rustic wisdom and cracker-barrel philosophy of the cartoon character. In the mid-1990s, Nashville promoted an annual "Abe Martin Festival" for several years, welcoming the county's weekend tourists with folk music by the local dulcimer society. Over time, the fame and appealing nature of the Abe Martin character combined with other positive aspects of Brown County's reputation—its cultural isolation, natural landscape beauty, recreational parkland, and the imprimatur of the artist colony—both to lure tourists to the area and to convince local businessmen that catering to tourists might become their economic salvation.

## Brown County Music and Dance before the Brown County Jamboree

The documentary record of folk and traditional music in the area is a spotty and brief one, despite the nearby presence of the Folklore Institute at Indiana University, twenty-five miles west of Brown County in Bloomington. Many university-trained folklorists turned their gazes upon Brown County through the years, but few looked deeply. Some, like longtime Folklore Institute director Richard M. Dorson, dismissed Brown County's apparent music, architecture, and craft traditions almost entirely, deeming them to be artificial and commercial lures for tourists, the very definition of Dorson's term *fakelore*. Others, like ballad collector Paul Brewster, sent letters to the local newspaper in a vain attempt to solicit old songs from Brown County residents.[21]

Yet local music traditions thrived in Brown County from the earliest days of settlement. Fife-and-drum corps regularly performed for political campaigns, and other sorts of music, from cornet bands to vaudeville troupes, were highlighted in the county's weekly newspaper from its inception in 1870. Building on the solid Brown County heritage of nineteenth-century fiddling and violin making, a group called the Brown County Fiddlers formed in the mid-1920s around several musical families or husband-wife teams—the Bisels, the Smiths, the Andersons, and the Walkers.[22] The group endured for years, playing for shows and dances, both within and outside the county, and were photographed in an apparent backstage setting during a vaudeville tour in 1926.[23] According to the remembrances of elderly locals, the Brown County Fiddlers provided musical accompaniment for frequent dances in Brown County.

Dance music—particularly square-dance music—was absolutely central to life in the county. The prominence of square dancing in the local entertainment spectrum in the 1930s is hard to overstate. Both the influence of "western" square dancing as shown in popular cowboy movies and also the strong heritage of local dance brought Brown Countians to many weekly square dances. Most dances took place in homes, with the living-room rug rolled up and neighbors providing the music. Others were held in commercial dance halls and dance pavilions that opened in and around Brown County in the 1930s and 1940s. The dance halls featured music by local bands, like the original Weed Patch String Band (named for Weed Patch Hill in Brown County State Park, the second-highest elevation in the state). The Weed Patch String Band played regularly for the Saturday-night dances managed by Marion Dooley at the Helmsburg Dance Hall in the mid-1930s.

One key network of old-time musicians in Brown County named themselves the Van Buren String Busters. In 1939 this group, then a four-piece band, consisted of local fiddler Louis Henderson along with Lonzie Gredy, Faun Clark, and Jack Hendricks.[24] In the early 1940s, the group's appearances were led by Adolph Beauchamp, known then and after as Doc Beauchamp. Membership in the band was flexible and adaptive. Jack Hendricks left, but others stepped in. Through the war years, Beauchamp's square dances were typically called to the accompaniment of fiddler Louis Henderson, the banjo of Wilma Anthony Spiker, and the guitar of Wilma's sister (and Beauchamp's wife), Hesper "Hep"

Anthony Beauchamp. Sometimes the Van Buren String Busters substituted other local musicians, such as guitarist Winona Lawrence. The group's repertoire was suitable for the many square dances they played in the area, being built around common standard fiddle tunes like "Soldier's Joy."

Complementing the traditional world of square dances and local musicians in the 1930s, radio brought a burgeoning universe of popular music to Brown Countians and millions of other rural or small-town Americans and Canadians. Radio entertainment was viable in the 1920s but became incredibly successful and important throughout the 1930s, when economic disruption brought Depression-era 78-rpm record production and distribution almost to a halt. Radio brought news and entertainment directly into even the most isolated areas and did not require ongoing purchases, like phonograph records. By the early 1940s, huge radio audiences across the country were tuning in to the Red and Blue networks and local stations and hearing an incredible variety of music. For the first time, many encountered classical orchestras, the popular "big bands," and more esoteric or specialized types, like "race" music, jazz, blues, and country, western, hillbilly, old-time, and "folk" music.

Although radio music and comedy competed with and slowly supplanted the live vaudeville-show circuit, radio imbued their audiences, urban and rural alike, with a burning desire to see their favorite new radio stars. A perfect format for such times was the radio barn-dance show, typified by the *Grand Ole Opry* on Nashville, Tennessee's WSM, the *National Barn Dance* on Chicago's WLS, and the *Boone County Jamboree,* broadcast on WLW in Cincinnati, Ohio. The stars of these programs, while seen live only at the big-city theaters that were their homes, could be heard hundreds of miles away, at no cost, on the radio. Moreover, the best-loved stars of any one major show traveled to other cities, to be presented as temporary "headliners" or featured artists at all of the other radio barn-dance shows.

From the mid-1930s on, radio listeners in Brown County were able to tune in regularly to stations in Chicago, Nashville, Cincinnati, and Indianapolis. They heard and adored groups like WLS's Lulu Belle and Scotty as well as the Girls of the Golden West, who after 1945 were based at Cincinnati's WLW. WLW's popular *Boone County Jamboree* show would go on the road periodically, traveling to other cities to put on special star-centered shows. Huge 1941 Indianapolis newspaper ads with publicity photos and large type proclaimed a regional appearance by Lulu Belle and Scotty: "Those Favorite Rustic Revelers of Radio Just as You Hear Them on Saturday Nights!"—but the ad noted two dozen other acts slated to appear in the live part of the WLW show following a movie. In the prewar years, the movie was typically a western that would appeal to the same listeners, like Caesar Romero as the Cisco Kid in the "bold romantic adventure" *Ride on Vaquero.*"[25]

The live radio barn-dance shows kept performers in front of their devoted fans, creating fast-paced shows that would also win new fans over the airwaves. Artists who had achieved national stardom could also easily be promoted to perform for packed houses in local live shows, minus any radio broadcast, on the strength of their name recognition.

From the mid-1930s on, the *Brown County Democrat* ran countless advertisements for such local and regional shows. Favorite radio stars could be heard every day and played live shows at theaters, school gymnasiums, and fraternal halls in Bloomington, Martinsville, Franklin, Indianapolis, and Cincinnati. At the close of the Depression years and the beginning of World War II, the radio barn-dance shows' influence was growing fast. The shows glittered brightly in the mind's eye, dazzling their beholders with numerous facets, blending the nostalgic yet modern musical acts smoothly with the theatrical, comedic, and sentimental trappings inherited from the shows' underlying roots in, and vestigial links to, earlier entertainment forms (minstrelsy, Tin Pan Alley, vaudeville) and contemporary motion pictures, particularly cowboy movies. The music itself might be labeled "western," "country," "old-time," or "folk," but it resonated through those prewar years with the right mix of familiarity and novelty for its enthusiastic audiences. In the emergent national "mediaspace" of the late 1930s, small local communities naturally began to develop local entertainment models based on what new media had brought to their collective attention.

In Bean Blossom, the new entertainment format took root. Despite the accelerating penetration of mass media in the lives of formerly isolated Brown Countians, local people in the late 1930s often expressed the idea that life there meant they had "nothing to do" for local entertainment. One summer day, all that changed.

**2**

# Origins of the
# Brown County Jamboree,
# 1939–41

According to oral sources, the Brown County Jamboree started one summer Sunday in the late 1930s or early 1940s.[1] Thirty years later, one of the key participants recalled the year of the Jamboree's founding as 1935, but most recalled that it probably began in the summer or fall of 1939.[2]

The oral sources are not supported by area newspapers; the first articles describing early Jamboree events appeared in the summer of 1941. The same newspaper articles imply that the first show leading to the establishment of the Jamboree actually happened in the spring of 1941.[3] Yet local newspaper articles cannot be wholly trusted, either; many contain evident errors of fact, and the disputed dates, even those reported in contemporary newspapers, were given to the papers by a variety of individuals. Despite the uncorroborated evidence for a pre-1941 origin, all sources do ultimately agree on what happened, and in what order.

A written account of the Jamboree's first days in Bean Blossom came from a key participant: a native son whose grocery-owning family, living in the area since 1853, directly participated in the Jamboree's early development. As Jack McDonald recalled:

> Sometime in the early forties when life in the country was a little slow, some men decided that Bean Blossom needed a little country music to lighten things up a bit. One person had an old station wagon with a sound system including a couple of big horn-type speakers mounted on the roof of the car. The car owner was Spurts Ragsdale. He hooked a small flatbed trailer behind the car, and another man by the name of Guy Smith and a third man whose name I can't remember, put on their satin cowboy shirts, climbed aboard the trailer, and as

they went through Bean Blossom and other towns, called out to those they saw standing near their path or sitting in yards and porches for them to "Come to Bean Blossom for a free music show!"

Now, a short time earlier, about a week or two, these same country music buffs had set a microphone and speaker system up on the grassy area in front of the local filling station on the South East corner of Road 135 and 45 in Bean Blossom. That filling station was owned by a father and son, by the name of Dan and Dan Williams Jr. In those days and nights were at a slow pace so a little thing like someone singing into a microphone and telling stories created a little excitement.[4]

McDonald dated the Jamboree to the early forties and named three key figures in the Jamboree's early history: Guy Smith, Denzel "Spurts" Ragsdale (known later as "Silver Spur"), and Dan Williams. A fourth candidate for the title of "founder" was the man McDonald couldn't remember, who may have been Guy Smith's friend and fellow music fan Riley Duckett. These local men helped to found the Jamboree, yet background information on them and their doings in the late 1930s is limited. Some information about Riley Duckett has been provided by two of his three sons, all of whom were regular performers on the early Brown County Jamboree. Ragsdale and Williams remain frustratingly shadowy. But Guy E. Smith—who seems to have been most central to the Jamboree's origination—can be presented more fully, through the recollections of his daughter and the scrapbook compiled by his wife.

Born in Kentucky in 1907, Guy Smith was a man of many talents. He never completed high school, having come to Indiana with his parents to take his place beside them working on their truck farm in Johnson County, just north of Brown County. Around 1936 he moved to Brown County and took a job managing Cotty's apple orchard near Spearsville. Apple and berry orchards were then prospering and increasing throughout the county. Smith, a gregarious man, lived in a house on orchard property with his wife and young family. In the late 1930s, he hosted frequent jam sessions involving local players like the Houchins brothers, and later on Smith's harmonica-playing friend Riley Duckett, who grew up in the country between the nearby hamlets of Trafalgar and Peoga, and who had himself fathered three musical sons. Among such fiddle-and-guitar-playing local talent, Smith always took the role of master of ceremonies and headed up several groups named for him. His groups' several names suggest bucolic, humorous, low-key local entertainment: Guy Smith and His Brown County Merrymakers, Guy Smith and His Brown County Entertainers, Guy Smith and His Hoosier Farmhands. With his band, Smith played several successful shows in

1938 and 1939 at the Shrine Temple in Indianapolis. He instigated and emceed square dances locally and was constantly involved with other active musicians and regional entertainers and promoters, notably the "Hillbilly Rhythmatician," W. LeRoy Wallace of Indianapolis.

Guy Smith was already a seasoned impresario when the Jamboree began. His 1940 business card trumpeted his ability to provide for "entertainment, dances, parties, clubs, mobile advertisement, loudspeaker, cowgirl or hillbilly bands." Later he earned a plumber's license and practiced that trade for a time, then served in the early 1940s as a deputy sheriff. After his serious involvement with the Brown County Jamboree came to an end around May 1942, he worked as a civil engineer, helping to construct nearby Camp Atterbury, which the army built that year in northeastern Brown County and a portion of neighboring Bartholomew County.[5] Later still, Smith sold real estate, operated a grocery store, and ran an electrical appliance store in nearby Nashville. Though he eventually moved to Florida, he and his wife also kept a home in Brown County until his death in 1964.

Denzel W. Ragsdale, another key figure, was from a farm just west of the modest town of Trafalgar, only a few miles north of Bean Blossom. Ragsdale was invariably called "Spurts" by area folks who knew him as a young man. About the time the Brown County Jamboree was founded, he began to wear conspicuous western attire, including a fine white cowboy hat, and adopted his preferred nickname, "Silver Spur."

Ragsdale was a remarkable local character—after Smith, he was certainly the most colorful of the Jamboree's original founders. Ragsdale was seven years younger than Guy Smith and probably looked to him for leadership in their joint promotional ventures. But Silver Spur stayed long beyond Smith, carrying on until his death in 1973, working first for Francis Rund and his sons Glen and Kenneth and later on for Birch and Bill Monroe (who both regularly pluralized his preferred nickname as "Silver Spurs"). For the thirty-plus years of his tenure at the Brown County Jamboree, he was a promoter, a soundman, an occasional rhythm-guitar adjunct to Jamboree acts, and—during the 1940s and 1950s—one of the Jamboree's principal emcees.

Ragsdale recalled the original Jamboree founders to be himself, Guy Smith, Dan Williams, and Carl Brummett.[6] A self-proclaimed soundman, Spurts loudspeakered his way into local fame with a series of special "ballyhoo cars" with sound systems: microphone, record player, and horn speakers mounted on the roof. By the mid-1940s, when the Jamboree was solidly established, Ragsdale's 1941 Chevrolet Suburban ballyhoo car was being used to advertise Ragsdale's

services, with painted notices reading "Sound Equipment for Hire" just above
the side doors and windows and "Silver Spur Ragsdale" on the driver's door.
"Brown County Jamboree" appeared in much larger letters down the side of the
vehicle. Guy Smith's daughter recalled the 1941 car: "It was sort of a station wagon,
a woody-looking station wagon with the speakers on top. And if something was
going to happen in Bean Blossom, well, they would come down through here,
they would go to Morgantown, and he would just broadcast that out over the
land, while he was driving along. Spit out the window occasionally—he chewed
tobacco," she said, laughing.[7]

Even before 1939, Ragsdale used a similar mobile system to promote auctions,
carnivals, dances, and other temporary attractions. Since his brother George had
an auction building adjacent to their farm and presided over many rural farm auctions, Spurts may have originally gone into the ballyhoo business to aid in those
vendues. With Silver Spur's ballyhoo car, Guy Smith's portable loudspeaker
equipment, and Dan Williams's gas-station and restaurant site, and more than
a bit of nerve, the original founders had the basic wherewithal to put on a show.
It was probably, by today's standards, a modest show, but it was entertainment,
and it was free. In the early days of World War II, and with memories of the Depression fresh on many people's minds, the free show would soon prove to be
an incredibly popular draw.

Smith's performance equipment at that first show was meager: one microphone on a stand and a solitary knee-high amplified speaker, both set up right on
the bare grass just a few feet back from Highway 135, on the southeast corner of
the intersection with Highway 45. The "free show," as Brown County residents
called it initially, featured both live and recorded music. Since the main performers were said to have been wearing satin cowboy shirts, they probably looked
every bit the part of hillbilly entertainers, even though, among them, only Guy
Smith had already developed a meaningful local reputation as a performer and
square-dance promoter.

Local people came to see the first free show and returned for shows each
following Sunday evening. This Sunday-afternoon and -evening time slot was
a constant through the entire life of the Jamboree. The Jamboree's scheduling
suggested an old-time rural context, the feeling that it was a Sunday-afternoon
after-church get-together with friends, family, and talented local entertainers.

Today, firsthand eyewitness accounts of these key "original" events are rare.
A good deal of the story was systematically recalled by Jack McDonald, then a
young boy. The grocery founded by McDonald's grandfather and modernized
by his father is located at Bean Blossom's crossroad center, within shouting dis-

tance of the original open-air "free show" site. McDonald attended the first of the free shows and many more. He and some other young friends even helped with the entertainment: "Guy Smith called out to us kids to come on up to the microphone and sing along. The only song that I could think of was 'You Are My Sunshine,' so I gave it a whirl. Wasn't the best attempt, but not the worst, either. This scene repeated itself for a couple of weekends until some of the local talent came along and the thought of a regular show became a reality."[8]

McDonald's song was inspired by the popular Jimmie Davis recording "You Are My Sunshine," made on February 4, 1940. Although Davis wrote the song a decade earlier, the 1931 release was obscure and inconsequential. However, the 1940 release became a national hit almost immediately. Jack McDonald's memory of singing this specific song therefore dates the free show in Bean Blossom to the summer of 1940.

As McDonald recalled, the next important change in the show was the addition of a stage: "The next week someone got a farm wagon and moved the event to a small area south of the filling station. A small restaurant was also located in this area. Less than 100 spectators watched the free show. As weeks went by an elevated stage built of native lumber was erected. The count of spectators grew."

McDonald remembered that the usual "open-air platform" was a flatbed truck pulled out onto a grease rack that paralleled the road, between the filling station and the Bean Blossom Lunchroom. The grease rack consisted of two heavy planks set into the hillside, supported by posts at the lower end. The grease-rack "elevated stage" provided a rudimentary focal point for shows, and local audiences kept coming.

## The Free Show and the Open-Air Platform, 1939–41

After their relatively unheralded beginning in 1939 or 1940, shows on the "open-air platform" grew quickly in popularity and attendance. As the show grew, so too did the number of artists and performers who played there.

Among the first performers were the three sons of Smith's friend Riley Duckett. The Duckett brothers—Cecil, Maurice, and Owen—began to play instrumental music before reaching their teens. They were impressed by the high-quality music they heard at Bean Blossom, particularly the banjo and guitar playing of two key musicians known now only by their nicknames: Kentucky Slim and Tennessee Red. As mandolinist and fiddler Maurice Duckett later recalled, "The way it started, we had been somewhere playing music, we had our instruments with us. And we were going through Bean Blossom for some reason or another, and there at the corner where 45 comes in, there's a fruit market—or it was one, but at that time it was a filling station. Next to it was a diner. I don't know who run the diner, I don't remember who run the filling station, but they had built about an eight-foot square platform out there along the road. And we saw that there was a couple musicians playing there, and we found out that it was Kentucky Slim and Tennessee Red."

The Duckett Brothers were already making a name in the area following their prizewinning 1936 debut at the American Legion amateur show in nearby Franklin. At Bean Blossom they played a few shows on the open-air platform with Kentucky Slim and Tennessee Red, concentrating on humorous or sentimental songs like "The Little Shirt My Mother Made for Me" and "Old Shep."[9] Their proud father promoted their music making, which proved fortunate for the nascent Jamboree.

The commercial possibilities of the enjoyable show, boosted by Brown County's prior reputation for cultural tourism, illuminated Dan Williams's thoughts in the early spring of 1941. Williams's commercial effort developed around his lunchroom beginning in March 1941. Williams printed detailed ads for his weekend events on the lunchroom's napkins, instructing visitors: "Drive in and park—and listen to snappy, peppy Brown County string band music on Friday, Saturday, and Sunday evenings." Such ads stressed the restaurant's ample parking and the featured drive-in service with "alert young women attendants to fill your orders quickly." The musical entertainments, already successful, were a new and potent attraction for the lunchroom.

Guy Smith, organizing and emceeing the shows, almost always included the Duckett boys, also known as the Hickory Ranch Boys, Hickory Ranch Ramblers, or Hickory Ranch Harmonizers. Riley Duckett worked closely alongside Smith, serving as the show's official manager during most of the first year.

The first documented performer at the incipient Jamboree at Williams's Bean Blossom Lunchroom was (perhaps unsurprisingly) Guy Smith. In May 1941, Williams's advertising began to proclaim free Sunday-evening shows by Guy E. Smith and His Hoosier Farm Hands, featuring Little Jack and His Swing Washboard. The shows, which ran from 6:30 to 9:30 p.m. in June and July, were held atop the Bean Blossom Lunchroom. Williams, who never missed a chance to trumpet the easy access for automobiles to his restaurant and the free shows, exhorted readers: "COME, PARK, LISTEN."

"Little Jack," the washboard player, may have been a local musician who worked with Guy Smith just once or twice in the summer of 1941. But "Little Jack" may have been an alternate short-lived stage name for an outgoing entertainer who soon burst onto the Bean Blossom scene from his home base in Indianapolis: sandy-haired Wilbert LeRoy Wallace, who promoted himself as "Washboard Wallace," "Scrub-Board Wallace," or "Professor Scrub-Board, The Original Hillbilly Rhythmatician."

Wallace was a brash, energetic promoter of his own musical career; his direct involvement with the Brown County Jamboree began in 1941.[10] A display ad in the *Jamboree*—a historical, ephemeral Indiana music magazine with no relationship to the Brown County Jamboree—listed him as "At Liberty" in early summer.[11]

Wallace became involved with Guy Smith as the Brown County Jamboree got under way. Expounding on his semiprofessional experience touring with the George "Tex" Hall Troupe of Hollywood Cowhands and Californians of Republic Pictures, Inc., Wallace wrote Smith, speculating on potential bookings and conveying a performer's-eye view of the right people to talk to and the right organizations to approach for Smith and the embryonic Jamboree to secure more entertainment work.

The open-air Sunday-evening show at Williams's gas station and lunchroom served for a short period—perhaps as brief as a single summer, but in any event no more than two years—as a key element in Williams's promotional efforts. The platform, like the highway frontage space in front of it, was truly open to the air and to the sight and hearing of anyone who could get to town by car or horse or on foot. Despite the makeshift stage and near-spontaneous origins of the "free show," the promoters—Ragsdale, Williams, Smith, and others—were all awed by the size of the audiences they drew and, as McDonald recalled, immediately began to both "sell" the event and try to find ways to profit from it:

> A woven wire fence was erected and tickets to the shows were sold for 25 cents each. The people running the shows began to pay a small amount to some of the performers to cover the cost of their expenses incurred in providing their talent and musical equipment for the shows. Spectators could stand outside the fence and see the show at a distance without buying a ticket. So to encourage spectators to buy a ticket the show organizers asked the local store owner—Herb McDonald, my father—to donate three baskets of groceries each weekend so the viewers would be encouraged to buy a ticket and get a chance on a drawing for the groceries. The Rihm's grocery in Morgantown also donated three baskets of groceries. The value of the baskets of food items was about 3 to 4 dollars each. These shows continued at this location into the end of the fall season.

Local merchants were critical to the show. Jack McDonald's mother stated, "The Bean Blossom merchants really started what turned out to be Bill Monroe's Jamboree, which draws country music fans to Bean Blossom from all over the world. Francis Rund was one of those who had the idea to provide free musical entertainment where Short's market is now. The merchants cooperated, to help bring in trade. It became so successful that they finally put up a tent and began to charge admission."[12]

Since the show could no longer be viewed for free by passersby—tickets were now twenty-five cents for adults and ten cents for children—the era of the "free show" and the "open-air platform" began to change. But the Brown County Jamboree was becoming a moneymaker. The free shows of 1939 or (more likely) 1940 were transformed into an intentionally commercial venture beginning in March 1941. By midsummer, Guy Smith and Dan Williams began to advertise and promote a named show at Bean Blossom to the surrounding region. They first called their show "Old Brown County Nights," advertising it as a weekend entertainment.

The inaugural Old Brown County Night show was held at Williams's Bean Blossom Lunchroom, on the Fourth of July, a Friday. An announcement in the Morgantown newspaper, likely drafted by Smith or Williams, called the show "a series of entertaining evenings featuring the kinds of fun and frolic that prevailed in Indiana's famous hills when Dad wore felt hats and Ma had rats in her hair."[13]

Within three weeks, an encouraged Williams began to seek commercial sponsors to help expand the venture. He invited local merchants to attend the Sunday, July 27, show and suggested to them in a printed circular that the Old Brown County Nights producers were planning to add radio broadcasts in the near future. A thirty-minute broadcast, said Williams, could accommodate from one to five sponsors; each sponsor would pay from $50 to $250 depending on the length of their sponsored segment of the show. The circular identified the weekly event as "a barn dance and amateur night combination that has grown, in the two months since its beginning, until it draws audiences estimated at 2,000 and up."

Performers on Old Brown County Nights included Guy Smith and His Hoosier Farm Hands; twelve-year-old "boy-wonder" ventriloquist George Scott with his "Talking Doll Tommy"; the Campbell Sisters; Indianapolis radio entertainer Lonesome Bill Jones, who had his own show on WIBC every weekday morning at 11:15; and the three "Hickory Ranch Harmonizers," the Duckett brothers, with their fiddle, guitar, and mandolin.

Another local band was the Van Buren String Busters, who brought to the free show both instrumental musical ability and the added draw of their square-dance promotions. Square-dance caller and band leader Doc Beauchamp remembered that they played often beginning in 1939 on the "open-air platform" on Highway 135 that predated the founding of the Brown County Jamboree.[14] In Beauchamp's own remembrance of the Jamboree's founding, forty years after the events took place, he emphasized the band's regular role: "We played there every Sunday as a drawing-card for a grocery give-away."[15]

The shows drew well, but contemporary newspaper notice lagged. Finally, in August 1941, the county newspaper gave the show its first notice in print, tersely reporting that "another large crowd was here Sunday evening attending the free show."[16]

Events following the launch of Old Brown County Nights proceeded quickly, driven by its success and the desire of Dan Williams to strike a bargain for regular radio broadcasts. Within two weeks, the newspaper noted the explosive growth of interest in the free shows, reported startlingly large crowds attending, and recorded the first appearance of the term *Brown County Jamboree* and the potential for a radio tie-in:

> Brown County talent may soon be heard over the air, and believe it or not it will be broadcast from Beanblossom, according to Dan Williams, proprietor of the lunch room at the south edge of Beanblossom. Mr. Williams states that representatives of Indianapolis broadcasting stations have been in Beanblossom several times in efforts to make satisfactory working arrangements to broadcast the programs which are being held there each Sunday night. Large crowds have been attracted to the place and each evening the performance has been staged the crowds have been becoming larger. Attendance was estimated at over 4,000 for last Sunday night.
>
> As soon as arrangements for broadcasting the program are completed a suitable building is to be erected that will house about 2,000 persons so that the programs which have been held in the open may be continued on through the winter, according to Mr. Williams.
>
> This Brown County Jamboree, which it has been commonly named, was not formally planned but just grew out of an evening when a passing truckman with a loud speaker system proposed that he connect it up and play records which he was allowed to do. The first performance proved so popular that it was repeated until local talent was added and the present programs are the result.[17]

Shows continued each week, with large crowds in attendance. As Gladys McDonald remembered, the successful free shows next attracted the attention of Francis Rund, a central Indiana grocer and entrepreneur, who with his wife, Mae, had bought some Bean Blossom farmland in 1938 from a widow, Ethel Ann Brummett. Rund's new landholding was just north of Bean Blossom, east of Highway 135 and south of the Spearsville Road. He quickly constructed a rural cabin retreat just off the highway for his family's weekend getaways to Brown County—but much more lay in store for Rund's land.

# 3

## The Rund Family's
## Brown County Jamboree,
## 1941–51

Francis Rund came from an old Brown County family.[1] He was named for his grandfather Franz Rund, who left Wittenberg, Germany, in 1848, settling near Bean Blossom about 1852. The Runds were soon linked by marriage to the McDonalds, whose first local ancestor arrived in Brown County in 1853. Succeeding generations of marriages and births bound the Runds to many other key families in Brown County Jamboree history: the Coxes, the Doyles, the Shehans, and the McDonalds.

The Runds and McDonalds ran grocery stores, and both families included successive generations of grocers. Kess McDonald, Jack's grandfather, was the last of the "huckster-truck" operators, driving weekly into the surrounding countryside to trade his truckload of "store goods" for local farm produce. Francis Rund operated two grocery stores in the suburban Indianapolis towns of Greenwood and Stones Crossing; his brothers, Forest, Roy, and Theodore, were also grocers.

In 1938, Francis Rund started developing his farmland at Bean Blossom, twenty-six miles south of his weekday home. He built a single-pen board-and-batten cabin just east of the highway as a weekend retreat. On Thanksgiving Day, the Runds hosted many friends and relatives, including cousins Herb McDonald and his young son "Jackie."[2]

Between 1939 and 1941, Rund bought more land in Bean Blossom and immediately sought to make it profitable. In August 1940, the newspaper observed, "Francis Rund, of Stones Crossing, is building tourist cabins near his lake here in Beanblossom." Three lightly framed cabins, much inferior to Rund's own house, were built near the northwest end of the property's small lake. Although

uninsulated, lacking running water, and heated only by "chunk-burner" woodstoves, they expressed Rund's vision of success through Brown County tourism.
The cabins endured for more than a half century, later sheltering Birch Monroe,
Bill Monroe, Monroe's Blue Grass Boys, and many others.[3] By June 1941, Rund's
purchase of a total parcel of land comprising more than sixty acres was complete.[4]

With his new tourist cabins and knack for promotion, Rund saw potential in
the open-air platform and the Bean Blossom Lunchroom's "Old Brown County
Nights" shows. The Runds' attendance at the primordial Jamboree in August or
September 1941 was noted by the county paper, which then published accounts
of even the smallest social happenings. Rund evidently struck a deal with Williams and Smith, for the newspaper announced near the end of September that
the Brown County Jamboree would "soon be moving to the Francis Rund place
north of town" and that Indianapolis radio station WIRE would take over the
show at its new site. In hosting the Jamboree on his own property, Francis Rund
helped it grow and prosper. While the Runds' Jamboree began as a narrowly focused local Sunday-afternoon show, the family laid the groundwork for the site's
expansion into a real rural country music park.

## Tent Show Days, 1941 to 1942

An unidentified newspaper article, contained in the scrapbook of Guy Smith's
wife, chronicles the transition:

SHOW SET IN TENT AT BEANBLOSSOM:
BROWN COUNTY JAMBOREE TO BE HELD
IN LOG AUDITORIUM DURING WINTER.

Beanblossom's outdoor Brown County Jamboree, which has been attracting
several hundred visitors each Sunday night since it opened early in March, will
move under a huge tent this weekend. Later a log auditorium will be built to
house the show through the winter months.

Dan Williams, Beanblossom service station operator, started the show when
natives of Brown County gathered at his station each Sunday evening to play
their instruments and sing. When families from the county were attracted by
the festivities, Williams provided a lot adjoining his place of business to take
care of the crowd.

Ministers in the county complained that the show was keeping their congregations from services, so Williams suggested that the clergymen hold services during
a fifteen-minute period midway in the show. Each Sunday one of the ministers of

the county conducts the services. Spurt Ragsdale and Guy Smith, both of Brown County, act as masters of ceremonies and help with details of the show.

The tent has been placed on the Frances Rund property adjoining Bean-blossom on the north. Pete French, of radio station WIRE, will act as master of ceremonies this week. Thirty-five acts are scheduled. The Farm Hands, of WIRE, will be guest artists and a quiz contest of the natives [is] being planned.[5]

The huge tent, 90 feet wide and 210 feet long, went up on Friday. A small secondary tent stood nearby for ticket vending.[6]

Decades later, those recalling the original Brown County Jamboree tent called it "an old circus tent," a reasonable description given its size and four-pole "big-top" construction. Despite the vastness of the Jamboree tent, crowds during its first fall season kept it filled to capacity.

On Sunday, September 28, 1941, around seven o'clock, Francis Rund hosted the grand-opening show. The premiere, emceed by Guy Smith, lasted three hours,

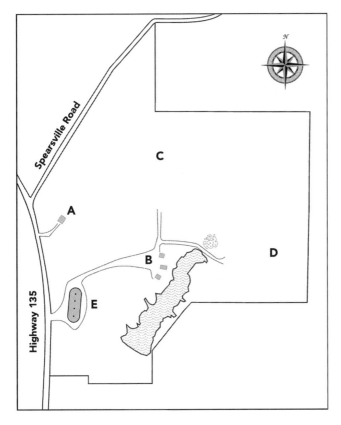

Francis Rund property, October 1941. A: Rund cabin. B: Tourist cabins. C: Wooded area. D: Upper field. E: Brown County Jamboree Tent (90' × 210').

with a roster of numerous original artists: Little June, the Hoosier Tigers, Sambo, the Hoosier Vagabonds, the Hoosier Rangers, Stuttering Jimmie, Jack Cox, Bill Ritter, Kentucky Slim, the Brock Brothers, Lane's Mountaineers, the Brown County Buckaroos, Lonesome Bill Jones, the Brown County Fiddlers, Margie and Dot (the Singing Cowgirls), the Brown County Sweethearts, Milt Allison, the Campbell Sisters, the Morgantown String Band, Chic Hacker, the Morning-side Revellers, the Day Sisters, the Nancy Lou Cowgirl Band, Fiddling Rufus and His String Band, the Nashville Ramblers, the Four Leaf Clover Boys, Roy "Scrub-Board" Wallace, George Scott, the Shelby County Farm Hands, Guy Smith and His Hoosier Farm Hands, the Starlight Rangers, the Hickory Ranch Boys, Tennessee Red, the Van Buren String Busters, and the Yodeling Trio. One of the Hickory Ranch Boys, Maurice Duckett, later recalled the music of most of these groups as a mixture of whatever was popular on the Grand Ole Opry and local square-dance instrumentals.

Roy "Scrub-Board" Wallace boosted the Sunday shows with laudatory notes he wrote to the *Jamboree,* a pamphlet-size Indiana fanzine that debuted in early 1940. Len Trissel published the *Jamboree* to support the efforts of hillbilly musicians and songwriters. A constant rationale for the little magazine was Trissel's folksy promotion of his newly founded American Composers and Entertainers Society, always abbreviated in the *Jamboree* as "ACES." The ACES intended to help amateur musicians present a united economic front, the better to resist the "song sharks" and "parasites of tinpanalley [*sic*]" who in Trissel's view were "racketeering their nefarious products among the jitterbugs and jukes." In the *Jamboree,* Wallace described the early Brown County Jamboree:

> The show, to date, consists of Nancy Lou and Her Cowgirl Band, a nice swell group of juvenile entertainers and one of the best that I have ever had the pleasure of working with on any bill. Then there is Bill Ritter and the Brown County Girls, featuring Sambo, the blackface comic, who can really hold his own and has a neat finale with a pair of bones. The Hickory Ranch Boys, sons of our manager, Riley Duckett, three very promising musicians that are really selling their act. The Four Leaf Clover Boys and their swing rhythm songs and gags, featuring Arizona Eddy, the mandolin player, with his fast, fancy rope spinning act.
>
> Margie and Dot, our singing cowgirls, always make a hit, and they have just composed a new song, "Cowboy Dream Girl," that has a wollop [*sic*] to it in a nice blended harmony. The Van Buren String Busters, two girls and a boy, fast workers, but sorry to say, with all their hot style and arrangements, yours truly has got the first time to see them live up to their name by busting their strings. Then there is Left-Hand Fiddlin' Rufus and his hot and sweet style, gives

you a real treat. Also we have George Scott and that wise-cracking, wooden-headed dummy of his. Why, only last night that dummy jumped up and down on George's knee, clapped his hands, paged the m.c., and said "Hey, Guy, you sure got a nice clean show around here, don't you?" Guy replied: "Well, we make it a policy to have a show as good for the kiddies as for the grown-ups." And the dummy then said, "That's exactly what I thot [*sic*], 'cause I see you still have that fellow way over yonder, hanging around with his washboards."

Wallace also described his own unique act:

Prof. "Scrub-board" Roy Wallace of Beanblossom, Ind., is now being featured on the Sunday night show now under canvas and just completed their 40th performance to a paid audience of 3200. . . . The show lasts for four hours, and is tops in Hillbilly entertainment. . . . Mr. Wallace is a tap-drummer and comedy man, also playing several different types of washboard set-ups. He has a complete style of his own while working a gag or monologue. He passes a string through his nose bringing it out the other nostril, causing a great burst of laughter. He also goes collegiate and gulps down several gold fish from a fish bowl, while working a drunk cowpoke routine, spins a rope, does a paper tear-ing trick, in fact, a very unusual magic routine while working a strict Hillbilly set-up, finishing up playing a Hot Style Washboard.[7]

Riveted by such entertainments, big crowds kept coming. Rund confirmed his dominance over the Jamboree that fall with the huge rented tent on his own property, surrounded by his open fields for parking cars.

Only one photograph of the Jamboree tent has turned up, taken a day after the grand opening by Frank M. Hohenberger, an esteemed professional Brown County photographer.[8] Hohenberger's photo offers a compelling, though strangely uninhabited, view of Rund's first Brown County Jamboree.

The tent extended roughly southwest to northeast, just east of Highway 135, unmissable by travelers. Jack McDonald recalled the first Jamboree setting: "To begin with a large circus-type tent was erected in the middle of the field. This time a large farm wagon was pulled into the tent and was used for the stage. Folding chairs were used for seating and also heavy boards were set atop rows of cement blocks for spectators and fans to sit on. A fee was charged for adults to get in and some children were admitted free with adults. On hot summer nights and evenings the side curtains of the tent were raised so air could help cool the performers and their fans."

In 1965, emcee Silver Spur reminisced passionately about the tent, exaggerat-ing its impressive capacity:

The first broadcast was carried from the big top tent, which was erected in 1940 and '41. The largest tent that's ever been in Brown County was placed right outside the barn here! The lumber for that tent was secured from the Art West Lumber Company of Helmsburg, Indiana. There were more seats—we had 3,300 paid admissions, average 3,000—besides the children that we raised the sidewall up and let 'em get in for nothing—were in the tent every Sunday evening. Neighbors, we didn't have no juvenile delinquency back then. That was the good old days! Along in later years, the Brown County Jamboree first appeared, so it was started on the open-air platform, the fine boys the Cook Brothers came along, put a big-top tent out in the garden, and it—ever' time the rain come, it leaked. . . . We operated under that for two years, and then later on we went back to the open-air platform. And then when 10,000 people appeared in 1940, in the town of Bean Blossom, 1939, there's so many cars that we couldn't park anywhere. They estimated a crowd of over 10,000 people. . . . It was moved to this present location, which now is the original home of the Brown County Jamboree where Francis Rund put the biggest-top tent that was ever in Brown County. . . . It was put out here, it was 198 feet long, and a hundred—uh, ninety-five feet wide. Everybody coming down the highway stopped to see that big tent. You could ride a horse in it at full speed![9]

For the Brown County Jamboree, links to the radio broadcast industry proved tenuous, and the relationship inconstant, unlike venues such as Renfro Valley, which was a radio show even before it became a music park. There was never a lasting radio home for the Brown County Jamboree, only a sporadic radio presence and a limited radio footprint. After the initial WIRE broadcast, many other stations broadcast the Jamboree for brief periods, principally WIRE's competitors, WIBC and WFBM, but also Bloomington's WSUA and Columbus's WCSI. The Jamboree's wobbly trajectory of commercial success, especially after World War II, resulted in part from its patchy media presence.

But radio brought a young Brown County native named Marvin Hedrick (1925–72) to the first tent show. In 1941 Hedrick was a bright, sensitive sixteen-year-old, who drove to the show in a 1936 Chevy along with his first cousin and pals from southern Brown County.[10] Young Hedrick played guitar and four-string tenor guitar, and he was obsessed with the hillbilly music he heard on the radio from his earliest years. Radio technology had ended the isolation of remote Brown County farm life and opened up Marvin Hedrick's life.

The Hedricks' Brown County farm was isolated, a self-contained, limited, unchanging world. But Marvin was, in the words of his son Gary, "a dreamer, a visionary, a complicated man, with intellectual curiosity," and a boy who "grew up on the farm but always had his nose in a book."[11] Marvin escaped a restrictive farm life through books and the miracle of radio. By his teenage years, Marvin had built his own first radios, setting up a huge antenna that let him tune in AM country music from distant locales. He installed car radios for others, tinkered with electric projects, and slowly rejected the idea of farming as his own future. Hedrick became a key participant of local musical networks, and many others named in this history, including Silver Spurs Ragsdale, Bill Monroe, Neil Rosenberg, Jerry Garcia, and Ralph Rinzler, knew him well.

Though Hedrick's family and neighbors listened to the Grand Ole Opry, Marvin exceeded them, immersing himself completely in distant sounds, from Chicago's WLS; Nashville's WSM; Wheeling, West Virginia's WWVA; and Richmond, Virginia's WRVA. He played guitar from his teenage years and carried his love of country music and that instrument ever after. Fainting spells left him medically exempt from military service, so during World War II he took radio and electronics courses at Chicago's DeForest Radio School. After the war, he married, settled in Nashville, and opened up a radio and television repair shop just east of town. He also resumed playing guitar and attending the Brown County Jamboree.

The 1941 Jamboree that Hedrick viewed must have been impressive, with emcee Guy Smith dressed in his satin cowboy shirt and huge western hat, along with forty-plus similarly costumed singers, fiddlers, and guitarists. Over the next months, Jamboree tent shows presented the same cast, including Smith, the teenage Duckett Brothers, Scrub-Board Wallace, and young ventriloquist George Scott. Also appearing were Chic and Ann Hacker, who sang western duets; Chic reputedly helped manage the shows for a short time, too.[12]

Although most original Jamboree acts, like the Van Buren String Busters, were local, the Jamboree rapidly initiated performances by radio artists from nearby cities, starting with Indianapolis. WIRE radio did not have a large roster of hillbilly stars, but competing station WIBC did, and WIBC performers like Lonesome Bill Jones and the Campbell Sisters soon became regular cast members.

The list of original Jamboree artists reflects the varied approaches to hillbilly entertainment that dominated in 1941. The show emphasized variety, with vestiges of minstrel comedy represented by "Little June," "Sambo" ("the Laugh of all black face comedians!"), and "Stuttering Jimmie." Brother acts like the Brock Brothers, the Houchins Brothers, and Jack and Alva Cox (the Hillclimbers) were prominent, as were sister acts such as the Campbell Sisters, the Day Sisters, Margie and Dot, and the Brown County Sweethearts. String-band traditions were represented by the Brown County Fiddlers, Left-Handed Fiddling Rufus and His String Band, the Morgantown String Band, the rousing banjo and fiddle duo of Tennessee Red and Kentucky Slim, and the Van Buren String Busters. Cowboy and western themes pervaded the early Jamboree handbills, presented by the Nancy Lou Cowgirl Band, the Starlight Rangers, the Hickory Ranch Boys, and the Yodeling Trio. Local pride was evidenced by groups named the Nashville Ramblers, Hoosier Rangers, Hoosier Tigers, and Hoosier Vagabonds.

Musicians from Brown County were always part of the show. For example, the Houchins brothers, Joe and Roy, were Brown Countians who sidelined in Guy Smith's Hoosier Farm Hands, later playing Jamboree shows in 1941 as the Brown County Buckaroos. Mandolin-playing Jack Cox (1925–2003) of Bean Blossom played in the tent several times in late 1941.[13] He and his guitar-playing brother, Alva, performed often at the Jamboree as the Hillclimbers, and their audiences always included family members and local neighbors. Jack was such a regular at the Brown County Jamboree that when he proposed to his wife, Jean, in 1943, she agreed to his idea that they be married there: "Me and my wife got married here, down in that little red house—cabin down here. And Lulu Belle and Scotty shivareed us. Well, this Irvin Weddle that worked for Francis Rund, had an old car. And there was an old manure-spreader used to set out here. So after the show one Sunday—Lulu Belle and Scotty was on the show, incidentally—they got it in their head that we had to be shivareed. So they put us on the seat of the old manure-spreader and Irvin had an old '32 Oldsmobile coupe, and he hooked onto it and pulled us around. And once in a while the old thing would engage, and it had beaters here on the back—-Sparks'd just fly!"[14]

No recordings of Jamboree shows from the 1940s are known to exist, but early participants recall covering popular hillbilly songs of the period, like "You Are My Sunshine," "Maple on the Hill," or "Life Is Like a Mountain Railroad." Fiddlers and instrumentalists drew also on common repertoires of square-dance, play-party, and fiddle tunes found in southern Indiana and much of the southeastern United States at that time: "Ragtime Annie," "Sally Goodin'," "Turkey in the Straw," "Liberty," and "Soldier's Joy." To such traditional repertoires the Jamboree performers added original songs and comedy skits. Scrub-Board Wallace mailed outlines and one-liners to Guy Smith, urging him to come up with new comic skits and song introductions. Brown County Jamboree shows were professional, fast paced, and entertaining. From the beginning, the music, comedy, and ambience of the site combined to present a nostalgic and entertaining whole.

Following the grand opening, capacity crowds returned every Sunday evening. But attendance diminished in early November with the onset of chilly weather. Moreover, the tents had been rented for only six weeks. Through late fall, WIBC sporadically broadcast the Jamboree from its studio. Breaking the pattern of

Sunday performances, most of these 1941 radio shows were on Saturday from 7:00 to 8:00 p.m.

By December, Smith and Williams arranged a winter home for the Jamboree at the nearby Martinsville High School. For the next thirteen weeks, the familiar fast-paced show continued there. A sample handbill listed twelve main acts and "many others," and advertised tickets at twenty-five cents for adults and ten cents for children, with sponsorship by the Martinsville VFW post. Free admission was offered to "ladies and girls" who brought pies or box suppers to be raffled off to the highest bidder. There were prizes for the prettiest girl (determined by the audience placing penny bids) and for the ugliest man. The handbill noted that other stunts would be pulled off as part of the show and that the evening's entertainment would culminate in a "round and old fashioned dance."[15] That winter, the Jamboree came to high school gymnasiums in New Marion, Shelbyville, Trafalgar, Whiteland, and other nearby towns. Ticket prices were typically between nine and fifteen cents for children and twenty-eight and thirty cents for adults.

The Jamboree operated under two different names in its first year. Dan Williams originally promoted the free show at his lunchroom as the "Brown County Jamboree." But when Guy Smith and Riley Duckett went on the road over the winter of 1941–42, they promoted the "Bean Blossom Jamboree." While details are scant, a column by Roy Wallace suggests an underlying controversy: "There has been a little dispute as to whether or not the show will return to the name of the Brown County Jamboree, as Dan Williams, the man who walked out on a nice show, without paying off, claims he has a copyright for the name of 'Brown County Jamboree,' and I am checking up on same to see if he has the name copyrighted or patented. If same is true, then another name will be adopted for the show."[16] When and why Williams "walked out on a nice show, without paying off," remains a mystery. But Guy Smith and Riley Duckett planned shows together through the winter months of 1941–42, and their advertising fliers cited the "Beanblossom Jamboree," in contrast to Williams and Rund's "Brown County Jamboree" usage.

*Both* Jamboree names appeared in lyrics on sheet music for the Jamboree's first theme song, composed in January 1942 by Roy Wallace and musician Pearl Clark. "The Brown County [Bean Blossom] Jamboree" established a light-hearted mood:

> How-de-do, we're the crew,
> Of the Brown County [Bean Blossom] Jamboree
> We'll put old gloom on the run

How-de-do, you and you,
At the Brown County [Bean Blossom] Jamboree

We hope you'll join in our fun
With our old-fashioned tunes
We will make the rafters ring
Let it snow, let it blow, carefree are we
How-de-do, there's our cue,
Call the Emcee and the crew
Of the Brown County [Bean Blossom] Jamboree.

[closing theme]
Goodbye Jack, Goodbye Joe,
It is time for us to go,
We will leave you with our theme song melody,
Thanks to you, from the crew,
Now a fond goodnight to you,
And the Brown County [Bean Blossom] Jamboree![17]

The show prospered through the winter. Smith and Williams reconciled suf-
ficiently to put on a party for the Jamboree cast at the Helmsburg Skating Rink
in February 1942. The cast by this time had added Bill Ritter's Brown County
Girls and also Mildred and Merlene, "the sweethearts of Brown County."

The Jamboree's success seemed ensured in its formative months, but there
were nonetheless tensions, reflecting the fundamental opposition between music
viewed as economically rewarding work and music viewed as neighborly play. In
early December, for example, when the cast assembled at the Martinsville High
School for a show, WIBC staff insisted that only union musicians perform on the
broadcast portion of the show. The broadcast Jamboree therefore featured new
entertainers. The Key Sisters and Doc Conover were "brought in" from Illinois,
and several string musicians performed under multiple group names during the
show, conveying the impression of a larger cast. Emcee duties were shared with
WIBC's new announcer, Bill Hadley, a friend of John Lair's who had been previously involved with Lair's Renfro Valley show. Amateur nonunion members
of the original Jamboree cast, mostly teenagers, were relegated to playing only
on the portion of the show that followed the actual broadcast, creating friction
between the newcomers and those who had been involved for the previous seven
months or more. These intertwined workplace issues—union versus nonunion,
newcomers versus established cast members, amateurs versus professionals—
likely informed Dan Williams's abandonment of the show and prompted Roy
Wallace to take a break as well.[18]

Despite the value of the Brown County Jamboree as a place to play, local musicians were not uniformly happy with its management. A chronic complaint was the piddling amount of money paid to local bands; another was the pressure to join the musicians' union. The Van Buren String Busters, who had helped inaugurate the "free show" by the side of Highway 135, played the tent several times for Francis Rund but stopped by mid-1942. Adolph "Doc" Beauchamp explained, "[He] paid us $1 to play there . . . When he told us we had to join the musician's union, we quit."[19]

Stage-clothing choices at the Brown County Jamboree consistently drew on two main tropes of country music representation: the cowboy/western and the hillbilly/old-time. Like Silver Spurs Ragsdale, most Jamboree performers played as cowboys and cowgirls. The positive status of the cowboy and cowgirl image in parts of the country far removed from the "authentic Old West" is well known, if not adequately explained by the legendary popularity of western movies among the generation that came to maturity in the 1930s and '40s. Why performers from southern Indiana, culturally tied to earlier generations of Kentuckians and immigrant Scots and German settlers, chose to present themselves as singing cowboys is a perplexing question. Undoubtedly, many loved the image of the cowboy, long viewed as the folk avatar of a respectable kind of freedom from "the pressures of home, family, or urban civilization."[20] It surely would have been *easier* for musicians in Brown County to perform as hillbillies. Though not as flamboyant or fanciful as the western theme, hillbilly costuming was easy to find. In Brown County, where the "Old Brown County Settlers" had been holding annual festivals since 1876 and the isolated rural past was still vividly familiar in the 1940s, exaggerated old-time rural costuming would have been more reasonable for the Jamboree cast members than cowboy hats, fringed vests, embroidered fancy satin shirts, and boots. Yet western imagery dominated the early Jamboree, as it did "country and western" music as a whole. The social upheavals occasioned by the Great Depression and World War II reshaped the imaginations of would-be performers and musicians, signaling increased acceptance of cowboys as American cultural heroes and the derivative idea of the cowboy-western performer as a living incarnation of the ideal, a sort of singing "noble savage."

The greatest local impact of the war resulted from the construction in early 1942 of Camp Atterbury, in the county's northeast corner. The forty thousand–acre military base was created from the northeastern corner of Brown County and the southeastern corner of Johnson County and a much larger tract in western Bartholomew County, northwest of Columbus. Camp Atterbury displaced nearly six hundred farm families and was built in just six months of frenzied work to provide for the training of up to thirty thousand soldiers.[21]

Right from the start, soldiers hungry for weekend entertainment found their way to Sunday Jamboree shows, hitchhiking when necessary. A new business, the Indiana Scenic Bus Line, began in October 1942 to run buses daily from Nashville to Indianapolis and back, with stops at Bean Blossom, Morgantown, Trafalgar, and Bargersville. A Sunday "Jamboree Special" bus offered shuttle service linking Bean Blossom and Camp Atterbury for soldiers desiring to attend Jamboree shows. Many did, for the base brought in trainees from all over the South and Southeast, and hundreds of southern soldiers in training brought a preexisting taste for hillbilly and country music that could best be satisfied at the Brown County Jamboree.

After Pearl Harbor, the war's effects became quickly evident. The rapid mobilization in 1942 shattered many bands, including the Duckett Brothers, as individual members enlisted or were drafted. New soldiers dispersed to military training camps across the country, and wartime migrations initiated an unprecedented period in which long-standing regional social traditions endured new cultural juxtapositions. Millions of men, suddenly taken far from home for their training, brought their own traditional tastes for diversion. Local USO clubs and dance halls or social venues like the Brown County Jamboree were inevitably provincial in character, and the influence of local or regional culture was felt most strongly in the areas that were most remote or inaccessible.

Around May or June 1942, Guy Smith stopped being involved with the Brown County Jamboree; he began instead to help build Camp Atterbury. The show permanently resumed its original "Brown County Jamboree" designation, and for a short time was held again at Dan Williams's Bean Blossom Lunchroom. Williams advertised in 1942 that the show was under new management, and he dropped the admission charges in order to again promote the "free show" concept. These short-term changes were likely due to Smith's leaving the Jamboree and probably related to the principals' contention for control of the successful show's profits. Additionally, the return to the lunchroom may have resulted from the arrival of spring and the fact that the big tent was no longer on Rund's land. Even a free show, after all, sometimes needs a sheltered venue, and bringing free shows back to the restaurant drew audiences to whom Williams could sell sandwiches, hot dogs, short orders, ice cream, and soft drinks. Yet by midsummer, the Jamboree returned to Rund's.

With many Brown County boys in military service, more Jamboree acts in 1942 were fronted by young women. Female Jamboree artists came from Brown

County and the ring of surrounding counties: Morgan, Monroe, Johnson, Bartholomew, and Jackson. Fern and Carol Logston debuted at the Brown County Jamboree around 1942, and local singers Anna Goud and her friends the Doyle sisters—Juanita and Nettie—joined the regular cast of the show, working closely with manager Kenneth Rund. The Doyle Sisters became mainstays of the mid-1940s Jamboree. At some point Juanita Doyle caught the eye of a Camp Atterbury trainee: fiddle-playing Oscar Van Shehan, whom she married in 1947.

"Shorty" Shehan was born in Erwin, Tennessee, in 1923.[22] A brilliantly talented fiddler, he was also proficient on bass and guitar. He started performing professionally in his midteens and worked intermittently for years at the Renfro Valley Barn Dance. Shorty often spoke later of John Lair's encyclopedic knowledge of folk and country music.[23] Shehan was a "trick fiddler," meaning that he could play hot fiddle tunes like "Back Up and Push" or "Orange Blossom Special" and could also play "Pop Goes the Weasel" or similar tunes with the fiddle moving through a dozen different positions: behind his back, between his legs, or holding the bow between his knees and rubbing the fiddle strings on the bow. In early 1942, Shorty joined a fluid East Tennessee group that included his friend banjoist Manuel "Speedy" Clark, who later became Renfro Valley's "Old Joe Clark."[24] To maximize bookings, the group comprised two named bands, the Moonlight Drifters and the Tennessee Pals. Shorty usually played fiddle leads with the Tennessee Pals, backed by a guitar and resonator guitar. Both bands traveled the region, playing baseball fields in coal-mining parts of southwestern Virginia. Both groups also enjoyed a radio base for a time in 1942, with a regular spot on the *Barrel of Fun* radio show on Johnson City, Tennessee's WJHL. Later in 1942, Shorty formed another group with friends; Jim Sizemore, Ray Atkins, Shug Mulkey, Speedy Clark, and Shorty called this venture the Lonesome Pine Boys.

But Shorty was soon drafted and sent for army training to Camp Atterbury. The precise date when Shehan first rode the Jamboree Special bus to the Brown County Jamboree is unknown, but by 1943 he was a regular Jamboree fan and occasional performer whose skill at flamboyant "southern-style" fiddling was evident.

Another early liaison between Renfro Valley and the Brown County Jamboree was fiddler Linda Lou Martin, a Virginian raised in Indianapolis. Martin complemented her grade school violin training with country fiddling in the styles of her musical heroes, Curly Fox and Fiddlin' Arthur Smith. Entering a contest at the Indianapolis Marat Temple, she tied for first place with professional performer Natchee the Indian, earning an appearance on the WIBC *Jamboree* and subsequent billings as "champion fiddler Linda Lou" at Renfro Valley, where she also doubled on steel guitar. After meeting John Lair in 1941, she went at his behest to perform in Atlanta but soon returned to Renfro Valley. There she met and married the famous one-armed banjoist Emory Martin.

Lair repeatedly sent Linda Lou, Emory Martin, and other Renfro Valley acts to Bean Blossom in the 1940s.[25] Over the next decade, more than twenty artists or groups affiliated with Renfro Valley and John Lair played on forty or more Brown County Jamboree shows. During the Rund years, the Renfro Valley roster included the Blue Mountain Girls, the Burns and Britton Comedy Act, Claude Sweet, the Coon Creek Girls, Emory Martin, Harmonica Bill, Homer "Slim" Miller, Uncle Juney, the Kentucky Corncrackers, Linda Lou, Rural Thomas and the 76 Quartette, Shorty Shehan, Red Foley, and Illinois sisters Millie and Dollie Good, well known as the Girls of the Golden West. The wartime Brown County Jamboree featured many acts sent by Lair, billing them always as "the Renfro Valley Barn Dance Cast."

Lair's Renfro Valley show, even from its inception, included many female performers. World War II enlistments altered the gender demographics of Brown County musicians, but there were always local female entertainers. However, little beyond their gender is known of early Jamboree acts like Leora & Marie (the Rangerettes), the Melody Ranch Girls, and Mildred and Merlene. Confusingly, local acts might adopt famous names, as in the summer of 1942, when there were several shows by a local female group called the Girls of the Golden West—*not* the Good sisters but rather an imitative local duo, "Vera and Marie." Their actual identities notwithstanding, one group of Girls of the Golden West made a lasting impression on Guy Smith's daughter, Guylia Lucille Smith, who vividly recalled them: "Now I'm not sure who they were, but I remember this one gal, she always had the shiny purple, like satin, shirt. And she sang 'Wabash Cannonball.' . . . She had lots of makeup on, and I just thought she was the most glamorous-looking person I'd ever seen in my life!"[26]

Despite a wartime spike in female artists, August 1942 brought the first of many shows by Ace Bailey and His Utah Trailers, all young Indianapolis men led by brothers Leroy "Ace" and Richard Bailey. They used evocative western stage names: Ace appeared onstage as Utah Slim; Richard, with a tenor banjo, was Banjo Dick; and the rest included Wanda "Little Lou" Arnold, Harry "Shorty" Waterbury, and Roy "Scrub-Board" Wallace. Given his promotional energy, it's likely that Wallace helped bring the Utah Trailers into the Brown County Jamboree circle.

By late August 1942, tent-based Jamboree shows resumed on the Rund property, and the local paper noted that the shows were as successful as ever:

The lid was blown off the most gala event of the season Sunday evening at the Brown County Jamboree when they featured Ace Bailey and His Utah Trailers and the Down Easters of WIBC Indianapolis opened its program before the biggest audience of the season. The Jamboree, managed by Cook Bros. of Martinsville, not only attracts hundreds of visitors to Bean Blossom but is also making rapid progress as a traveling show. In addition to the regular Sunday night performances, the entire troupe has made matinee and evening performances each week in Greenwood, Mooresville and Paragon. Veteran local entertainers include the master of ceremonies, Spurts Ragsdale, the Melody Ranch Girls, Yodelin' Joe from Mexico, Chic and Little Ann, the Hawaiian Buckaroos and many others.[27]

## The "Old Barn"

Within a month of the grand-opening show, the principals began thinking of a permanent building. A Nashville architect, William Exner, envisioned a ten thousand–square-foot structure to be built on Rund's land, to seat three thousand fans. The plans were detailed:

> The auditorium will be 80 feet wide and 124 feet long. It is to be of all native wood construction with the main span 40 feet wide with twenty-foot sheds on both sides. Walls of the center section will be 16 feet high. The front is to have three six-foot doors and each side will have four doors of the same size allowing a capacity crowd to gain an exit from the building in less than ten minutes.
>
> At a later time according to Mr. Exner a 16 by 40 foot stage is to be added with large dressing rooms on either side. Eighty-four hinged windows of barn sash type are to be placed all around for ventilation.
>
> Government approval is now being sought to begin the structure. Present plans are to side the building with native lumber and tar paper covering the walls later with slab wood for a rustic effect.
>
> The Jamboree given each Sunday night has attracted large crowds from far and near with cars from sixteen different states bringing customers last Sunday night.
>
> The management of Radio Station WIRE have shown an interest in the development of the jamboree with references being made to it in its programs many times. While it has not been officially announced it is expected that later the programs at the Jamboree will be heard over this Indianapolis station.[28]

Though Exner's specific plans were never realized, Rund knew that a permanent building was essential. So in 1942 Rund bought the partial remains of an old barn, purchased additional materials from a Helmsburg lumber company, and began to build a venue for Jamboree shows. The building loosely resembled Exner's vision, since it ended up being 44 feet wide and 140 feet long.[29] The structure was longer and lower than most farm barns in southern Indiana but was called "the barn" or "the big barn" from its earliest days and—perhaps because much of the structure had been rebuilt from used materials—quickly became qualified conversationally as the "old barn."

The barn was painted white at first. Though not sheathed in wavy-edged slab wood, it still evoked the "rustic effect" planned by Exner, congruent with the deliberate rusticity characterizing Brown County architecture. The barn's roofline ran almost parallel to the north-south line of Highway 135. A ventilating cupola and crisp signs on the roof's peak proclaimed "The Brown County Jamboree." Just to the southeast was a concrete-block restroom building, where porcelain toilet fixtures could actually be flushed, if water was first pumped up from the five-acre lake. A fence running beneath an east-west hedgerow separated the barn and restroom from a farm field and small horse barn to the south.

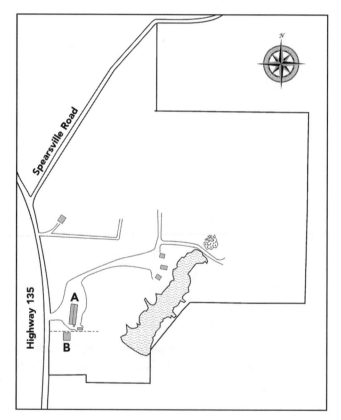

Francis Rund property, fall 1943.
A: Brown County Jamboree barn with concrete-block restroom.
B: Horse barn south of the fencerow.

The Jamboree barn was built over two years, mostly by local part-time farmer-carpenters and helpers not otherwise involved with the war effort. Rund hired Wilbert Kegley, a part-time carpenter, to begin building the barn. In 1942, the southern third of the building was put up, with the rusticated stage and back-stage areas and a small gravel-floored audience area. The next year, the barn was extended northward to its full final dimensions. Kegley's small crew of helpers included his son Jack. Kegley was paid in cash for his work, but "not very much," recalled Jack Kegley, though the family got free Jamboree tickets for a couple of years.

The barn's long roofline on a north-south axis made its full impressive length and rooftop sign unmissable by drivers on Highway 135. Ample parking space was available in the open fields just north and east of the barn—sometimes Kenneth Rund helped park cars there from horseback—and the barn's sheltered audience entrance lay close to the parking lot, in the building's northern gable end.

Next to the double-door entrance was a glass-fronted booth where patrons bought tickets from Mae Rund. On entering, visitors saw the curtained stage at the distant southern end of the barn, at the far end of a center aisle of seats.[30] Side aisles resulted from two long rows of posts, about ten feet apart, supporting the one-and-a-half-story central section of the barn's roof. The side aisles, with additional seating, were lit by ten small windows and two propped-open barn-size doors in each of the long sides of the barn. Seven small "potbellied" iron woodstoves stood in the side aisles in various locations near the barn's long walls, where their flues penetrated the barn's outer skin of board-and-batten construction and vented into tall, narrow brick chimneys. The side aisles, which like the center aisle could accommodate folding chairs or other seating, were only one story high at the building's eaves.

In the tall central section, old wagon wheels hung horizontally from roof beams, supporting electric lights. In the barn's recycled framing, a variety of mortise slots and notches remained visible. The floor of the central section was one step lower than that of the two side aisles, particularly in the southern third of the barn's length, near the stage. Visitors had to step carefully from the gravel-and-cinder surface of the center aisle (later covered with concrete) to the smooth concrete foundations of the side aisles.

At the northwest corner of the building, near the ticket booth and main entrance, lay a small screened-in area that served as the barn's kitchen and concession stand. Centrally located at the back of the barn was a raised and inclined section of bleacher seats, permitting the last couple dozen members of a full house to see down the long rows of seats to the stage. Along the northernmost end of the barn

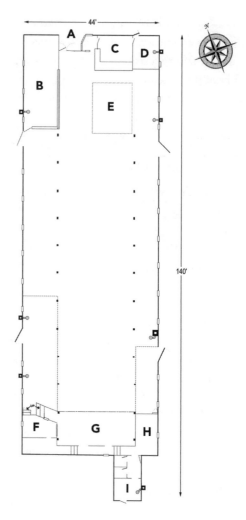

Scale plan of the Brown
County Jamboree barn.
A: Entrance. B: Concession
kitchen. C: Concession area
behind counter. D: Bedroom.
E: Bleachers. F: Control
room. G: Stage. H: Backstage
warm-up rooms. I: Performer
entrance and partitioned
changing areas.

was another vending area, for soft drinks and cigarettes, with a narrow counter
for selling souvenirs or programs. A small room in the northeastern corner of the
barn had its own door to the outside and its own potbellied stove. Used most often
in later years for general storage of signs and small items, the northeast-corner
chamber was a bedroom for at least one early manager or helper at the Jamboree
and was also said to have been used as a bedroom in the Monroe years as well.

Audiences at the front of the new barn sat in old wooden theater seats, with
seat numbers painted on the backs. Extra folding chairs were available in the side
aisles. Over years of use, more folding chairs eventually replaced the deteriorat-

ing theater seats, but the early Jamboree's numbered seats could be reserved for seventy-five cents to a dollar, depending on location. Many weekly attendees kept their reserved seats for more than one season at a time, and seats could be informally retained from week to week by regular patrons as well. Jack Cox and Sandy Rund, Francis's daughter-in-law, both described the reservation process:

> It was just as local as local could be. And everybody reserved seats. "A dollar? Well, I'm gonna give you a dollar. I'll be back next week. Save that seat for me."
>
> Mother did [sell tickets], Mae did that. And people would call at [Rund's grocery store at] Stones Crossing all week and make reservations, "I want seat so-and-so, and row so-and-so," and some people had the original seats. Every week, every Sunday, they had their regular seats. There was all—I can remember these people, they came every Sunday that I can ever remember being there. I can't think of it. Yeah, the front row, the first three rows was always booked, no one [else] could have 'em.[31]

The stage stood about two feet above the auditorium floor. It was built to suggest the porch of a small log house, with two doors opening onto the stage from the back, both sheltered beneath an overhanging pitched roof. The stage cabin's "front porch" roof was adorned with icons of bygone rural life: a mounted deer's head, a grain cradle, an old-style ladies' sidesaddle, and some kerosene lanterns. The front of the stage was rusticated, too, with uneven vertical puncheon slabs rising a few inches to conceal footlights and an old farm dinner bell hanging at the right end of the stage as seen by the audience. The dinner bell was rung frequently by emcee Silver Spur to encourage audience response after—or even during—performances. Some performers recalled Ragsdale's incessant use of the bell as "annoying." Jack Cox remembered, "Spurts would—no matter what was going on, [even a] religious number—he'd ring that bell. . . . He would ring that bell [even] if it's a religious number, a quiet number. So we took caps from cap pistols and lined the inside of it. He rang that, and it really got him! We put axle grease on the clapper, [and] we threatened to throw the clapper out of it in the ol' restrooms, toilets that used to be outside here."[32]

The stage occupied the central third of the barn's southern end. Left of the stage was a slab-sided blank wall that concealed a backstage warm-up room, used occasionally in the Rund years for a makeshift photography studio with painted canvas backdrops and later on by Jamboree artists as a "tune-up" room. Several small dressing rooms separated by flimsy neck-high partitions filled most of a tiny one-room entrance addition to the barn's southern end, with a covered backdoor entrance for performers.

A sign of Rund's hope for a radio liaison was the "control room" at the stage's right side, partly visible to the audience. The control room had no outside entrance, but featured large glass windows so technicians could see the stage and the audience. Behind the control room was another warm-up space, with handy access to the stage itself through one of the two stage doors.

World War II brought gas and rubber rationing. Rationing took effect locally in late 1942, but audiences never abandoned the Jamboree. Weekly attendees from inside the county sustained the show through the war and the following years; that pattern remained unchanged until late-1960s bluegrass festivals began to draw national and international fans. Wartime gas rationing fostered reliance on close-to-home entertainment, so for indigenous fans, the Jamboree remained a viable venue for amusement and diversion. Auto owners virtually never drove to the Jamboree alone—the trip always involved a car filled with family and friends. Even with rationing and higher prices, it was a bargain to take a car or truck full of people to the Jamboree for an afternoon and evening of varied entertainment. Jack McDonald lightheartedly observed that the main effect of rationing was to keep people from driving *away* from Bean Blossom.[33]

In late 1942, the Jamboree changed, despite settling into a regular routine. Some original artists, like twelve-year-old ventriloquist George Scott, left after the summer of 1942, but new ones arrived. In September, a large crowd saw a show with several performers affiliated first with WIBC or Lair's Renfro Valley Barn Dance: George Arthur, fiddle star Linda Lou, and the Blue Mountain Girls, Bernice Scott and Virginia Sutton, who played guitar and bass themselves and often performed on WIBC with George Arthur as the Blue Mountain Trio. Weekly shows resumed in the spring of 1943 with a mix of local and regional acts appearing in the half-built barn and on the WIBC airwaves but announced as taking place on "WBCJ" (that is, using the initial letters of *Brown County Jamboree*), noted in the newspaper as "a mythical identification."

Advertising for the Jamboree was sparse in 1943, perhaps because of the accelerating war effort. WIBC stars Ace Bailey and His Utah Trailers and Bill and Evalena continued their Jamboree appearances, and more acts seeking exposure on the successful Jamboree shows came along as well after Rund announced the "grand re-opening" in promotional ads for a July 4 show.

On September 26, 1943, a gala show was held for the "dedication of the new barn." Performers included fiddler Casey Clark's Lazy Ranch Boys and Judy Perkins; both were later featured on Indianapolis's WIBC, Cincinnati's WLW radio, television's *Midwestern Hayride* show, and even later Detroit's WXYZ and WJR Saturday-night radio shows, *The Lazy Ranch Boys Barn Dance.*

A memorable debut at the Brown County Jamboree came in October, just after the "new barn's" dedication. West Virginia–born James C. Dickens, with an impressive stage presence and a remarkably short stature, arrived at the Brown County Jamboree already known by the name he would use for the rest of his career: Little Jimmy Dickens. The twenty-three-year-old was already a major attraction, having served a radio apprenticeship in his home state before coming to WIBC. On Indianapolis radio, he worked shows alongside guitarist Hugh Cross, Byron Taggart, Bill and Evalena, and comedian Ray "Quarantine" Brown, self-billed as either "the handsomest man" or "the ugliest man" in radio. In October and November 1943, these popular entertainers played the Jamboree's barn; they drew large crowds, with the newspaper noting that Little Jimmy Dickens's second appearance, on Halloween night, attracted more than fourteen hundred people.[34]

Performances in 1944 brought together local acts, those associated with WIBC and those sent by John Lair from Renfro Valley. Advertisements in this period sometimes included a catchphrase associated with emcee Silver Spur Ragsdale: "on the beam." The motto seemed to reinforce the connection with radio: "The Brown County Jamboree Puts WIBC Stars on the Beam!"

Ragsdale used the phrase broadly; he often enjoined performers during shows to "get on the beam" and would note happily on exciting evenings that the show was really "on the beam!" The phrase came from postal and U.S. Army Air Force navigation in preradar days, when pilots of military planes were taught to stay "on the beam" between two radio beacons that continually broadcast the Morse-code letters *A* (dot-dash) and *N* (dash-dot) along perpendicular axes from an airport. When the pilot could hear both broadcasts simultaneously, and with equal strength, the signal merged into a steady tone, indicating that the plane was "on the beam," that is, lined up properly on a navigation route for landing in nighttime or poor weather conditions. By extension, a performance or performer who was "on the beam" was really *ready* for broadcast. Ragsdale's constant use of the phrase was a reminder to all that the Brown County Jamboree shows, even when they were not broadcast, were supposed to be worthy of a public offering on the radio.

Despite the convenience of the completed show barn, the Jamboree continued making special appearances on the road. A particularly meaningful show for Francis and Mae Rund, whose son Glen was then serving in Italy, was staged at Camp Atterbury on July 3, 1944. A few days later, the Runds put on a fish fry at the barn and around their cabins for the whole Jamboree cast, to celebrate a successful season: "'Spurts' Ragsdale, jovial master of ceremonies, kept everything 'on the beam' while Ray Selch, chief cook, served the entire Jamboree personnel and several other guests. A short business meeting was held, and the group discussed their last week's personal appearance at Camp Atterbury. Mr. Rund expressed his appreciation to all who had participated in the show for the soldiers, and as an afterthought added, 'I surely wish Glen could have been there.'"[35]

By late summer of 1944, the Sunday shows offered ever more prominent hillbilly stars. Notable was T. Texas Tyler, who appeared with Little Jimmy Dickens, entertaining the large crowd between shows as they rode their horses around the grounds.

That summer brought the first of many Jamboree appearances by WLS stars Lulu Belle and Scotty. Originally from North Carolina, both Lulu Belle (Myrtle Cooper) and "Skyland" Scotty Wiseman enjoyed separate successful performing careers on radio before joining the WLS's Chicago-based *National Barn Dance* in the early 1930s. They married and soon became known as the "Sweethearts of Country Music," singing romantic duets like "Have I Told You Lately That I Love You?" or "Remember Me" and varying their show with nostalgic, rollicking numbers like "Homecomin' Time in Happy Valley" and "Mountain Dew." The couple made themselves at home whenever they appeared in Brown County. They socialized often with the Rund family and other members of the cast and impressed Francis's daughter-in-law Sandy because they never "put on airs" with the local talent.

The same could not be said of another wartime *National Barn Dance* star, invited to Bean Blossom only once. "Smiley" Burnette, billed as the "hilarious co-star of Gene Autry and Roy Rogers," was really more of a comic sidekick. Burnette brought to the Jamboree his program of cowboy comedy, including "songs of the range, western instrumental music, and laugh provoking novelties." Though his September performance was a crowd pleaser, the Runds never forgot his blunt disdain for the barn's poorly appointed backstage area, which he deprecated as beneath his dignity as a major screen star.

Around 1944, Francis Rund began making the Jamboree grounds available for the annual "meets" of the Southern Indiana Fox Hunters' Association. Previous fox hunters' meets had been held at Nashville's baseball park, but once the barn was completed, the association was eager to use the Jamboree park for their thirty-third weeklong meet. Rund also staged Jamboree shows for fox hunters' entertainment, not just on Sunday night but also on Thursday, following the day's fox hunts, races, and bench shows.[36]

The Runds frequently rented out the park grounds and barn to Democratic or Republican political candidates for campaign rallies. Dozens of political events were held at the large barn over the next decades, no doubt because music shows, normally held only on Sundays, left the place available at most other times. Wisely,

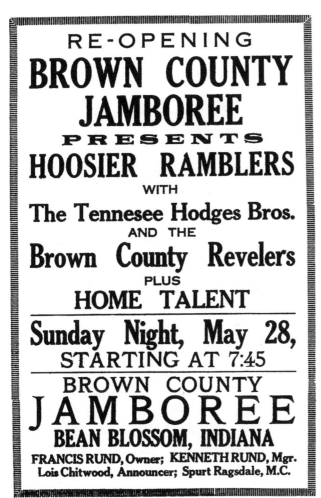

RE-OPENING

# BROWN COUNTY JAMBOREE

**PRESENTS**

## HOOSIER RAMBLERS

WITH

### The Tennesee Hodges Bros.

AND THE

## Brown County Revelers

PLUS

### HOME TALENT

### Sunday Night, May 28,
STARTING AT 7:45

BROWN COUNTY

# JAMBOREE

**BEAN BLOSSOM, INDIANA**

FRANCIS RUND, Owner; KENNETH RUND, Mgr.
Lois Chitwood, Announcer; Spurt Ragsdale, M.C.

Brown County Jamboree advertisement for the first show of 1944, in the *Brown County Democrat*, May 25, 1944. Throughout the Rund era, newspaper advertisements were generally run as large, carefully composed "display ads," even when the featured talent was mostly local.

most political candidates took advantage of available Jamboree talent, keeping their own orations short and staging free campaign shows with "radio entertainers and local talent," motion pictures, and free food.

Except for sporadic political rallies or fox hunts, the Runds' music park remained underused. Francis and Mae worked long weekday hours at their grocery in Stones Crossing. Rund occasionally offered his acreage for farming, offering partnership with anyone wanting to raise a crop of tomatoes "on shares." During the late 1940s, Kenneth Rund would ride his motorcycle from Stones Crossing to Bean Blossom to care for hogs that the Runds also kept on the grounds. On most Saturday nights, the Runds headed to Bean Blossom for a getaway. Spending the night at their cabin, they were then ready to supervise afternoon and evening Jamboree shows.

As time passed, the burden of operating the park as a secondary family business grew heavier, and Francis Rund sought outside help. In the summer of 1948, accordionist and bandleader Pee Wee King started to help operate the park. *Billboard* magazine observed, "Pee Wee King, Victor disk artist, whose 'Tennessee Waltz' is a top-rider in Southern jukes, has taken over as house band leader and director at the Sunday jamborees at Bean Blossom, Ind. Pee Wee reports that the Brown County Jamboree will utilize the King group as well as an outstanding array of guestars [*sic*]."[37]

King may have helped influence some other Opry acts to play the Brown County Jamboree, but despite the commanding title, "house band leader and director," he remained involved mostly as a featured performer. Emcee Silver Spur usually introduced King and his Golden West Cowboys and habitually asked if they would back him on a vocal number. One such instance led to a standing joke in the band. King's pedal-steel player, Roy Ayres, recalled it:

> [Silver Spur] was a really nice, congenial guy, but wasn't the world's best musician. He was a singer, and played rhythm guitar. Our band (The Golden West Cowboys) always backed him up when he sang on the show. I recall one time that he was planning to sing a song we hadn't heard before, and was telling us what the chord pattern was. After reciting the sequence of chords, he added, "And any time you're in doubt just go to G." That became a standard "inside" joke with the members of the band. Any time after that, when one of our guys would ask what chord was to be played at a given spot in a song, someone would yell out, "Any time you're in doubt, go to G!"[38]

WSM Grand Ole Opry stars like King played the Jamboree in the summer of 1948, including comedy acts like Lonzo and Oscar, Whitey Ford (the Duke of Paducah), and Uncle Dave Macon, as well as popular Opry musicians Curly Fox and Texas Ruby and their Fox Hunters. Stars from distant regional radio stations appeared, too, including Gene Autry's cousin Bob, then a regular on WPFB in Middletown, Ohio; the Campbell Quartet from Louisville; and from Findlay, Ohio's WFIN the Hoosier Corn Huskers, winners of a 1947 national hillbilly contest.

While 1948 Jamboree shows reprised some longtime Jamboree performers like Jack and Alva Cox, new acts also debuted. The Kentucky Boys were two brothers, Bob and Bub Thompson, originally from Cub Run, Kentucky, who had moved to Brown County in 1938. They attended the Jamboree nearly from its beginnings and finally started performing there with their cousin Geraldine

Coop and two other friends, brothers named Turner. The Kentucky Boys were a typical prebluegrass string band, playing familiar songs and tunes on fiddles, mandolin, banjo, and guitar.[39] The 1948 season also included the Sunrisers, the duo Art and Delores, and Miss Gene Campbell's All Girl Accordion Band. A new nearby group was the Kentuckiana Ridgerunners, with several key musicians from Columbus, Indiana: ace fiddler Pirtle Allman, his sons Bob and Dick Allman, and their friend Carlton Duncan, father of fiddler Glen Duncan.[40]

New performers constantly turned up locally, in part because they emerged from the ranks of longtime Jamboree fans and perhaps also because of the influence of visiting stars like Pee Wee King. For instance, a Brown County farm boy, Loren Parker, began as a fan but became an enduring cast member. Parker attended Jamboree shows intermittently during the tent-show days. While in high school, Parker often listened to Little Jimmy Dickens's noontime broadcasts on WIBC and attended every Dickens shows at the Jamboree. After learning guitar and playing some country music in Japan with a small band of fellow soldiers, he came home and found employment at the nearby Cummins diesel-engine plant in Columbus. There he met Bob Bartley, another musician, who impressed Parker with his nice "western-style" clothes. They began playing at weekly jam sessions and continued to attend Jamboree shows. They never missed seeing Pee Wee King, who like many other big Opry stars remained friendly and approachable when they were at Bean Blossom. In 1948, Parker broke his arm and attended one of Pee Wee King's shows in a cast; to his great delight, Pee Wee asked him two years later how his arm was doing!

In 1949, twenty-three-year-old Parker debuted as a Brown County Jamboree performer. He often sang duets with his wife, Maxine Montgomery, whom he had first heard sing on a Seymour, Indiana, radio station. Loren and Maxine befriended Shorty and Juanita Shehan and Jack Cox and another Jamboree musician named Tex Watson, and they played the Jamboree in various combinations that year.[41] Though Loren's Jamboree appearances slowed in the early 1950s, his friendships with other players endured, and he returned to the Jamboree stage in 1956 and 1957.

After World War II, Brown County continued to reflect in microcosm the accelerating pace of social changes occurring across the nation. Marvin Hedrick's newspaper ads began emphasizing the new technology of television, supplanting his prior emphasis on radio. The populations of troops in training at Camp Atterbury diminished, so the Indiana Scenic Bus Line ended the "Jamboree Special."

But interest in country and western music kept growing, even as new artists planted seeds of musical change. Hank Williams's late-forties radio hits "Move

It on Over," "Honky Tonkin'," and "Lovesick Blues" signaled the beginning of a new era and a new direction for country and western music. As late as 1950, Brown Countians still staged minstrel shows at the Nashville High School gymnasium, but the radio waves were increasingly filled with new sounds, including those of black artists who were transforming the older acoustic "race" and blues traditions of earlier years into electrically amplified rhythm and blues.

In April 1949, the Runds ran a classified ad seeking outside help to run the popcorn concession and usher Jamboree fans to their seats. They began to neglect advertising for the Jamboree shows themselves, running only a single 1949 print ad, and that for a nonmusical group, the Burns & Britton Comedy Act.

Just prior to the 1950 season, another Rund ad sought "4 girl ushers" to help for the entire summer. Shows were played in 1950 by Rural Thomas and the 76 Quartette, Pete Weaver and his Corn Huskers, and the familiar "Renfro Valley Barn Dance cast" who performed with the "Brown County Jamboree cast." The last show of 1950 was special. Roy Acuff and His Smoky Mountain Boys, who had played Bloomington's Harris-Grand Theater in 1949, came to Bean Blossom. Acuff traveled to Indianapolis in his own DC-3 airplane, *The Great Speckled Bird*, bringing along several other Opry acts for a rare *Monday*-night Brown County Jamboree show.

As if the Runds were somehow distracted, no articles or advertisements heralded the Jamboree's 1951 opening. Indeed, no ads appeared at all until the end of July, when the Jamboree suddenly announced shows by the Hoosier Sweethearts, the Martin Sisters, and the Monroe County Ramblers. All these groups had previously appeared on Bloomington's WTTV television, on Robert "Uncle Bob" Hardy's pioneering *Happy Valley Folks* show, which was widely viewed in south-central Indiana after its 1949 debut. Since WTTV's transmitting antenna was actually located at Trafalgar, the *Happy Valley Folks* show was viewable in Brown County and incredibly popular. When Bob Hardy left for another broadcast position, the *Happy Valley Folks* show was taken over by Freddy Helms, and later by Jack Noel. *Happy Valley Folks* continued successfully as a television show and a traveling musical act, even after Bob Hardy returned to WTTV and founded a competing country music television program, the *Hayloft Frolic Show*. Among Bob Hardy's friends were several musically talented residents of Monroe County, Indiana, including guitar wizard Joe Edwards and an eager young singer named Bobby Helms, Freddy's brother. Both would later go on to play 1950s-era shows, usually unadvertised, at the Brown County Jamboree. Edwards later moved to Nashville to develop his career as a studio musician and member of the Grand

Ole Opry house band. Bobby Helms went on to achieve national fame with his 1957 hit songs "Fraulein," "My Special Angel," and "Jingle Bell Rock."

The entire spectrum of American business was in flux by 1951. Both the burgeoning medium of television and conspicuous shifts in popular radio music foretold a new era. Sixty-one-year-old Francis Rund and his hardworking family had run the Jamboree for a decade or more; perhaps their energies were flagging, or maybe Kenneth and Glen Rund were increasingly focused on their own young families. Whatever direction Francis Rund's thoughts about the Brown County Jamboree took at that time, the perspective from more than a half century later shows that he was ready for a change, and profound changes lay just ahead.

# 4

# Bill Monroe's Brown County
# Jamboree Park, 1952–57

In April 1952, a tiny article on the front page of the *Brown County Democrat* announced:

JAMBOREE UNDER NEW MANAGEMENT

The famous Brown County Jamboree at Bean Blossom has new owners. Mr. and Mrs. Francis Rund, founders and owners for 13 years, have sold the Jamboree Hall to the Grand Ole Opry entertainer, Bill Monroe, of Nashville, Tennessee.

The Rund family started their Jamboree in a tent in the Fall of 1939, and built the permanent hall in 1943. The show operates every Sunday night from the first Sunday in May until the first Sunday in November.[1]

When did Monroe actually buy the park? Though answers in oral tradition range widely, the newspaper corroborates Monroe's functional acquisition of the Jamboree in the spring of 1952. The actual deal to buy Rund's Brown County Jamboree, reached in the last days of 1951, was such a watershed event in the history of bluegrass music that most bluegrass artists and fans—even those who befriended Monroe in the early 1950s, like Sonny Osborne—came to the park with the assumption that it had no significant history prior to Monroe. Sonny put it simply: "Was there *anything* there before Monroe?"[2]

Monroe's first documented performance came surprisingly late in Jamboree history, on October 21, 1951, near the end of that season.[3] Former Blue Grass Boy Jimmy Martin avowed that Bill played there "many times" before buying the park. Jimmy said Rund was eager to sell to Monroe and claimed Rund had even lowered his original price to facilitate the deal. Could Monroe have played

the Brown County Jamboree before October 1951, without advertisements, stories, or comments appearing in the county paper? Perhaps Bill Monroe never
played the park earlier because he had just never made the connection with the
Runds before, or they with him. Sandy Rund speculated that during the Rund
era, Monroe might have been, like Eddy Arnold, too big and expensive a star for
a small venue like the Jamboree.[4] But Bill had been in central Indiana just a year
before, playing a Labor Day show at Shady Acres Ranch, the music park created
in 1946 by former WLS musician Curley Myers near Mulberry, Indiana.

Birch Monroe—Bill's oldest brother and former musical partner—recalled
that Bill's first visit to the Jamboree gave the Opry star an immediate and positive impression of the place.[5] Bill quickly began discussing a possible purchase
with Rund and concluded a verbal agreement to purchase the property under a
land-contract arrangement.[6] The contract called for monthly payments to Rund
and was evidently signed between Christmas and New Year's Eve in 1951.[7] As
conclusively as can now be said, therefore: Monroe bought the property in late
1951 and began to operate it with the 1952 season. But *why* did Bill Monroe buy
the Brown County Jamboree?

Birch's memory of a "positive impression" was echoed in later stories about
Monroe's successful first Bean Blossom appearance. Glen Duncan, a Blue Grass
Boy in the mid-1980s, explained Monroe's purchase decision this way:

> He went up there and played, and had a huge crowd, and thought, "Oh, boy! I
> have got it! This is great!" And when I was with him, he still had this in him. We'd
> go play a place one day, and have a huge crowd, and he already started talking
> about wanting to come back: "Now, next year, we need to play two days." That
> was still his thinking, left over from the forties, and it wasn't right in the forties.
> Actually, you need to keep your supply a little more limited, but he didn't think
> that way. He still was from the—"Hey, there's a lot of people willing to pay." So
> he bought the place and, as it's been told to me by the locals, never ever had
> that kind of crowd again![8]

Monroe's motivations may have included Roy Acuff's 1948 purchase of Dunbar
Cave, a music-park attraction with a lake and motel, near Clarksville, Tennessee.
Acuff used Dunbar Cave as a home base for his band, who both performed there
and also "helped with any kind of chore, from painting equipment to feeding
Roy's prize collection of fancy fowl." Reflecting on Bill's purchase of the Bean
Blossom property, his friend Hazel Smith agreed: "He probably did it because
they [Acuff and his band] did it, don't you imagine? You know, they always si-
lently competed with each other."[9]

Another likely factor in Monroe's decision was his emotional reaction to the park's topography and landscape. Like others close to Monroe, Glen Duncan felt that Rund's land and the Brown County hills resonated with the formative landscape of Monroe's childhood: "If you think about it, Rosine and all—Brown County's more rocky and hilly, but around where Bean Blossom is, you know, you got those big rolling hills and stuff, and it probably did something that made him think more of when he was a kid, or something. 'Cause he was that way. He would have liked things that made him think of when he was a kid. That would have appealed to him."[10]

Monroe's decision to buy the Jamboree was also encouraged by key local individuals. Three men top the list of facilitators: emcee and soundman "Silver Spur" Ragsdale, fiddler Oscar "Shorty" Shehan, and local businessman-entrepreneur and square-dance music fan Carl Brummett.

Charlie Cline, who was one of Monroe's prominent multi-instrumentalist Blue Grass Boys in the early 1950s, stated unequivocally that Silver Spur Ragsdale "got Bill to buy the park." Monroe would certainly have made Silver Spur's acquaintance at the barn when he played his first show there, and Ragsdale would have known if Francis Rund wanted to sell the Brown County Jamboree. But fiddler Shorty Shehan also would have known that, and he was a key figure in the sale because he evidently hoped to become a partner with Monroe in purchasing the park.[11]

The date of Bill's first meeting with Shorty Shehan is unknown, but when guitarist South Salyers replaced Carter Stanley in September 1951, Shorty was already in the band.[12] On the October 21 Jamboree show, Monroe's guitarist was probably Edd Mayfield. Shorty played bass and warmly welcomed another artist featured on that show: his old friend, Renfro Valley's Old Joe Clark. A week later, Shehan played on the recording session that produced "Christmas Time's a-Coming" and "The First Whippoorwill."[13] As a respected musician, a Blue Grass Boy, and a Jamboree regular, Shorty was perfectly positioned to inform Bill that the Runds were ready to sell the park.

The third oft-named facilitator was Carl Brummett, a Bean Blossom businessman—owner of Brummett's grocery and saw shop, the Bean Blossom Wrecker Service, and the Brown County Dragstrip, located less than a mile east of the Jamboree park. Brummett's contribution may have been mostly financial; in later years, in the presence of Monroe and others, Brummett made the unchallenged claim that he had loaned Bill Monroe the money required to buy the park from Rund.[14] Bill's longtime girlfriend and bass player, Bessie Lee Mauldin, also asserted years later that she had invested her life's earnings in Bill's property, and

Monroe biographer Richard Smith interprets that to mean that she may also have helped pay for the Bean Blossom park.[15]

For Bill Monroe, another powerful motivation to buy the Brown County Jamboree would have been the fox hunters' meet held on the Jamboree grounds that same weekend. Rund had long allowed the Brown County and southern Indiana fox-hunting associations to use the Jamboree barn and park for regular conventions. The "meets" were large events, with hundreds of dogs and dozens of hunters involved on Saturday night and Sunday morning. Saturday evening was the competitive "bench show" of dogs, held on the barn's stage in front of record-setting numbers of visitors and spectators.[16] Late Saturday evening, an actual fox hunt would begin, lasting well into Sunday morning. Fox hunts in the rural upland South consist mainly of the hunters sitting around an outdoor nighttime fire, listening to the hounds roaming about the countryside, and taking pride in recognizing each hound's individual voice and estimating where the hound is and what he's up to. Bill Monroe, arriving for his first Bean Blossom show, would have experienced the familiar final hours of a large fox hunt. Given Bill's (and his brothers') well-known love of fox hunting, he was surely delighted by the lively local fox-hunting tradition.[17] Fox hunters at the Jamboree barn would have made Monroe feel very much at home. Cline and Monroe often took dogs on long road trips, expecting to go hunting when they arrived in a new place for a show. Whenever Bill traveled from his home near Nashville, Tennessee, to Bean Blossom, he hoped to bring his own foxhounds along to run them in Indiana.[18]

In March 1952, the county surveyor mapped Monroe's park. In addition to showing the three parcels of property making up the site, the map also notes the approximate location of the lake and shows both the "Jambory Builden [*sic*]" and the short drive leading in an S curve from Highway 135 past the old barn's north-end entrance. The site also included a horse barn and several other small outbuildings, the three tourist cabins overlooking the lake, and the neglected semiruin of an outdoor stage that Rund had crudely constructed and rarely used. For the next forty-five years, Bill, his oldest brother, Birch, and his son, James, would be the park's owners and stewards, and instigators and overseers of its many music shows.

When Bill opened the park in May 1952, the fox hunters returned with Monroe's blessing. They held a bench show and fox hunt on Saturday night, May 3, and Bill and the Blue Grass Boys provided free entertainment before and after.[19] Blue Grass Boy Charlie Cline, also a fox hunter, recalled that "they had stands for the dogs, and a competition for the one that could get the fox first. The dogs had numbers painted on their sides, like race horses!"[20] On Sunday, May 4, Monroe headlined the first regular Sunday show of 1952. The band likely included Edd Mayfield, Charlie Cline, Larry Richardson, and possibly Shorty Shehan on bass.

Monroe paid a significant amount for the property, purportedly between thirty-two and thirty-eight thousand dollars.[21] Bill's purchase was made through a land contract with Francis Rund that was legally set up in the name of Birch Monroe. This arrangement may have been reached because the plan was for Birch to take charge of the property, or perhaps to protect it from any potential claims by Bill's first wife, Carolyn Monroe. The purchase may also have represented Bill's strategy to provide for Birch. Whatever the rationale, it was a workable arrangement. Birch moved into one of Rund's drafty cabins overlooking the lake and soon established himself as manager of the Brown County Jamboree, a position he filled, with a few significant lapses, each season for the remainder of his life.[22]

In the following years, monthly payments had to be made on Rund's land contract. The money wasn't always at hand, perhaps because of the economic downturn that all country and hillbilly musicians increasingly suffered as rock and roll began its relentless ascendance. A recurrent theme in oral histories of the Brown County Jamboree in the 1950s is the loaning of money to Bill or Birch to sustain the park during periods of low attendance and revenue. Carlton Haney said that in 1955, he borrowed money from his father to help the Monroes make an overdue payment of five hundred dollars to Francis Rund. Local entrepreneurs and businessmen Carl Brummett and Herb McDonald also said they provided intermittent financial aid during problem periods.

As manager, Birch supervised the park and grounds, cleaned and maintained the show barn, and hired help for concessions and local talent for the Sunday shows. Birch was a key player in the entire subsequent history of the Jamboree and the park, making many positive contributions, such as the weekly Saturday-night "Big Round and Square Dance" that he originated and hosted for decades.

But Birch also provoked some negative commentary along the way for his sometimes small-minded frugality and spotty record as manager of the previously successful Brown County Jamboree enterprise. Compared to the energetic, well-integrated management efforts of the Rund family, the Monroes seemed often to demonstrate poor business skills, muddled communications, and doubtful decision making as they became stewards of the Jamboree and the park.

The balance of the land-contract debt was paid off one month at a time over the next eight years, with the warranty deed to the fifty-one-acre property finally being executed in August 1959, proclaiming the property's ownership had then been formally transferred to Birch.[23] Bill took on full legal ownership of the site in his own name after another deed transfer, in May 1976.

The Jamboree gave Bill a home base in addition to the Opry. Monroe began immediately to call the whole place the "Brown County Jamboree Park" and used the venue to fill in his own performance calendar. Jimmy Martin explained the new situation succinctly: "Bill would play it at least two or three times a year, and sometimes two or three times in the wintertime. Every time we didn't have nothing to play, we'd head to Bean Blossom."

From his first appearances, Bill was greeted repeatedly at Brown County Jamboree shows by crowds of dedicated and constant local fans, people who lived in the vicinity. The most memorable of these, from Monroe's point of view, were musicians like Marvin Hedrick: aspiring pickers from central Indiana who had already been won over to the bluegrass sound by hearing Monroe's music on the radio.

In the audience at Monroe's 1952 Jamboree shows was just such a local fan: Harold Lowry. Lowry first heard Monroe's sound on the radio about a year before and was transformed:

> One night I was going on a date, as a matter of fact, when I was sixteen, to a town called Hope over here, about twenty miles away. Driving down 9, and I was listening to WSM, the Grand Ole Opry, as a matter of fact. Which my folks had always listened to, and all that, you know, and that's how I come to love music, I think.
>
> But at any rate, I heard—I never had heard of Bill Monroe. Came on WSM and started playing "Uncle Pen," and it just knocked me out! Back in those days, you know, the two-lane highways and all the power lines and everything? I stopped at a place where it was coming in real clear, and I stopped and listened to that. And I set there—I think it was one of those fifteen-minute shows, and I set there and listened to "Uncle Pen," and then they came back and did, uh, "Footprints in the Snow." And I sat there the whole time, and I was late for my date, matter of fact, because—well, that was just something that knocked me out, I don't know any other way to describe that.[24]

After Bill's Opry announcement that he would be appearing at Bean Blossom, Lowry planned to attend. The experience created vivid lifetime memories of the Blue Grass Boys, especially Jimmy Martin and Gordon Terry, who made a great impression in their "Kentucky riding breeches" outfits and hats. Their musicianship won him over as well. Already an aspiring guitar and bass player, Harold performed on the radio in those years with his banjo-picking friend Jack Perry from Seymour, Indiana. Over the next three years, Lowry developed a friend-ship with Birch and Bill. Lowry was also was the first local person known to have used the term *bluegrass* to name the style, having termed it that in a conversation recalled later by Marvin Hedrick and cited by Neil Rosenberg.[25]

Most of the year, Bill was back in Tennessee playing the Grand Ole Opry or doing the myriad midweek road dates he booked, typically for a percentage of the gate, at schoolhouses, fairs, parks, and concert halls. But he always returned to his base at Bean Blossom for the spring opening and the fall closing of the park. Most years, Monroe and the Blue Grass Boys performed many more weekend shows at the Jamboree as well. Some were advertised, most not.

Indeed, the pattern of advertising established by the Runds changed under Monroe ownership. Ads for Jamboree shows had given Rund's phone number all through the final shows of 1951 but provided no telephone number at all in the early Monroe years. Monroe's newspaper ads in the *Brown County Democrat* immediately became smaller and appeared less regularly than they had before. Instead, Birch relied increasingly on the hand distribution of inexpensive four-teen-by-twenty-two-inch "boxing-style" show posters.[26] Always wearing his trade-mark white shirt and tie, Birch carried these personally to local grocery stores, gas stations, and small storefront shops whose owners he individually asked to help advertise the next Jamboree show to local customers. Similar "Hatch-style" show-print posters had been used sporadically during the 1942 Guy Smith–Dan Williams era of the "Bean Blossom Jamboree," but from the early 1950s on, Birch's posters increasingly became the Brown County Jamboree's main form of ad-vertising.[27] Some (known as "showcards") were designed with blank areas for performance details; such posters could be filled in as needed and hence used for many different shows. Other Jamboree posters forecast a month's worth of shows at once. The gradual abandonment of newspaper advertising may reflect Birch's familiarity with, and preference for, a less expensive but still effective form of regional publicity.

Monroe's first Bean Blossom season established lasting patterns. Bill opened each season and played frequent shows in the barn and also used the park for other non-Jamboree events, especially those involving favored rural pursuits like fox hunting, farming, driving with horses and mules, and even, so it is rumored, clandestine cockfights.

Some changes at the park came quickly. By July, the Monroes constructed a small unshaded platform stage northeast of the barn, in an open field not far from the woods. That month, Bill and the Blue Grass Boys played a very successful show on the new platform. As Jimmy Martin recalled, "He had a little small piece of a stage over there in them trees, you know. And so we—just a little old one-horse stage over there, and if it was a pretty day, why, we'd just go over there and play. I remember—seemed to me like the first time we played it over there, it was with Wilma Lee and Stoney Cooper."[28]

Birch quickly moved into the regular duties of his new position. He booked local bands, advertised the shows, and put up showcard posters to promote the Jamboree. He oversaw minor maintenance of the property—lawn mowing, mostly, and periodic cleaning of the barn's interior—and he directed the workers in his concession stand and ticket booth. He emceed most Jamboree shows, often making a guest appearance with the featured artist of the week. If opportunity presented, he might also perform his own modest set of old-time fiddle tunes.[29]

Birch relied mostly on Bill for contacts involving booking Opry stars, but he found many artists and groups in the local musical landscapes of south-central Indiana. Over time, Birch interacted with many players and groups, hiring local artists to open the show for "name" artists headlining the Jamboree shows. Talented local musicians occasionally also rose to become headliners or featured artists. It was typically local players, often organized by Birch, who manned most Bean Blossom "house bands" or "staff bands." House bands in the early Monroe years were especially fluid in their makeup and relations with other named groups or organizations. Jake Lambert, who worked as a deejay at Columbus, Indiana's WCSI, recalled heading up his group, the Cumberland Mountain Boys, who he said were "regulars" at the Jamboree one summer in the early 1950s, disbanding by fall because of receiving no pay from the Monroes.[30] Local musicians, including those who increasingly showed up and picked in the parking lot, remained key to Sunday Jamboree shows.[31]

Some groups appearing at Monroe's park had previously worked for the Runds. The Logston Sisters and the Van Buren String Busters both played briefly during the Monroe era. Years later, Doc Beauchamp, leader of the Van Buren String Busters, blamed their departure from the Jamboree on the low pay that he claimed Monroe offered, though he may have misremembered the responsible Jamboree managers, confusing Monroe with Rund. Others who returned after appearing during the Rund years included Linda Lou and her husband, the renowned one-armed banjo player Emory Martin, Claude Sweet, and Old Joe Clark, all from Renfro Valley, Kentucky. Jack Cox, the former Hillclimber, performed alone several times on the Jamboree before 1955 as Cowboy Jack Cox. Afterward, Cox's musical career took him for a short time to other venues, including WKRC-Cincinnati television and the *Cornhusker's Jamboree* show, which featured a mixture of regional artists and country music legends like the original Carter Family and Mainer's Mountaineers. Cox worked briefly in Cincinnati, singing duets on stage with a young woman, Evalina Stallard. After Jack gave up the role of traveling musician, he returned permanently to the Brown County Jamboree as a fan, picker, occasional performer, and electrician employee of Monroe's.

Radio stars with national reputations played for both Francis and Kenneth Rund in the 1940s and then Monroe in the 1950s. This roster certainly included Pee Wee King, Roy Acuff, Grandpa Jones, Stringbean, Lonzo and Oscar, and WLS's Arkie, the Arkansas Woodchopper.

New acts began to surface occasionally as well, including up-and-coming local singer Bobby Helms, who eventually recorded the huge national hits "Jingle Bell Rock" and "Fraulein." Contemporaries recall Helms practically begging Francis Rund, and then Bill Monroe, to be allowed to play on the Brown County Jamboree, since in its region it was a proven and reliable country music venue.

Lattie Moore, an early harbinger of the rockabilly and rock and roll revolution, came first to the Jamboree with the Renfro Valley Gang in 1946 or 1950 and eventually played the show from the late 1940s to the mid-1950s, "under Kenny Rund, John Lair, and Bill Monroe." He starred on a November 1951 Brown County Jamboree show, only a month after Monroe's own first show there.[32] As a guitarist, singer, and songwriter, Moore contributed to the early momentum of the rockabilly wave whose mounting rock and roll crest bore Elvis Presley suddenly into national view in 1956 and signaled changing fortunes for all forms of country music.

The 1951 billing for his only *advertised* Jamboree appearance mistakenly read "Laddy Moore and the Allen County Boys." Lattie's musical background and orientation were hillbilly, western, and honky-tonk. His biggest hit, "Juke Joint Johnnie" (Speed 101), was released in 1952.[33] Moore liked Monroe's "Little Girl and the Dreadful Snake," which he requested on shows he played with Bill in the early 1950s. A 1953 Lattie Moore release, "I'm Not Broke but I'm Badly Bent" (King 1228), would eventually become well known in bluegrass circles. Lattie's show demonstrated the kind of driving honky-tonkin' country-boogie sound that was already his hallmark.

The first house band of the Monroe years began in 1952 under the telling name Brown County Fox Hunters. Birch was always involved. Over time, the changing roster included banjoist Larry Richardson, Texas guitarist (and Blue Grass Boy) Edd Mayfield, musician and comedian Harry Weger, Jack Perry, and Red Ritchie.

An exceptional show took place in early November 1953, when the Jamboree featured not only Bill and the Blue Grass Boys but also his brother Charlie and his daughter, Melissa. Since Birch was also there with the Brown County Fox

Hunters, the Monroes realized that they could stage a unique quartet performance with four blended Monroe voices. Jimmy Martin, then lead guitarist and singer, recalled a story about Birch Monroe's funny comment during their rehearsal:

> Melissa's gonna sing the high part, and Bill's gonna sing the baritone, I guess, and Charlie sang lead, and Birch sang bass. And I can hear it right now, Charlie laughed, great big, "hee, hee, hee," he laughed great big. And he says, "Brother Birch," says, "about what key would you—"—well, he's gonna do "A Beautiful Life," I think—and he says, "Brother Birch, uh, what key would you like to do this in?" And Birch kind of cleared his voice, "Uggghhmmm," he said. "Well, my throat's pretty clear, I don't think—just any key you all want it. You can't get 'em too *high* for me." [Martin laughs] And he's singin' *bass!*[34]

Birch quickly met and befriended other musicians in the area. At a local cock-fight, he encountered Kyle Wells, a transplanted Virginian who had labored in the coal mines of eastern Kentucky and then migrated to Indiana in the fall of 1953 to work for a company that manufactured mine-pumping machinery. Wells remembered:

> I got acquainted with Birch around then. He had some game chickens, and then he invited me to come over there, and I went over to the Jamboree. That's the first time I think I ever saw him.
>
> My dad had some chickens that he'd turned out into what they called a "walk," and let these chickens get out, you know, and raise little chickens, and he had 'em there on the farm.
>
> But they was Birch's, really, the chickens. But he's just keepin' 'em over there for Birch. And Birch come over and talked to me and invited me down. I went down there and then got a-playin' music down there with Birch. I got started pickin' with Birch then.

Kyle and Birch got along well, and their friendship grew as they discovered their shared passions, not only for game chickens and foxhounds but also for old-time and bluegrass music. Kyle usually played guitar and mandolin, sometimes trying his hand at the fiddle. He recalled Birch's fiddling, too: "He'd play square-dance music, there, and waltzes, you know. Some of the tunes that Birch played was 'Carroll County Blues,' and 'Florida Blues,' and he played—he had one he'd play, 'Boatin' Up Sandy,' 'Down Yonder,' 'Boston Boy.' A lot of them old fiddle tunes."[35]

The Monroe-era roster of Jamboree headliners booked in 1952 included WWVA stars Wilma Lee and Stoney Cooper and the Clinch Mountain Clan, whose July 27 show on the platform stage was noted in *Billboard* that summer:

"Stoney and Wilma report that Bill Monroe, the Decca biggie, is operating the old country music park at Bean Blossom, Ind., which was operated only on a small scale until it was taken over by Monroe this year. They played the park last week."[36] There were also Opry stars that summer: Lonzo and Oscar appeared with Cousin Jody, Tommy Warren, and the Winston County Pea Pickers.

Before the first season ended, Birch established a new regular Saturday-night event sustained with the help of local musicians like Kyle Wells. This was the weekly "Big Round and Square Dance," commonly highlighted on Jamboree show posters for the next three decades. Birch saw the Saturday-night dances as one of his main contributions to the park's offerings and a real supplement to the Sunday shows. By emphasizing dancing, Birch tapped into a deeply rooted and popular tradition, important in his childhood in Ohio County, Kentucky, and vibrant in the early 1950s in Brown County.

The descriptive phrase "Square and Round Dancing" was in common use in the area by the 1930s to characterize these popular events. Dancing was among the most well-liked forms of public entertainment in Brown County before the mid-1950s, and weekly public dances offered by entrepreneurs and organizations took place at Kelp's Grove; the Oak Grove Barn; George and Mary's Dance Pavilion; the high school gymnasiums in Nashville, Helmsburg, and other surrounding towns; and the Brown County Dance Land, a mile east of Bean Blossom. The phrase "square and round dancing" highlights two familiar old American dance forms with many variations. In square dancing, two or four couples, or multiple groups, dance a series of figures that are verbally cued by a figure caller, who may dance while calling. With the mid–nineteenth century's dramatic waves of immigration, newer European dance forms like the waltz and polka increasingly displaced square-dance traditions, leading to a series of revivals of the "old-fashioned" art of square dance. However, in "round dancing," any number of couples perform the same basic figures, steps, or routines, moving around the dance floor at the same time. The simplest phases of round dancing, typical of the Saturday-night round dances at Bean Blossom, included common underlying steps like the country-western "two-step" or the waltz. These figures could be danced, without requiring a caller, to the vast majority of the old-time string-band instrumental repertoire in southern Indiana, as well as to solo or accompanied fiddle playing of local fiddlers like Thurman Percifield, Louis Henderson, or Birch Monroe. More complex forms of round dancing like fox-trots, tangos, cha-chas, rumbas, quicksteps, and swing dancing were probably rare at the Brown County Jamboree's Saturday-night dances. While square dancing was the most popular at the Jamboree in the early 1950s, change would eventually overtake the dances. From about 1959 to 1962, the Brown County Jamboree also hosted rock and roll ("twist music") at the Saturday-night dances, in a bid to attract a new generation of fans and park attendees. By the late 1960s, when the square-dance tradition began again to diminish in importance in local entertainment, the term *old-time* became more prominent in public dance advertising. Pee Wee King, for instance, returned to the park at the end of August 1952 with his Golden West Cowboys. The performance included King's prolific cowriter, Redd Stewart, and a "western variety show" highlighted by "beautiful girls" and dancers. King, who knew Monroe well from the Grand Ole Opry, was by then a regular artist on WAVE-TV, based in Louisville.

Another Opry artist presented in that first Monroe season was banjo-playing Louis Marshall "Grandpa" Jones, with his fiddling wife, Ramona. The Grandpa Jones and Ramona show surely featured Jones's hit songs "Old Rattler" and "Mountain Dew," as well as some of the gospel material he had become known for in his postwar years with the Brown's Ferry Four.[37]

In September, the Monroes brought in another popular star, cowboy singer and movie star Rex Allen, advertised as "the Nation's No. 1 Cowboy Star." Allen, famous for his 1950 Republic Pictures B-western *The Arizona Cowboy*, had been lured to the *WLS National Barn Dance* in 1946 by stars Lulu Belle and Scotty, after which he became one of the first country and western artists on the then new Mercury record label. Between 1950 and 1954, he starred in nineteen more singing-cowboy movies with a roster of sidekicks who included Buddy Ebsen, Fuzzy Knight, and Slim Pickens. At his first Brown County Jamboree performance, Allen undoubtedly wore his full-plumage western clothes. He surely manifested his trademark "look," with guns holstered backward, and he undoubtedly reprised his successful Mercury releases, like "Afraid" and "Sparrow in the Tree Top."

Late summer saw an "Opry double-header" featuring two well-known artists. First was Manuel D. "Speedy" Clark, Shorty Shehan's old friend and bandmate, known by then as "Old Joe Clark." For the bulk of his career, over a period of more than fifty years, Clark was most closely connected with the Renfro Valley Barn Dance, but he also played occasionally on the Opry with Monroe and Grandpa Jones.[38] His onstage persona, developed in part at the suggestion of John Lair, was that of a grouchy old man with a grumpy attitude and the verbal mannerisms of a yokel from mountainous East Tennessee.

Second on the show was Robert Lunn, advertised for this show as "the Talking Blues Boy."[39] Lunn's show was always built around his popular number, "The Talking Blues," a rambling performance he made famous on the Opry. By the time he played Bean Blossom, Lunn had added a hundred new (often topical) verses to the original song as he had learned it, and he surely included some new verses in this, his first and only Brown County Jamboree show.

A week later, the Jamboree again turned to performers from Renfro Valley. The October 26 show, opened by the Brown County Fox Hunters, was built around three Renfro Valley performers: guitarist Claude Sweet, fiddling Linda Lou, and Linda Lou's husband, "the World's One and Only One Arm Banjo King," Emory Martin.

The Monroes perpetuated another practice established by the Runds: renting out the barn for political rallies and other large public events. While Democrats significantly outnumbered Republicans in Brown County, both parties used the big barn frequently until the mid-1970s, typically occupying it on a weekday night—a Wednesday or a Friday, and often within a month of each other—for their public events. In the early years, Birch and the Brown County Fox Hunters entertained at many such events, which also characteristically offered a "bean dinner" or a "pitch-in supper" to attendees.

In June 1952, fourteen-year-old Kentucky-born banjo player Sonny Osborne traveled to Bean Blossom in the company of Jimmy Martin to meet with Monroe. Though they didn't play a Jamboree show at that time, Martin and Osborne were immediately hired by Monroe, and they were soon performing together on the Opry.[40] Several Blue Grass Boys were hired or fired at Bean Blossom later on, and the park's entire story includes dozens of key encounters and career-changing meetings among later generations of pickers and fans.[41]

Some tales from the early days center on certain Blue Grass Boys, like Charlie Cline, known for his "pulling pranks and carrying on, acting like one of the Three Stooges." In one account by Garry Thurmond, Cline got back at three other musicians:

> I remember Darvin Byrd [a Georgia musician] telling the story about the old cabins at Bean Blossom. Y'all were all staying together and Charlie got to snoring so bad that the three of you picked his cot up and set him outside so you could sleep, and then locked the door so he couldn't get back in. It was on down in the fall, so they had a fire in the woodstove and Charlie decided he would fix them up. He climbed up the side and on top, and got a burlap sack and stuffed it in the stovepipe, and smoked Gordon [Terry], Red (Taylor) and (I think it was) Bobby (Hicks) out. Then Charlie ran inside and locked the door and wouldn't let them in.[42]

Bill Monroe and his "road girlfriend," Bessie Lee Mauldin, survived a devastating early-morning head-on collision with another car in mid-January 1953, following a nighttime foxhunt. Bessie, who had ducked down at the last moment, suffered only minor injuries, but Bill required months to recuperate from nineteen broken bones, a concussion, and other serious problems.[43] While Bill remained in Nashville Memorial Hospital, his wife, Carolyn, sent their daughter, Melissa, to Danville, Virginia, where a young man named Carlton Haney met her at a dance featuring Clyde Moody. Haney began to date Melissa around the end of February and began to pay attention to Monroe's music after hearing him sing "Little Girl and the Dreadful Snake" on the radio in July 1953. Haney had heard Monroe before, at a show in Danville in 1948, a week after Scruggs left the band, with Blue Grass Boys Tommy Goad, banjo; Benny Martin, fiddle; Cousin Wilber, bass; and Lester Flatt, guitar. Bill came in late to the show, and when he played, Haney found that he really didn't care for the sound of his music, saying later that it sounded like "squealing" to him. When Carlton told Melissa he didn't like Bill's old-time music, Melissa replied, "Daddy don't play old-time music; he plays bluegrass music."[44]

In September 1953, Monroe came to play a show at Walnut Cove, North Carolina. Haney, still dating Melissa, met Bill then and renewed the acquaintance several times through the next two months. In November, Bill called and asked Haney what he did for a living, an overture to asking him to come to work for him. Two weeks later, Haney gave notice and left his battery-plant job just before Christmas. When he got to Nashville, Bill first tried to make a bass player of him. But after three weeks, Haney told Bill he didn't want to play anymore, so Bill then asked him to try booking some shows. That inaugurated a period of intense involvement between the emerging promoter, Haney, and the Opry star, Monroe. It was the initial basis of their complex lifelong relationship.

Haney began by booking Monroe into movie theaters in North and South Carolinas, where he already a reliable following. Bill approved and began to sense that Haney had more ability as a manager and promoter than as a musician. In the summer of 1955, Bill sent Haney to Bean Blossom and—according to Haney—asked him to run the place. With rare exceptions like the Stanley Brothers show of June 27, Birch was relying heavily on local music, and the place was not doing well.

Haney brought in more Opry acts and arranged with WIBC to once again broadcast Jamboree shows. The broadcasts required that they string phone lines to the Jamboree and send an announcer to Bean Blossom each week to do the show. Haney jumped at every chance to promote the Jamboree on the radio. He personally emceed many nonbroadcast shows and also began to get to know some local musicians. He helped find or rediscover local talent, too, including the Logston Sisters, who often performed novelty numbers like Jimmy Dickens's "Out Behind the Barn."

Veteran Jamboree performer Loren Parker said Carlton Haney's turn as manager at Bean Blossom brought big changes, including a revitalized radio presence: "Carlton Haney came up there and here he got 'em on the map. He went up one day by WIBC and they had a program every day. Started out fifteen minutes, then went to half an hour, and then had an hour every Sunday night. Now, he really had 'em on the map. And they advertised all day long, even on the pop shows, who was gonna be there. I think that was fifty cents. Boy, he really put her on the map. We was playin' somewhere about every night."[45]

Haney worked closely with radio announcer Jack Morrow to build a mutually beneficial promotional relationship. Using the broadcast power of WIBC, Haney advertised promotional appearances and reorganized the Rund practice of staging wintertime Brown County Jamboree shows at venues all over Indiana, Kentucky, and even into Tennessee. One of Haney's live announcement spots, typical of that day, makes the heightened midfifties level of Jamboree activities over a single week abundantly clear:

> Thank you, Jack Morrow. Tuesday of next week we'll be down in Hindman, Kentucky at the Hicks Theater with the Brown County Jamboree; and we want all the folks out in that part of the country to come by, and be with us. Wednesday at West Liberty, Kentucky, at the Rex Theater, all the folks down there can see the Brown County Jamboree, Wednesday of next week. Thursday we'll be back at the Maple Croft Drive-In, on Highway 40, eight miles from Plainfield, Indiana, with our big show starting at 6:30. All the Brown County Jamboree Boys will be there, at 6:30 for the big show. The movie and the show, all for the price of one. Friday we'll be in Newcastle, Indiana, with our big Jamboree at the Little Ryman Auditorium. Starting at 8:00, and any of the folks over thataway that pick and sing, we'd be glad if they'd come out and be on our Jamboree show, over there at Newcastle, Indiana. Saturday at North Vernon, Indiana for a big round and square dance at the National Guard Armory, sponsored by the National Guard. And we want all the folks to come out, and we'll show you a big time, we'll have dancin' up until 12:00. That's at the Armory in North Vernon, sponsored by the National Guard. Sunday of next week we'll be right back at Brown County, with the Brown County Jamboree, and our guest stars, Homer and Jethro.[46]

An enduring Haney contribution was the introduction of a new musician to the region: Roger Smith. Originally from near Mount Airy, North Carolina, Smith was a banjo player and fiddler. Haney brought him in to help in the Jamboree's house band and introduced Smith to Marvin Hedrick, then regularly hosting

Wednesday-evening jam sessions at his radio and television repair shop. Hedrick recalled meeting Roger Smith there:

> First time I ever met him, he came walking in the front door of the shop, in we'll say May 1955. In come Carlton Haney. Now I'd met Carlton Haney a few days, a few weeks, before, over at the Jamboree. Through Birch. Birch introduced me to Carlton Haney. In comes Carlton Haney with this long, tall fellow, with bad teeth, and prematurely bald, obviously about my age. And—here was an ole boy from down in North Carolina that was interested in bluegrass.... And they started, the next week, they had a contract on WIBC, they played every day at noon. 12 to 12:30. Half hour. And I listened to a lot of those broadcasts—every day, I listened to them. They'd tell about the show, and then they had a sponsor-paid part of it. Roger would play a fiddle tune, then he'd play banjo for 'em—a banjo tune—and then they'd sing and Tex'd sing and they'd have a steel guitar number.[47]

Smith's talent on fiddle and banjo made him critical to the Jamboree and to Monroe and signaled a stronger bluegrass tradition there. Smith soon began, too, to teach dozens of young musicians in central Indiana, including the sons of Marvin Hedrick and the talented children of Columbus's Bill Banister, who all grew up attending Bean Blossom shows in the 1960s. In his own proud and demanding way, Roger Smith taught them all how to get it *right* as bluegrass musicians.

Haney's tenure as manager of the Jamboree lasted only one season, in part because Birch and Carlton did not like one another. Not only had Haney displaced Birch as manager of the Jamboree, but Haney's brash manner and constant ferment of new ideas about promotion also upset Birch, who was conservative, reserved, and parsimonious. According to Carlton, the clash reached a head when he asked Birch for money "to eat on," and Birch offered him only spare change pulled from a box in the trunk of his car.

In 1955, Bill showed up at Bean Blossom to see what was going on. After observing the show anonymously from the audience, Bill told Birch to let Haney take over running the show. In the aftermath, according to Carlton, an angry Birch Monroe chased Haney with an ax; the latter wisely retreated, hiding out behind a locked door in one of the cabins by the lake. Soon after, Haney left Bean Blossom, returning home to Reidsville around Christmastime. He began booking Don Reno and Red Smiley and eventually produced "package shows" of bluegrass and country bands and singers. Though he never resided there again, he returned to Bean Blossom on many occasions.

In September 1955, Bill brought a strong group to the recording studio. With guitarist Charlie Cline and banjoist Joe Stuart and the soaring fiddle trio of Gordon Terry, Vassar Clements, and Bobby Hicks, Monroe recorded three cuts, one being his own composition "Brown County Breakdown." Another tune Monroe named for a local place was "Stoney Lonesome," taken from a well-remembered rural neighborhood at the far-eastern edge of Brown County.[48]

A West Virginia native and lifelong bluegrass musician, Melvin Goins was around Bill a lot in those years: "I met Bill back when I was a young boy, I worked with the Lonesome Pine Fiddlers. We came here and played the old Brown County barn over here. 1954, and Brother Birch was here—that's when we stayed in the little log cabins over here. Birch would get up of a mornin' and cook breakfast for us. And he was a good cook; he could really fry eggs and bacon. And make good gravy and good biscuits. 'Cause we didn't have the money to eat out. A flat rate was a hundred dollars, then. That's what you got to come play, one hundred dollars, for a band. And we would come here, and work for Bill." In Melvin's nostalgic, rapid-fire public recollection, the thinly framed tourist cabins by the lake are misremembered now as *log* cabins, but Melvin's enthusiastic recollections vividly recall the early days. His stories acknowledge Birch Monroe's crucial role and occasionally also highlight the clashes that occurred when Bill found fault with Birch's managerial judgment:

> Birch was in charge. And when it was cold weather we had to get out there, they did, and Birch'd take a crosscut saw and a double-blade ax and cut these hickory trees and white oaks down for firewood to heat the old Brown County barn. Sometimes that smoke kindly got rough. You'd cry your eyes out; that smoke'd really get rough on your eyes. Bill went back there one day. Birch had put some wet wood in the stove. And boy, he had the smoke a-boilin.' And Bill said "Birch, you're gonna have to put some dry wood in there," said, "that wet wood ain't gonna get it," said "it's choked me to death." He said, "Well, Bill, that's all I had." "Well, you get out and hunt some dry wood sometime, so we'll have some wood to burn here." That was the only heat we had.[49]

The Brown County Jamboree began the 1956 season with shows in a "winter quarters," the Columbus, Indiana, Eagles Hall. These winter shows presented a series of country stars like Martha Carson, Justin Tubb, and Ferlin Husky, punctuated by bluegrass music shows by Monroe. A Jamboree show in January had Bill playing the Nashville High School gymnasium with the Blue Grass Quartet, the Brown County Boys and Girls, and comedian Old Joe Clark. The turnout was probably poor; there were no further advertised Brown County Jamboree shows until July, when Monroe returned for weekly Jamboree shows with Lew Childre, Rose Maddox, and Cousins Jodie and Odie and Their Country Cousins. One curious ad for a show in July 1956 relegated Monroe's name to tiny type at the very bottom of the ad, highlighting instead the announced show by Cousins Jody and Odie and Their Country Cousins and the day's main entertainment, an appearance by daredevil thrill driver Crash Brown, billed at the Jamboree that day as "The Human Bomb." Brown's "casket of death" was a box built to come apart easily; he would put dynamite beneath it, get in, and have the explosion touched off.[50]

## Rural Music Parks as Fan Scenes

From the beginning, rural country music-park audiences included fans who were themselves aspiring performers. They would bring their instruments along to shows in order to play informally—sometimes for hours—before the show was due to begin, between shows, or after the whole event ended. Since music shows at Bean Blossom increasingly featured bluegrass performances throughout the 1950s, the number of bluegrass musician-fans increased, and the practice of meeting others to play music in the warm summer parking lots around the old Jamboree barn took hold. Players arrived planning to "pick in the parking lot." In ephemeral small-group jam sessions near parked automobiles, new faces were also welcomed, and—given the semiformulaic nature of both traditional and "new" bluegrass music—it proved easy for strangers to meet and play music together. Today's common term for this sort of music making is *jamming,* but that term also carries overtones of improvisation and open-endedness that were not always present in "parking-lot picking" sessions at the Brown County Jamboree.

An amateur banjo picker, Ron Teofan, was invited to Bean Blossom when Monroe noticed him playing backstage at the Grand Ole Opry. In July 1957, Teofan joined in with a capacity crowd at the Brown County Jamboree. Birch was running the place, and Bill's show was the highlight. Teofan was excited by the great banjo picking of Don Stover, then in the midst of a six-month 1957 stint as a Blue Grass Boy.[51]

Many other dedicated players began to frequent Bean Blossom around this time, including Robert "Red" Cravens and Francis Bray, from near Champaign, Illinois. Along with Francis's talented brothers, Nate and Harley, they were about to advance their musical educations at Bean Blossom in a big way.

# Survivals, Revivals, and Arrivals, 1958–66

Two revolutionary mid-1950s music-industry developments affected Bean Blossom. Rock and roll music, bursting forth in the first half of the decade, forced changes in country music and all other popular music genres, and the folk song revival of the second half-decade provided new audiences with a worldview in which bluegrass's distinctive sound and folk roots marked it as separate from the Nashville sound that increasingly defined "country music."

Kenny Baker, who first worked as Monroe's fiddler in 1957, recalled the effect of rock and roll on artists who would not or could not adapt: "There was a few years there about the time that this rock and roll came in. It wasn't only bluegrass music, but all of country music shot its wad. Why, they just disbanded left and right down there in Nashville. Of course, Bill kept an outfit, but he damned sure didn't make no money with it. There just wasn't any money to be made in bluegrass or country music then."[1]

Bill opened the Jamboree on April 20, 1958, with a pulled-together group. Fewer shows had diminished the prosperity of his sidemen and led to rapid turnover. Eddie Adcock, Monroe's newest banjo player, stayed only three months, until lack of work and money drove him off. Plenty of fill-in or short-tenure Blue Grass Boys followed Adcock on banjo that year, including Bobby Atkins, Joe Drumright, Bob Johnson, Buddy Pennington, Earl Snead, and local "fill-in" Roger Smith. The April 20 show drew 450 people, and that probably felt to Bill and Birch like a reasonable success amid the country music–market erosion.

A week later Monroe hosted another successful Jamboree show, featuring fiddler (and former Blue Grass Boy) Gordon Terry and also steel-guitar icon Don

Helms and the Carlisles, led by "Jumping Bill" Carlisle. The next morning, Silver Spur cleaned up the barn with his helper, Warren Day, and a five-man crew. They finished around nine thirty, but by midafternoon a serious fire broke out near a chimney. The fire was quickly extinguished by fire departments from Nashville, Fruitdale, and Morgantown, but the fifteen-year-old barn was heavily damaged by flames, smoke, and water. A large section of the roof in the northernmost third of the structure was completely destroyed.[2] Warren Day announced that the Jamboree would carry on in tents, but repairs took only three weeks. Burned sections were hauled off and a portion of the roof replaced. Several lightly charred rafters were left in place.

With hasty repairs complete, the Sunday shows resumed on May 18, with Bill Monroe hosting a big "reopening" show starring then new Opry member Porter Wagoner and His Wagoneers, along with the Wagoneer Trio, and comedian Curly Harris. From the start, Monroe frequently hired fellow Opry artists, either on percentage or for modest guarantees, to play shows at Bean Blossom. But the country music mainstream was shifting. Partly in response to the generational awakening of postwar youth to rock and roll, country music abandoned the hard-edged honky-tonk sounds of the early fifties for the smoother "Nashville sound" conceived by Chet Atkins.

Moreover, by 1958, Bill Monroe's unique "Blue Grass sound" was becoming a recognized style.[3] Although the Stanley Brothers had played Jamboree shows in 1954 and 1956, before 1958 there was not much bluegrass—other than Bill's own music—at Bean Blossom. The emergence of new bluegrass bands, whom Monroe initially saw as competitors, surely increased his appreciation of his park in Indiana, where audiences were always particularly friendly to him and receptive to his music, if not always as large as he hoped. But in and after 1958, there seemed suddenly to be more bands than ever playing bluegrass. Despite his competitiveness, Monroe began to see that his sound had spawned a genre and that other bluegrass bands were not just potential competitors but also prospective acts that he and Birch could book.

Monroe's former agent Carlton Haney, then booking Reno and Smiley, may also have tempered Bill's famous artistic protectiveness and his preference for limiting the term *bluegrass music* to his own artistry. Carlton likely helped Bill see that he could benefit from the growing interest in bluegrass music, and he booked Reno and Smiley there that summer.

So while Monroe's 1958 Brown County Jamboree still presented Opry acts like the Carlisles, Porter Wagoner, and Kitty Wells, it increasingly began to feature the emerging bluegrass genre. Don Reno and Red Smiley & the Tennessee Cutups appeared in June 1958, and in late July the Stanley Brothers returned to perform at Bean Blossom along with Bill and the Blue Grass Boys.

Bill himself brought in another band as fill-in musicians: Red Cravens and the Bray Brothers, from Illinois.[4] Guitar-playing Robert "Red" Cravens grew up in Tuscola, Illinois, listening to country music on Illinois radio. His guitar style was first shaped by the sound of WDZ artist "Bluegrass" Roy Freeman (nicknamed for his native Kentucky, not for his style of performance). Around 1954, Red Cravens met the Bray brothers—Nate, Harley, and Francis—who played mandolin, banjo, and bass, respectively. Together they began playing live radio shows around Champaign, Illinois, occasionally with young fiddler John Hartford.[5] In 1957, Nate and Harley Bray enlisted to avoid the draft, serving a short stint in postwar Korea. Francis Bray was ineligible for military service due to health problems. Red Cravens then began going to Bean Blossom regularly. Cravens admired the guitar work of Red Smiley, whom he saw in June, and from whom he learned "the D-run and the G-run." In 1958, he and Francis began to jam there with another Illinoisan, banjo player Jerry Waller.[6] The Brays typically drove over on a Friday, staying overnight with Waller's adoptive father, fiddler and guitarist Kyle Wells. Wells moved Birch Monroe into his own home around this time, too, because Birch was ill and living in one of Rund's drafty cabins. Cravens remembered sharing a bed with Birch Monroe at Wells's home, but noted that Birch was usually out Friday nights, coon hunting and fox hunting. Saturday night was Birch's "Big Round and Square Dance," and on Sunday, they would all attend the Jamboree shows. Later on, Red helped Birch "run things" at the Jamboree and donated money to keep the Jamboree afloat after unprofitable shows.

Red, Birch, Jerry Waller, and Kyle Wells soon began playing as an occasional and unofficial "house band." They sometimes made up a name like the Boys from Martinsville, but more often were simply introduced as individuals.

By midsummer of 1958, Cravens had befriended Bill Monroe. Red also found a kindred spirit in Monroe's guitar player: returned Blue Grass Boy and Texas cowboy Edd Mayfield. Edd's picking featured punchy transitional bass runs like Cravens himself played. Admiring Mayfield, Cravens exclaimed, "I've met my match!"

In July 1958, when Harley returned from military service, Red brought Francis and Harley over to Bean Blossom to work as fill-in Blue Grass Boys. The July 20, 1958, show on which the Brays first backed Monroe actually featured the Stanley Brothers and the Clinch Mountain Boys, then based at WWVA, and also legendary Grand Ole Opry comedian Rod Brasfield. Before playing, Bill asked Red

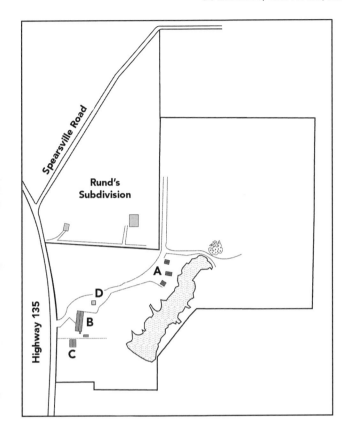

Bill Monroe's Brown County Jamboree Park, ca. 1958. A: Cabins. B: Jamboree barn and restroom. C: Horse barn. D: Open-air dance platform.

only one question about Harley's banjo work: "Does this boy know my stuff?" Cravens answered "Yep," and they played the show.

That muggy July day the show was held outdoors, on the unshaded open-air "dance platform" that Bill had built about fifty feet northeast of the barn's ticket booth.[7] The platform was roughly twenty feet square, surrounded by a single two-by-four railing. The hot, humid weather soon gave way to light rain. Harley Bray later recalled the scene: "That day cars were parked all around it and Bill was there with a fiddle player from Nashville, and Red, Francis and I played with him. It was sprinkling on and off and so Bill told everyone to stay in their car and instead of applauding, honk their horn! That was the strangest feeling! I was really nervous and Bill asked me what instrumental I wanted to play and the only thing I could think of was 'Bluegrass Breakdown,' so I started it out, and boy, I played it fast!"[8]

Subsequently, whenever Bill played the Jamboree, Red and Francis drove over in Francis's old Studebaker. Once they had a flat tire along the way and put on their spare tire. Two miles from the Jamboree, the spare went flat. Nonetheless, they finished their trip, bursting onto the music park's graveled entrance road "riding on the rim, with sparks a-flying," provoking Monroe's laughter. Cravens also remembered Jamboree shows that were illuminated with coal-oil lamps when summer storms interrupted the electricity.

Other events brightened 1958 and 1959 for the Bray brothers: learning the tune "Kickin' Mule" from Roger Smith, who played it at furious tempos, or attending when Johnny Cash played his one popular date at the park. Birch long remembered Cash's show and the relatively low fee he paid: "Some of the biggest stars got their start here, you know. Johnny Cash played here when he only had about—Well, I guess he played for about 75 or 80 dollars, maybe a hundred. Now you couldn't—He wouldn't talk to you for less than 50 thousand, I don't guess!"[9] Cash's show drew a huge crowd, and as a consequence was held "in the woods," perhaps on the last remnants of a platform in the woods built by Francis Rund.

By April 1960, Harley and Nate Bray completed all military obligations. The Bray Brothers came to Bean Blossom with Red to play the opening show. They returned every Sunday afterward and quickly became the regular house band under their own name: Red Cravens and the Bray Brothers.[10] Often that summer, Monroe traveled from Nashville, Tennessee, to the Jamboree accompanied only by a fiddler, usually Kenny Baker or Bobby Hicks. He would then front a band with Cravens on guitar, Harley Bray on banjo, and Francis Bray on bass.

The Brays and Cravens eagerly threw themselves into the Jamboree's growing bluegrass jam scene. Red joined afternoon jam sessions that coalesced behind the Jamboree barn between shows or in backstage rooms after the evening show. There were marathon jams lasting until well after midnight, bringing Red into extended musical contact with Monroe's Blue Grass Boys and other musicians, particularly fiddlers like Lowell Denman, Kenny Baker, and Joe Stuart. Baker appreciated Red's powerful rhythm playing, and they would pick together for hours. Though the Brays and Cravens were paid, they did not make much, but cash did not motivate them. Red memorably spoke for them all: "We didn't care about money in those days. If we did, we wouldn't have went there. Bean Blossom was the University of Bluegrass."

The Bray Brothers' repertoire emphasized old songs and tunes of anonymous origin that were explained to college audiences as bluegrass "folk songs." This presentation was congruent with the spreading notion among new urban audiences that bluegrass was not really commercial country music; rather, it was a kind of folk music, "mountain music," or "roots music." Seeing bluegrass as folk music helped legitimate its acceptance by new young urban mass music audiences.

At Bean Blossom, Birch Monroe slowly adapted to new entertainment realities. His 1959 Jamboree ads proclaimed that Saturday-night dances would feature "Square-Round Dancing, also rock-roll." Later on, Birch also advertised "twist music." Through the summer of 1962, the regular Saturday-night dance at Bean Blossom advertised such dual programs: for example, "Square dancing [and] Waltzing with the best fiddling and guitar players in the country" (Birch Monroe, Kyle Wells, Stanley Miller, and Jim Key), and "Rock 'n' Roll and Twist Music by a hot rhythm band—the Three Spades from Martinsville (Paul Day, Pete Young and Ronnie Owens)."

Since repertoires of the first generation of recording bluegrass artists included many textually traditional and anonymously authored songs, it was easy for new fans to simply regard anything done in the emergent bluegrass style as "authentic folk music." This sensibility was immeasurably aided by the October 1959 publication of renowned folk song collector Alan Lomax's *Esquire* article, in which he labeled bluegrass "folk music with overdrive."[11]

Neil Rosenberg has explained how the generic bluegrass *style* was created and named after Bill Monroe's particular "Blue Grass" *sound* began to spread.[12] As Monroe's own music evolved into a separately named genre, not purely folk song based, and less identified as a kind of country music, precise definitions of bluegrass became increasingly arguable. The most restrictive definitions of bluegrass limit it to music made by Bill Monroe and his Blue Grass Boys, or music that is closely comparable, in that it draws principally on the same body of familiar recorded songs as a classical canon and demands that its players hew close to the instrumental and vocal approaches of classic Monroe bands. But looser definitions abound; for some, any song accompanied by a five-string banjo is bluegrass, and the banjo's resurgence among purveyors of popular 1950s folk music helped connect the ideas of "folk music" and "bluegrass."

Just as the late-1950s phase of the folk song revival exploded into national visibility, several individuals who came to bluegrass music from different backgrounds entered the life of Bill Monroe. They began to make decisions that would powerfully influence the history of the Brown County Jamboree.

One towering personality of the folk song revival was Ralph Rinzler (1934–94), a college-educated New Jersey suburbanite whom Neil Rosenberg identified as the key figure among city bluegrass followers in starting the bluegrass festival movement.[13] Rinzler helped redirect the course of Bill Monroe's career, and his influence on the Monroes' 1960s management of the park at Bean Blossom was profound.

In his midteens, Ralph began listening to songs from the 1952 Folkways *Anthology of American Folk Music* compiled by Harry Smith. In 1953, as a Swarthmore College freshman, Rinzler saw Pete Seeger at a folk festival concert and was inspired to take up the banjo.[14] Rinzler soon met and befriended Mike Seeger, Pete's half brother, who was also then beginning to explore and chart both older southern musical traditions and their hybridized offshoots. By 1954, Rinzler and Seeger started journeying to rural music parks to see musicians they liked, including Monroe, Reno, the Stanley Brothers, and Grandpa Jones. Although Sunset Park and New River Ranch were nearby—less than ninety miles from Seeger's home near Washington, about fifty miles from Philadelphia and only thirty miles from Swarthmore—Rinzler found that for him, "it was like going into another world. I was fascinated by the totally different life-style—dinner on the grounds, different speech patterns—a whole different way of life."[15]

In 1957, Folkways Records publisher Moses Asch asked Mike Seeger to compile an album of banjo players who were fluent in the modern three-finger "Scruggs style." Rinzler wrote the album's liner notes, using the new term *bluegrass* to name the typical style that provided a band context for Scruggs-style picking.

Seeger and Rinzler were performers as well as avid students of old-time and bluegrass music. In 1958, when the frenzy over the Kingston Trio and their mass-market success with "Tom Dooley" was at its peak, multi-instrumentalist Mike Seeger joined two other revival musicians, John Cohen and Tom Paley, to form the New Lost City Ramblers. They made many concert appearances reinterpreting and presenting music they had learned from old recordings and their own fieldwork and tried to bring fans of a newly commercialized and mass-marketed "folk music" to a deeper appreciation of older sounds of tradition.

In 1960, Rinzler—a mandolin player like Monroe—also blossomed as a performer, becoming a founding member of the Greenbriar Boys along with guitarist John Herald and banjoist Bob Yellin. The Greenbriar Boys were skillful "citybilly" musicians and entertainers. They presented audiences with music taken from aural and recorded tradition while acknowledging their own urban origins, but they played in a manner more closely tied to bluegrass than the New Lost City Ramblers.

In the early 1960s, Seeger and Rinzler made more trips to Sunset Park and New River Ranch, where they particularly admired the music of Bill Monroe. Their close ties to other city-bred and well-educated fans of folk music soon put them in a position to strive to increase the number, prestige, and remuneration for appearances by folk artists, including Monroe.

The northeastern urban folk-music scene included others who were coming to appreciate Monroe's music. Some knew that Monroe had originated a new string-band genre, but few at that time appreciated that he had adamantly refused to change his own music in the face of the new Nashville-sound imperative and consequently was suffering financially. Jim Rooney and Bill Keith, who first saw Monroe without any regular band of his own at Watermelon Park in 1960, began to better understand Monroe's economic situation when Keith became a Blue Grass Boy and had to ride in the same decrepit Oldsmobile station wagon that Monroe had driven to Watermelon Park.[16]

Rinzler and John Cohen, whose own fieldwork ventures led them to rediscover older string-band artists like Kentucky's Roscoe Holcomb, Tom "Clarence" Ashley, and Arthel "Doc" Watson, decided in 1960 along with Mike Seeger and *Sing Out!* publisher Israel Young to create an organization called the Friends of Old Time Music. The FOTM promoted urban concerts featuring relatively unheralded rural performers of an earlier generation. Bill Monroe headlined a Friends of Old Time Music show in 1963, reflecting the growing bond of trust between Rinzler and Monroe.

Still, Monroe was typically withdrawn, taciturn, and not easily approached by strangers. When Rinzler in June 1962 asked Monroe for an interview, in order to write a *Sing Out!* article to help restore Monroe's name to its deserved place of historical prominence, Monroe brusquely acknowledged him as someone he had previously noticed (along with Seeger) making audiotapes by the side of the parks' stages but diverted Rinzler's request with the blunt, angry, and ultimately misleading suggestion: "If you want to know about bluegrass music, ask Louise Scruggs."[17] Rinzler persisted, and with the help of the Stanley Brothers, Mike Seeger, and Bessie Lee Mauldin, Bill agreed in August 1962 to let Ralph interview him for an article that appeared late the following January.[18]

Rinzler began booking Bill into new venues, more lucrative and more satisfying to Monroe than the package tours he had been playing for Nashville's music-row booking agencies. Rinzler pursued a deliberate strategy with Monroe, as he had begun to do for Doc Watson and Tom "Clarence" Ashley: "My strategy for attracting an urban audience . . . had two parts. The first was to legitimize them by demonstrating the historic links and relationships between the two of them and musicians already acknowledged to be our nation's prime recording artists in their field. The second was to validate the 'folkness' of their roots through detailed biographic notes and articles."[19]

In January 1963, Rinzler became Bill Monroe's manager.[20] By month's end, Rinzler presented Monroe as a headlining act at the prestigious University of Chicago Folk Festival. For Monroe, it was the first of a long series of folk-festival and college concert appearances and clearly the opening step of Rinzler's plan to see his music discovered by new audiences.

On the opening night of the University of Chicago Folk Festival, Rinzler gave Bill and Bessie the newly issued *Sing Out!* with his picture on the cover. Titled "Bill Monroe—Daddy of Bluegrass Music," Rinzler's article tried to set the historical record straight for growing legions of bluegrass fans who were beginning to be excited by the sounds of Flatt and Scruggs, but who had not necessarily heard of Bill Monroe. Although Rinzler did not coin the phrase "Father of Bluegrass Music," the *Sing Out!* essay went a long way toward spreading that honorific's acceptance and eventual adoption by Monroe himself. The article argued for the restoration of Monroe's rightful place as the bandleader whose group's name had become the accepted term for the style and whose former sidemen were cresting the wave of bluegrass popularity in the early 1960s. Rinzler also gave Monroe a copy of the notes to the first Greenbriar Boys album, which recounted the story of bluegrass music and affirmed Monroe's central role in it. Overnight, the relationship changed. Rinzler wrote, "From that time forward, the curious distance bordering on hostility never reappeared in my relationship with Bill."[21] By mid-March, Ralph Rinzler moved to Nashville as Monroe's full-time manager and booking agent.

Monroe soon began to meet city musicians who were learning his music. Since Monroe then frequently used local fill-in musicians, he asked Rinzler to help line them up as he played in new regions. They were drawn from groups like the New York City Ramblers, with banjoist Winnie Winston and fiddler Gene Lowinger. Rinzler called in Winston to play banjo with Monroe in 1963 at the Swarthmore Folk Festival, and Lowinger also became a Blue Grass Boy that year.

Rinzler knew of the park at Bean Blossom, but did not go there until 1962 or 1963. Given his familiarity with both emergent urban scenes and the Pennsylvania country music parks, Ralph probably saw the Brown County Jamboree as a place that would not aid his search for *new* Monroe audiences. He also understood that the Monroes, despite their importance in American music, were ineffective managers of the Indiana venue. Ralph soon took steps to improve the business situation there. Those steps involved several more key figures who found their ways to Bill Monroe and Bean Blossom.

Neil V. Rosenberg was already a fan, but he directly entered Bill Monroe's orbit in 1961, when he began graduate studies in folklore at Indiana University. Rosenberg was born in Seattle, Washington, but by his tenth birthday had moved to Berkeley, California. Neil grew up playing the violin and later learned guitar, mandolin, and banjo. He immersed himself in folk, country, and—eventually— bluegrass music. After being a founding member of the first important West Coast bluegrass band, the Redwood Canyon Ramblers,[22] Rosenberg attended Oberlin College in Ohio and joined the budding bluegrass music scene there, honing his skills on banjo, mandolin, and guitar. In Bloomington, Neil began exploring local musical networks; within a week, he heard about the Brown County Jamboree from a next-door neighbor. In June 1961, he made the first of hundreds of trips to the Brown County Jamboree. There he found a musical scene that was vital and fascinating to him as a folklorist, although he saw the park as a disappointing example of Brown County's tourism industry: "In 1961, the Brown County Jamboree was not one of the county's tourist attractions. A seedy, rundown place, the Jamboree was an embarrassment to those members of the local chamber of commerce who knew about it. Its owner, Grand Ole Opry star Bill Monroe, had a loyal following, but he and the Jamboree had fallen on hard times."[23]

As a musician, Neil was welcomed immediately by Jamboree musicians. Shorty and Juanita Shehan, then the "house band," auditioned him as a banjoist. After Neil played "Bury Me beneath the Willow" in front of Bill, they encouraged him to return. Within two weeks, he had been accepted as an unpaid member of the house band.[24]

From the start, Neil contended with the divide between his university-centered academic studies and his Bean Blossom–based musical interests. Richard M. Dorson, the dominating, opinionated chairman of Indiana University's Folklore Institute, was uncomfortable with the intersection of folk and popular culture as it applied to American folk song and folk music. Dorson's widely known diatribes against "fakelore" reveal his sense that aficionados of the folk song revival, especially "folk musicians," were not involved in anything that academic folklorists should take seriously.[25] Dorson was not in the least supportive of Rosenberg's interest in the Brown County Jamboree.

Dorson's failure to encourage work on bluegrass led to a division of Rosenberg's energies during his stay in Bloomington, which lasted until July 1968. He was drawn to the Jamboree and accepted there as a musician, but while his professors believed in fieldwork's value in discovering the workings of culture and tradition, they disagreed with Rosenberg's immersive tactics, which involved his operating as a sort of apprentice musician himself, playing with and observing a wide variety of other musicians at country music shows and clubs, square dances, and weekly jam sessions like the one at Marvin Hedrick's shop. Dorson's bias altered the course of Neil's own subsequent dissertation scholarship and writing, but through his many popular fanzine articles, liner notes, journal publications, and especially his seminal 1985 book, *Bluegrass: A History*, Rosenberg emerged as the foremost scholar of bluegrass music.

Also entering Bill Monroe's life in 1961 was a thirty-three-year-old Indiana State Police Training Division sergeant: Jim Peva. Peva was born in rural southern

Indiana, near Evansville, and knew a boyhood life of farm animals, outhouses, kerosene lanterns, and Saturday-night baths in a galvanized washtub. As an adult, he joined the Indiana State Police Department, eventually retiring as a colonel. In 1961, he was assigned to arrange entertainment for an annual invitational pistol-match banquet. He knew of Bill Monroe from listening to the Grand Ole Opry but had never heard his music in person. One Sunday, Peva drove from his home in Plainfield to Bean Blossom and talked to Birch, who was putting up posters for an impending fiddle contest. Birch told Peva when Monroe would next be playing the Brown County Jamboree, and Peva attended with his whole family:

> I made it a point to be there so I could talk to him about playing for the banquet. I had my wife and three small daughters with me. None of us had ever attended a live music performance before. When Bill and the Blue Grass Boys took the stage and played "Watermelon Hanging On The Vine," the hair stood up on the back of my neck! Something about that music and the high-pitched fiddle activated a genetic memory deep within my DNA! I was hooked! I talked with Bill after the show and we agreed he would play the Wednesday-night banquet, (which happened to be on his 50th birthday), for $250, with an extra $50 to bring a comedian/impersonator, Rusty Adams. Following that initial exposure to live bluegrass music, my family and I seldom missed a Bill Monroe show in the Jamboree Barn.[26]

Peva's friendship with Bill Monroe grew warmer through the years.[27] Bill would always welcome the Peva family by name, and the Pevas offered him hospitality at their music-park campsite many times over the next few decades. Peva selflessly volunteered to help Birch and Bill with Jamboree and festival shows at Bean Blossom in any way he could. An enduring consequence of Peva's admiration for Monroe's music has been the legacy of his photographs and tape recordings of historic shows at the park. Since in the 1960s the Indiana State Police encouraged troopers to become completely familiar with their large-format evidence camera, Peva often took the Speed Graphic camera to Bean Blossom. His carefully composed and luminous photos of Monroe, the Blue Grass Boys, Neil Rosenberg, Roger Smith, the Hedrick family, and many other Jamboree performers have frequently been published or reprinted in recent years.

Both Jim Peva and Neil Rosenberg thus became "regulars" at the Brown County Jamboree. They attended whenever Monroe appeared. Rosenberg often played in the ad hoc house band with Shorty and Juanita Shehan and with others drafted for a given show. He observed throughout the remainder of 1961 and 1962 that—despite being an open laboratory of vernacular musical culture where young musicians could meet and learn directly from those who had shaped the

recorded traditions of hillbilly and string-band music—the park was not a successful or well-run place. Neil saw "piddling" audiences, the consequence of
chronically poor management and marketing decisions by Birch or the appalling
series of Bill's or Birch's friends who worked as fill-in managers.

Birch supervised these transient managers but usually in a disorganized and
ineffective way. With little prior planning, Birch did not properly advertise,[28] or
even announce the acts who would be playing each Sunday; that failure in turn
contributed to poor attendance. There were other management gaps as well.
For instance, in the summer of 1962, fans came from as far away as Chicago for
a Bill Monroe show, but the person helping Birch run the park that summer, a
record-store owner from Terre Haute, Indiana,[29] had unsuccessfully tried to
book Bill Monroe for the show with only a week's notice. The Barrier Brothers
of Crown Point, Indiana, performed instead, but Rosenberg felt that next to Bill
and the Blue Grass Boys, the Barrier Brothers were a "comparatively colorless
group," whose substitution disappointed those who had driven long distances
to see Monroe. Rosenberg saw a continuing pattern of such "little screw-ups"
happening at Bean Blossom, dissuading potential customers from troubling to
drive to the park.[30]

Aware of such problems, Ralph Rinzler asked Neil Rosenberg in early 1963
to manage the Brown County Jamboree and asked Monroe to consent to the
change.[31] Neil agreed to run the park, but only for that year's season, and only
with the hands-on help of Marvin Hedrick. He consented mostly to please Rinzler
and Monroe, whom he regarded as friends and fellow musicians. Although Neil
took his management job very seriously, he continued scholarly observations of
Jamboree activities, and as a participating musician he kept playing in the parking
lot and on Jamboree shows. In the May 1963 banjo-picking contest, he took first
place and fifty dollars in prize money. Neil quickly expanded the park's advertising, supplementing Birch's posters with newspaper ads run in Brown County
and Indianapolis and with limited regional radio spots.

The 1963 season began in late April with Bill Monroe's show. The Blue Grass
Boys then included innovative Massachusetts banjoist William Bradford Keith
(known by his middle name "Brad," since by Monroe's informal decree, there
would be only one "Bill" in the group).[32] Monroe's band also included Bill's girlfriend, Bessie Lee Mauldin, on bass, Kentucky fiddler Kenny Baker, and banjo
player–turned-guitarist and lead singer Del McCoury. John Wright of Northwestern University visited the Jamboree around this time and noted Monroe's
vigorous performance to a small crowd: "My wife and I were lucky enough to
see the Bill Keith edition of the Blue Grass Boys at a Sunday afternoon show at

Bean Blossom in the summer of 1963. As I recall the audience consisted of three or four graduate students from Indiana University (including Neil Rosenberg, who was responsible for our being there) and a half a dozen Hoosier farmers. Needless to say, despite the tiny audience, Mr. Monroe played his heart out."[33]

In subsequent correspondence, Wright observed that Monroe at that time was "obviously a very angry man, and he didn't care who knew it. He opened the show with a quick number or two and then snarled out, 'Well? Any requests?' The tone of his voice clearly indicated that any proper audience would have inundated him with song titles by that point."

That season's offerings included a heavier mix of bluegrass than ever, and connections between bluegrass and folk music were stressed more. Both Rosenberg and Rinzler envisioned Bean Blossom as a center for bluegrass music, so ads Rosenberg placed each week in the *Indianapolis Times* proclaimed the park "Bluegrass and Folk Music Headquarters in Indiana." Bill kept resisting, though:

> Bill saw it as a country music park, and he thought of bluegrass as *his* music. And he wasn't really that certain that he liked the idea of calling it "bluegrass." And he definitely—He knew that people were calling it "bluegrass," but he didn't think that it was a good idea to have a whole bunch of bluegrass bands at the park. Certainly not at the same time, and even not from one Sunday to the next. He would have some acts in there, bluegrass acts, that he knew, but they would book in mainstream country artists. And of course, Bill being on the Opry, he could always get a pretty good price from people. So that's the way they ran it, and we kept saying to Bill, "listen, you ought to make this the bluegrass headquarters."[34]

The 1963 bookings make clear this difference of opinions. Bluegrass bands appeared amid plenty of Opry and other country music acts. Early in the season came shows by Don Reno and Red Smiley & the Tennessee Cutups, Charlie Monroe, Ernest "Pop" Stoneman, Scott Stoneman, and the Stoneman Family. Later came Little Jimmy Dickens, comedian Whitey Ford, Jean Shepherd, Lefty Frizzell, Archie Campbell, Loretta Lynn, Martha Carson, Roger Smith and Vernon McQueen, Stonewall Jackson, the Carlisles, Carl and Pearl Butler, Cousins Jody and Odie, Opry pianist Del Wood, Bob Krise and the Indiana Playboys, Ken Marvin (a former "Lonzo" of the group Lonzo and Oscar) and Red Murphy, Justin Tubb, Melissa Monroe, the Osborne Brothers, the McCormick Brothers, Jim and Jesse & the Virginia Boys, and of course Birch Monroe and the Brown County Boys and Girls. Rosenberg and Rinzler soon added a new feature at the "Bluegrass and Folk Music Headquarters": a "local talent hootenanny," staged between the afternoon and evening shows.

Managing the Jamboree was a heavy load for Rosenberg on top of his graduate work at Bloomington. He wrote frequently to Rinzler, detailing the cost of each show, noting persistently low attendance even for headline artists, and bemoaning the chronic lack of money in Jamboree accounts to pay advertising costs, light and water bills, and even the agreed-on guaranteed fees for artists.[35] Rosenberg told Rinzler about the challenging relationship he and Marvin Hedrick had with Birch, who despite being displaced as manager kept running his own part of the Jamboree operation, the Saturday-night dance. As in the Carlton Haney days, the 1963 arrangement between Bill, Ralph, Neil, and Marvin diminished Birch's authority. Neil reported that Birch's Saturday-night events had acquired a reputation for being unsavory and out of control, and instead of enhancing the park's desired reputation for "good old-time entertainment," the Saturday dances suggested "an image of teen-age rioting and booze."

All that year, Marvin Hedrick worked with Rosenberg and also played music locally in a group called the Weedpatch Boys. The name derived from Weed Patch Hill in the Brown County State Park, and also evoked the earlier Weed Patch String Band, which played for dances back in 1936. The newspaper claimed that the new Weedpatch Boys were all "descendants of Brown County folks." One Weedpatch Boy was not local at all, though; William Bernard Lee was a traditional fiddler transplanted by army duty from Mississippi. Born a sharecropper's son in 1921, Lee grew up hearing fiddle music by Mississippi recording artist Willie Namour and also blues played by his neighbor "Mississippi" John Hurt. The other 1963 Weedpatch Boys were Charles Percifield on mandolin, Loren Parker and Marvin Hedrick on guitars, Jim Bessire on bass, Jack Weddle as dance caller, and Hedrick's sons David and Gary on five-string banjo and tenor banjo. Throughout most of the state park's tourist season, the Weedpatch Boys played for dances held each Saturday night in the new "dance pavilion."

In June 1963, the Weedpatch Boys released a 45-rpm record on the "Brown County Records" label, with their new composition "Brown County Autumn," backed with the fiddle standard "Ragtime Annie." A pressing of a thousand was released and sold at live appearances of the group. The Weedpatch Boys often played fill-in roles at Sunday Jamboree shows, exemplifying the Jamboree's dependence on local musical networks. Though the musicians were all personally loyal to the Jamboree, they were often able to find better-paying gigs elsewhere.

Despite his hectic Weedpatch Boys schedule, Marvin Hedrick worked hard at the Jamboree through the summer of 1963. As an experienced radio and television repairman and recording aficionado, Hedrick advised Bill and Birch to improve the decrepit sound system at the Brown County Jamboree, which still featured

1940s horn speakers and other equipment brought in by soundman Silver Spur for the Runds. Hedrick arranged a deal with Bill: he would modernize the barn's sound system in exchange for a mandolin, which Bill promised to bring up from Nashville. Hedrick spent nearly five hundred dollars on changes. He put in a new 90-watt Bogen amplifier, new boxed speakers for the barn's interior, a new outside horn speaker to help ballyhoo shows to passersby on Highway 135, a new turntable for the "radio control room," and a new Shure microphone. Hedrick completed the installation by late June or early July, and near the end of July, Bill paid Marvin off with a Gibson F-4 mandolin, serial number 34142.

In August, Neil Rosenberg went on vacation, leaving Hedrick to fill in. Hedrick reported to Ralph Rinzler, detailing his efforts: mowing the unkempt meadow in front of the barn, cutting weeds, cleaning up barrels of beer cans and liquor bottles, and removing a huge pile of trash that Birch had simply dumped behind the barn. With the help of Roger Smith, who emceed Jamboree shows in Neil's absence, Hedrick installed new outdoor sockets and lights at the Jamboree's entrance and hauled advertising posters to Columbus, Seymour, Brownstown, Scottsburg, Austin, Bloomfield, Bloomington, Trafalgar, Morgantown, Martinsville, Mooresville, Edinburg, Shelbyville, and Indianapolis. Hedrick reported continuing problems with Birch and the Saturday-night dance:

> After thoroughly cleaning the inside [of the barn] last Tuesday, then going in on Sun. and finding it a complete mess I decided that some other arrangement had to be made. After Sat. night's dance we picked up in excess of 40 beer and whiskey bottles on the grounds. According to the Brown County Sheriff and other sources, they had a drunken brawl and fight Sat. night. . . . As a Brown County businessman I shudder to think what an impression a tourist would get if he made the mistake of going on Sat. night and got involved in a drinking brawl of the type that is taking place there. The Sat. nite dance used power, gas, advertising and general facilities including rest rooms, toilet paper, soap, water and towels, which are wasted. I can't find where they pay any percentage into the account and it is my intention to take out rest room supplies and hold them until Sun.'s show to curtail this cost.[36]

More fans discovered Bean Blossom and the Brown County Jamboree in 1963. In the fall, Frank Neat—a transplanted Kentuckian then living in Indianapolis—made his first trip to Bean Blossom to hear Monroe. He was excited to be there, completely focused on Bill Monroe. Neat began learning the art of banjo building while living in Indiana. Though he later returned to Kentucky to build banjos full-time, in the midsixties he frequented Bean Blossom, eventually playing banjo for Bryant Wilson's Kentucky Ramblers when they were the house band. At Bean

Blossom, Frank befriended many great banjoists like Ralph Stanley and Sonny Osborne. Eventually, he repaired their personal instruments and built hundreds of new instruments to sell under their own brand names, like Ralph's "Stanleytone" and Sonny's "Osborne Chief" banjos. In the 1990s, Neat also built several fine banjos to sell under his own name from the wood of old walnut trees removed from the park's wooded amphitheater.

When the 1963 season ended, Neil told Ralph and Bill he could no longer spare enough time to manage the Brown County Jamboree, so Ken "Lonzo" Marvin, an intermittent fill-in agent and manager, took over to manage the 1964 season.

In 1964, Bill and the Blue Grass Boys played four advertised Jamboree shows, and likely many more that never made the newspaper. The Blue Grass Boys underwent more changes that year, with four different banjo players, three different fiddlers, and three different guitar players. In 1964, Bill was starting to pay less attention to his longtime girlfriend and bass player, Bessie Lee Mauldin, and by the end of the year, she had been replaced in Bill's band by his son, novice bass player James William Monroe. Complicating matters, Ken Marvin's management was less conscientious than Neil's, and once again many shows weren't being advertised except with the familiar posters. Performers that year ranged from old-time fiddler Arthur Smith and champion fiddler Curly Fox to Opry stalwarts Kirk McGee and Jim & Jesse and the Virginia Boys, along with guest artist Ray Pillow, who would join the Opry several years later. August 9 brought the Osborne Brothers, newly added to the Grand Ole Opry roster. Monroe's own shows brought in supporting artists like Ken Marvin, Melissa Monroe, and fiddler Benny Williams, who was an on-and-off Blue Grass Boy through the early '60s, often alternating shows or sessions with Buddy Spicher.

Some dedicated new fans and pickers made long pilgrimages to Bean Blossom in 1964. In May, two Californians, members of the San Francisco–based Black Mountain Boys—Sandy Rothman and his friend Jerry Garcia, who would help to found the Grateful Dead about a year later—crossed the country in Garcia's white 1961 Corvair.[37] They brought their instruments and a reel-to-reel tape recorder and planned to immerse themselves in bluegrass. They visited their former Berkeley friend Neil Rosenberg, who was not the Jamboree's manager but was still closely connected. Neil brought Rothman and Garcia repeatedly to Bean Blossom, where they recorded live shows. They also arranged to copy audiotapes from the large collection of Marvin Hedrick, in whose basement they stayed for a few days.

Hedrick and his family gave Garcia and Rothman an entrée into local networks of musicians, and admired their evident musicianship, but regarded them as outsiders—as they had Neil Rosenberg when they first met him. One of Hedrick's sons recalled Garcia's 1960s hippie look, which made him seem to them to be "an unwashed crudhole."[38]

Jerry Garcia hoped that his banjo-playing skills, using the new melodic fiddle-tune style popularized by Bill Keith, might suffice to earn him a spot as a Blue Grass Boy. Rothman wrote perceptively of that hope: "All bluegrass musicians wanted that musical apprenticeship with the Father of Bluegrass, and Garcia by his own admission was no exception. I felt that Jerry would have been a good choice for the Blue Grass Boys at the time. Monroe liked the Keith style—having admitted that a Yankee, and not a southern musician, had been the first to figure out a way to play fiddle melodies note-for-note on the banjo—and was looking to keep that sound in the band after Bill Keith left at the end of 1963. Garcia could do it. He would have been adept at interpreting Monroe's tunes in the style. . . . Jerry was confident, but he was still too shy to push himself on a hoss like 'Big Mon.'"[39] So the audition Rothman and Garcia anticipated never took place. Although Rothman played banjo as a Blue Grass Boy later that year, Garcia moved on to his destiny with the Grateful Dead.[40]

The 1964 Brown County Jamboree ended late in the year, with Monroe shows on November 8 and 15. At both shows, Monroe was present not just as an entertainer but also as a businessman dealing with an interesting new proposition.

## The Brown County Music Corporation

Early in 1964, four Jamboree regulars envisioned a change. Familiar with both Brown County's long-standing attractiveness as a rustic tourist destination and the folk song revival's emphasis on authenticity and tradition, they hoped to take over the park and improve its operation. To ensure their own attention to detail and to prove to Monroe and others the earnest seriousness of their decision, the four men—Roger Smith, Marvin Hedrick, Jim Peva, and Carroll McClary—pooled a thousand dollars of their own money and created a business corporation with themselves as sole stockholders and officers. The Brown County Music Corporation first met on August 9, 1964, to develop formal bylaws and to create a proposal and contract that the Monroes might approve, permitting the BCMC to operate the music park. They wanted their control to be continuous and absolute, and for the full 1965 year they planned to offer the Monroes a rental fee of $1,300, based on $150 per month during the season from April to November, and $25 a month for the rest of the year. They also sought an option to buy the property, with a mutually chosen appraiser to set the price, and signaled their intent to offer Monroe himself an equal corporate share.

ROGER SMITH, PRESIDENT
CARROLL D. M⸱CLARY, VICE-PRESIDENT

ROUTE 2
NASHVILLE, INDIANA

JAMES R. PEVA, SECRETARY
MARVIN HEDRICK, TREASURER

With its rustic typeface, musical notes, stylized guitar and banjo, and a map showing Brown County's location within the state of Indiana, the letterhead of the Brown County Music Corporation (1965) suggested its main interests. (Courtesy of Jim Peva)

Bill Monroe immediately demanded changes in the contract. He asked for almost $500 more in annual rental, said he himself would name the price of the park if he *ever* wanted to sell, and showed no interest in becoming a shareholder in the Brown County Music Corporation. After such changes were ironed out with Bill, the contract was signed on November 23 by Birch Monroe, still the park's legal owner.

Over the winter, the ambitious officers of the BCMC made new management decisions. They changed show times from 3:00 and 8:00 p.m. to 2:00 and 7:00 p.m., and decided to continue the "local talent hootenanny" between the shows at 5:00. They authorized passes for a core cadre of supporters and key personnel, had name cards printed, sent out invitations to artists, built a bulletin board, had a pay phone installed, began work on a brochure, obtained liability insurance, and investigated the old barn's preparedness for fire and other emergencies. Jim Peva moved his daughters' former playhouse to a spot in the dusty road near the barn's northwest corner, to use as a ticket booth. They installed new flooring and linoleum in the barn's concession-stand kitchen and acquired a popcorn popper, a sink, an orange-drink dispenser, and a used gas stove with an oven and grill top. They worried about serious repairs needed for the barn's seating, floors, roof, and the concrete-block restroom behind the barn and decided to talk to Monroe about such basic improvements. They modified the stage's central microphone with fittings suspending it from above, to minimize the loud booming noises that floor stands always picked up from feet tapping on the stage's sagging wooden floor. The officers decided that the new season would include a fiddle contest, a banjo contest, and two talent contests. Finally, they began to book artists. The 1965 shows would include Bill Monroe, Merle Kilgore, the Glaser Brothers, Charlie Louvin, and the Osborne Brothers.

Despite careful preparations and hard personal work, by May 1965 the Music Corporation had lost money on all shows and had exhausted their corporate nest egg making improvements. Although the group pluckily moved ahead with the shows they had booked, they knew by June that they would have to terminate their lease with Monroe at the end of that month, just after his June 27 Jamboree show and prior to the July 4 "Big Banjo Pickin' Contest." On paper, the Brown County Music Corporation lasted until the next January, but that summer and fall it was clear that despite the dedication of Smith, Hedrick, Peva, and McClary, the Brown County Music Corporation had failed, and the Jamboree was still in trouble.

In September 1965, Monroe's former manager Carlton Haney hired Bill, the Stanley Brothers, Don Reno, Red Smiley, the Osborne Brothers, Mac Wiseman, Jimmy Martin, Clyde Moody, and several other key musicians like Doc Watson to put on the first multiday bluegrass festival at Cantrell's Horse Farm, near Fincastle, Virginia, less than twenty miles north of Roanoke. The nascent festival movement signaled the dawn of a new age for bluegrass music and musicians.

The festival idea had simmered in Haney's mind for some time, based partly on input from Ralph Rinzler and the memory of earlier one-day multigroup bluegrass shows staged at Virginia country music parks, notably at Watermelon Park in 1960 and at Oak Leaf Park in 1961. Eddie Adcock later recalled that Haney approached the Country Gentlemen with the notion of a festival as early as 1962. Though the Country Gentlemen did not play Haney's first festival because of a prior commitment, they recognized that a festival performance might be a big improvement over the country music-park shows they had been doing: "Carlton had discussed with us the possibility of a multi-day bluegrass festival, and we all thought it would be a workable thing. Previously, most big bluegrass bands had been accustomed to playing outdoor shows at country music parks, so an all-bluegrass show seemed like a neat idea. At last, we wouldn't get drowned out by loud country bands before and after us!"[41]

The first bluegrass festival was a critical success, though only a thousand or so fans attended. Those who came—a notably mixed crowd of "citybillies" and rural country folk—paid six dollars each for a weekend ticket, and there were reported problems with traffic, toilets, food concessions, and water supply. The dedicated followers who converged for the 1965 festival, many of them musicians, were nonetheless impressed by the bluegrass shows presented there.

Familiar elements in the first bluegrass festival were music contests, reminiscent of fiddlers' conventions, and instrumental workshops, which owed a direct debt to Rinzler's productions at the Newport Folk Festival.[42] Several new ideas emerged as well, including a Sunday-morning all-gospel bluegrass concert and Haney's historic retelling of "The Story of Blue Grass Music," which stressed Monroe's role as the genre's founder.

At Haney's festival, Bill Monroe was surrounded by other legends of first-generation bluegrass, with one notable absence. Though Haney had approached the hugely popular Flatt and Scruggs about playing, their asking price was higher than that of all other acts combined, and Haney could not afford them.[43] In their absence, Haney presented Bill Monroe as the central iconic figure representing the genre he had founded.

Though Haney's festivals made a lifelong impression on Monroe and flattered him by putting him at the narrative center, Bill did not embrace the festival idea right away. He spent the rest of 1965 and 1966 in the usual way—driving seventy thousand miles or more on the road, playing the Opry, and recording in the wintertime. But he had observed the relative ease of staging a festival in a campground and saw that the festival and the Monroe-centered "Story of Bluegrass" pageant planned by the mystical Haney and the scholarly Rinzler reinforced his place as "the Father of Bluegrass." It did not hurt his pride when fans at Haney's first festival formed the Bill Monroe Fan Club and began to publish periodic newsletters. The first powerful impact of the festival movement on Monroe and the park at Bean Blossom would prove to be economic. As Glen Duncan later reflected, "Festivals hit, then all of a sudden you had what has become an *industry*. You had places for these guys to go play. And Bean Blossom, instead of being that—sixty or seventy-five, or forty-five—paid people on a Sunday afternoon, all of a sudden was thousands. And instead of Bill getting a few hundred dollars for playing on a Sunday, he's got that place full of thousands of people for ten days. 'Cause it was an *event*. It was a *happening*."[44]

Following CBS's 1962 network debut of *The Beverly Hillbillies* television series, huge new audiences who had never before heard of bluegrass became familiar with the approachable music of Flatt and Scruggs. Most of the new audience did not have rural or Appalachian backgrounds and apprehended the cultural side of their new musical attraction as outsiders. Perhaps in part because of their palpable sense of wonderment at the sound and story of bluegrass, such new converts often became effective missionaries for the style.

One important new fan was Norman Carlson, who found his way to Bean Blossom and soon began to write focused and laudatory articles about the park. Carlson's writings appeared in his own intermittent mimeographed newsletter called the *Bluegrass Handbook,* the *Ralph Stanley International Fan Club Newsletter,* and *Bluegrass Unlimited,* which began as the first true national bluegrass music fanzine in July 1966.[45]

Norman Carlson discovered hillbilly music on Chicago's WJJD radio in the latter 1950s, but when he went to college and then graduate school, he really got involved. He was surprised to find that most students in the Country Music Club at Cornell University, in Ithaca, New York, had already heard of bluegrass and considered it a type of folk music, yet knew almost nothing about other types of country music. Arriving in Lafayette, Indiana, in 1965 to attend graduate school at Purdue, he heard about Bean Blossom and ventured there in November for that year's closing show. His account reveals the impact on him of both the music and the place: "Bean Blossom was the hillbilly heaven I feared I had missed by being born too late and too far north. The shed-like building and rough grounds, the stoves, the posters, the audience, the performers and the music were a 1955 rural idyll, my personal paradise. Roger Smith's house band working two big microphones amplified by vacuum tubes was the best thing I had ever heard. How could this be just a warm up? Don Gully and the Pinnacle Mountain Boys and Dave Woolum and his band followed, equally good. When Bryant Wilson came on, I was beside myself. Here was the ultimate of intense, deep in the hills, bluegrass. All that was only a prelude to an hour and forty-five minutes of Bill Monroe."[46]

In the first key months of *Bluegrass Unlimited*'s existence, Carlson published reviews and reports of his noteworthy observations of the Jamboree and its impact. His national reporting explained the place and its attraction: "The Brown County Jamboree is owned by Bill Monroe and managed by his brother Birch. Performances are held in a ramshackle barn that can be heated by a variety of old time chunk stoves. Every week some of the best bluegrass and old-time music in the country is heard there in an ideal atmosphere. Each week Birch Monroe manages to play his fiddle with part of the visiting band or some of the local performers. He also sings bass on some gospel quartet numbers. Both his rich traditional sound and his serene look from the obvious enjoyment he derives from his performance completes the spell in this purists paradise."[47]

A subsequent report amplified Carlson's view of the place and what it meant to him:

> Brown County Jamboree is a folk institution in the truest sense of the words. The building is a somewhat rundown shack of plywood and miscellaneous lumber. Part of the floor is concrete and part is gravel. Most of the seats are folding chairs, some are like old-fashioned school seats. On cold days the building is heated by several coal stoves of assorted rustic shapes. All this contributes to an atmosphere that transcends any other commercial park. I will always remember sitting around the warm stove in the back room, a dusty anteway with a crude creaky floor. Also sitting there were Carter and Ralph Stanley and Birch Monroe singing "Boat of Love." Another memorable incident, impossible to duplicate elsewhere occurred as Shorty Sheehan was playing "Orange Blossom Special."

He worked in this comment, "see the conductor, only today he's the fireman. Shovel in a little more coal, Birch." Over to one side by a stove was Birch dressed in a suit and tie for MC'ing the show but with a coal bucket in one hand and an old glove on the other, throwing coal into the fire. There is a minimum of formality and no polish at Beanblossom. Country music isn't merely "performed there," it is lived. It sounds better that way.[48]

Bryant Wilson—always a Norman Carlson favorite—had played the Brown County Jamboree on and off for twenty years before Norman first saw him in 1965, but he was then starting a two-year period in which he and the Kentucky Ramblers played nearly every weekend as the house band. Wilson played a concentrated, commanding style of bluegrass. As a successful local songwriter and recording artist, he had attracted notice by other central Indiana pickers for years. His band in the mid-1960s included locals Elmer Rooks and Hiram Gist and young Frank Neat from Kentucky. Later that decade, Columbus, Indiana, teenager Glen Duncan made his first appearance as a fiddler at the Jamboree while sitting in with Bryant Wilson. But in 1965 and 1966, Norman Carlson was listening reverently to Wilson's group and focusing on Wilson's singing and repertoire. Carlson called the band "the best of the bedrock-traditional bluegrass bands frequently heard at Beanblossom," and particularly appreciated Wilson's own compositions, "Steppin' in Daddy's Tracks" and "Meet Me Up Yonder."[49]

Carlson often returned to Bean Blossom over the next few years and published detailed letters and reviews in the fan-club newsletters. He was a no-nonsense advocate for the kind of "intense, deep in the hills" bluegrass that was played by the first and second generations of bluegrass musicians and had little tolerance for those willing to compromise the old style for modern sounds in the pursuit of wider popular acceptance.

On Halloween evening 1965, the Jamboree presented "Old-Timer's Day," celebrating the Jamboree's rich history. Artists from the 1940s and 1950s were invited to take part in the show, as were surviving members of the Rund family. In an emotional speech, Silver Spur presented "a little history," stating that the Brown County Jamboree was the oldest country music show in Indiana and recalling that "it was originated by a fellow by the name of Guy Smith, myself, Dan Williams, and Carl Brummett." Silver Spur also claimed, misremembering the correct date, that the Jamboree was then thirty years old, having started, as he claimed, "in 1935 on the open-air platform." Old-Timers' Day brought back many venerable Jamboree acts: Shorty and Juanita, Loren Parker and Maxine Montgomery, the Weedpatch Boys, and Jack and Alva Cox (the Hillclimbers), accompanied by Neil Rosenberg and Gary Hedrick; nostalgia ran deep.

That fall, while the park at Bean Blossom was limping along under Birch's desultory management, Bill was booked for some shows in New York and New England and needed a band. Rinzler found Bill some local musicians in the Northeast, with a fiddler named Benjamin "Tex" Logan hired to work the tour. Tex shared the series of shows with his successor, New Yorker Gene Lowinger, the first northern fiddler to become a Blue Grass Boy. Tex worked only part-time as a fiddler, since in his day job he was Benjamin Logan, Ph.D., a mathematician and engineer at Bell Laboratories' Communications Theory Department. But he was a genuine West Texan, with deep roots in his home state's fiddling traditions.[50] He had honed his skills playing with the Lilly Brothers when he was a graduate student at the Massachusetts Institute of Technology.

By late summer in 1966, Tex Logan and Bill had become close-enough friends that Bill and the Blue Grass Boys (with guitarist Peter Rowan, banjoist Lamar Grier, and James Monroe on bass) began attending the first of a series of annual September "Monroe birthday parties" at Tex's home in Madison, New Jersey. Tex served "homemade barbecue, beans, Texas chili, homemade cornbread, and sweet tea."[51]

Bill opened the 1966 Jamboree season early in April. Blue Grass Boys Rowan and Grier, like their counterparts before and after, found that Monroe expected of them a good deal of hard farmwork. They noted Monroe's constant trial of their ability to perform physical labor at his own high level: "Pete Rowan & I went from Nashville to Beanblossom to deliver hay into the barn that was there [a small gable-end-opening barn located in the field just south of the Jamboree barn]. I remember when getting there that Bill went up into the top of the barn, at a second story door opening, to receive bales of hay that Pete & I would hand up from Bill's stake bodied truck. I easily succumbed to the physical energy of picking up those hay bales & throwing them up into the air so Bill could grab them to stack them in the upper barn. Pete & I couldn't keep up with Bill's energy. Bill was telling us to give him some more bales to work with & I was developing energy loss in that exercise. I felt 'whooped' when it was all over."[52]

That summer the Jamboree alternated country and bluegrass acts and also juxtaposed local groups with famous radio and recording artists. Ever more bluegrass was being added to the mix, with shows that year by the McCormick Brothers, the Osborne Brothers, Charlie Moore & Bill Napier and the Dixie Partners, Don Reno & the Tennessee Cutups, and, in October, the Stanley Brothers. Locally, Bryant Wilson still filled the house-band slot, and there were many shows with Birch's persistent Brown County Boys and Girls. At July's banjo contest, Marvin Hedrick's banjo-playing son David took first place. For Saturday nights in 1966,

Birch advertised his Saturday dance sometimes as a "teen hop," with music provided by the Nomads, from nearby Morgantown.

The October 16 show put on by the Stanley Brothers was recorded and eventually released on LPs on the Joy and Rebel labels. In their second set, Carter told the audience of the group's plans for 1967, with a blunt reminder of the nation's situation: "While we're speaking of war songs and the like—I know most of you probably have some connections, either friends or relatives, that are stationed in or near Vietnam. I'd consider it a real favor if you'd write to 'em and tell 'em that the Stanley Brothers are coming to South Vietnam in January. The latter part of January, we'll be in that country, in and around there, for six weeks. So if you do have friends or relatives that you think would enjoy our down-home playing and singing, drop 'em a line."[53]

But the Vietnam tour was not to be; after the last Jamboree show, the Stanleys went to Nashville for the annual deejay convention, where they saw their old Brown County Jamboree friend "Brother Silver Spur." They played a few songs at a show the next Friday in Hazel Green, Kentucky, but Carter's illness ended the show early and prevented him from ever performing again. He died at Bristol Memorial Hospital in Bristol, Virginia, on December 1, 1966. Carter Stanley was the first major bluegrass performer of the first generation to pass away, and it marked the end of an era for bluegrass and for Bean Blossom.

# 6

# Building the Festivals, 1967–68

The 1967 season of the Brown County Jamboree opened April 2 with a show by Bill Monroe, the Shenandoah Valley Trio, the Famous Blue Grass Quartet, and—according to the poster—"a host of others."[1] Birch let the "host of others" remain unnamed until showtime, promising only that Bill would once again open the season. From the late 1940s on, Bill's show often began with a short opening set by the Shenandoah Valley Trio, who were simply the Blue Grass Boys, wearing hats but performing without Bill. Bill's show also included a segment by the Famous Blue Grass Quartet—also the Blue Grass Boys, but with hats off as they sang gospel quartets like "A Beautiful Life" or "Wicked Path of Sin."

In 1967, Bill and Birch's Jamboree again presented a variety of country music acts and square dances, plus occasional hootenannies and "twist music" shows. But after Monroe's April opener, four bluegrass shows came in rapid succession. First was Byron Berline, Red Allen, and James Monroe, then a show led by Ralph Stanley with his newly minted solo act, fronting Clinch Mountain Boys Melvin Goins and Curly Ray Cline. A successful country music show by Kenny Price came next, but more bluegrass followed, with Don Reno, Bill Harrell & the Tennessee Cutups, along with Shorty and Juanita Shehan, and the house band at the time, Bryant Wilson and His Kentucky Ramblers.

Musicians at Bean Blossom for the June 11 show did a radio promotion over a Martinsville radio station; the ad hoc band included Don and Ronnie Reno, George Shuffler, Roger Smith, and Mike Seeger on bass. A week later, the Jamboree presented another strong headlining act—Jim and Jesse with Bobby Thompson, Jim Buchanan, and Ray Kirkland—on a show opened by a secondary Jamboree house band of that era: the Stoney Lonesome Boys, with fiddler Roger Smith, guitarist Vern McQueen, mandolin player Osby Smith, and on banjo and bass, respectively, Neil and Ann Rosenberg.

A week later, on the last weekend of June 1967, a new era began at the old park with a modestly advertised but momentous event: Bill Monroe's first bluegrass festival. Bluegrass festivals ushered in a new era at the old country music park, as they did for bluegrass music generally. Monroe's bluegrass festival, like his music, was a unique realization of a modern idea built on many traditional precedents.

In mid-twentieth-century America, the concept of music festivals was reinvigorated by George Wein's Newport Jazz Festival in 1954 and its offspring, the Newport Folk Festival, in 1958. The Newport festivals emphasized the presentation of musical genres through an annual multiday event with multiple performers, groups, or acts. At Newport, festivals were also self-consciously educational, if only in the sense that festival producers knew they were exposing new audiences to unfamiliar music. Therefore, from the beginning, the Newport festivals complemented main-stage performances with "workshops," where artists on smaller secondary stages explained and demonstrated styles or techniques to small audiences.

Earlier multi-act one-day bluegrass shows had been staged by promoter John U. Miller at Watermelon Park, near Berryville, Virginia, in August 1960, and also by bluegrass singer Bill Clifton at Oak Leaf Park in Luray, Virginia, on July 4, 1961. These events have sometimes been held to constitute the first bluegrass festivals, but they lacked several key elements of later festivals: they did not use workshops to educate a newly receptive public about the music or performers, and they did not centrally involve camping overnight.

When Carlton Haney staged his first multiact, multiday festival on Labor Day weekend in 1965 at Cantrell's Horse Farm, near Fincastle, Virginia, the modest audience of about thirteen hundred people included some tent campers and some who slept in their cars.[2] The Fincastle festival, now commonly accepted as "the first bluegrass festival," came along just when the folk enthusiasts who most revered "authenticity" at the revived Newport Folk Festivals were being driven away by the perceived transformation of "folk" into "folk rock." Haney saw the wisdom of filling time between concerts with workshops but invested most of his own energy into presenting a series of onstage reunions of Bill Monroe with several generations of former Blue Grass Boys, thus telling "The Story of Blue Grass Music," much as a mindful minister makes sure his flock knows the story of the gospel.

With Carlton Haney's successful 1965 and 1966 festivals fresh in his mind, Bill Monroe decided to stage his own festival. Monroe planned his bluegrass festival at Brown County Jamboree Park for two days on the weekend of Saturday and Sunday, June 24 and 25, but it actually opened on the twenty-third, with a small Friday-night show and a dance. Louisville musician Harry Bickel, who attended that night, brought his banjo but found few pickers in the parking lot.[3] All of the first festival's shows took place inside the Brown County Jamboree barn, built twenty-five years before. Those who camped overnight found plenty of unimproved open space in the fields to the barn's north and east, and a few tent campers were in evidence. Many fans slept in cars or pickup trucks in the first year or two of the Bean Blossom June festivals; it was not until the mid-1970s that special recreational vehicles, soon called RVs, arrived in noticeable numbers. Whatever their accommodations, attendees stayed overnight in the park, eating picnic meals, shopping for basic groceries at McDonald's IGA, and playing or listening to parking-lot music as it happened.

In advertising the 1967 event, Monroe avoided using the term *festival.* The poster called it a "Big Blue Grass Celebration." Haney had already used *festival* to describe his own bluegrass events, a minus in the competitive mind of Monroe. *Festival* also suggested similarities to the then prevalent folk festivals, from Newport to the National Folk Festival to the college folk festivals held at Berkeley, Chicago, and many more colleges in the 1960s.

The "Big Blue Grass Celebration" poster listed just a few headliners: Monroe and the Blue Grass Boys, Ralph Stanley & His Clinch Mountain Boys, the Country Gentlemen from Washington, and "Hilo [*sic*]" Brown and Red Allen.[4] The actual lineup also included Benny Martin, with former Monroe banjoist Rudy Lyle playing electric lead guitar, the McCormick Brothers, Bryant Wilson and His Kentucky Ramblers, the Moore Brothers, the Texas-based Stone Mountain Bluegrass Boys, Carl Johnson and the Kentucky Mountain Boys, and Shorty and Juanita Shehan.[5]

Monroe's band then included his son, James William Monroe, on bass and featured several other new members, notably newly minted guitarist Roland White, fiddler Byron Berline, and young Joseph "Butch" Robins on the five-string banjo.[6] Butch had joined the band only a couple weeks before, but being a Blue Grass Boy at Bean Blossom was not entirely positive:

> Early Tuesday morning we left for Bean Blossom. We went early to get the park ready for the festival. My first impression had nightmarish overtones. Birch had been in charge of maintaining the park (classic Monroe thrift mode) and it had fallen into a horrible state of disrepair. The wooded part of the park had been closed since the 50's. The performances had been held in the barn for several

Brown County **JAMBOREE**

Bean Blossom, Ind. Presents

# BIG BLUE GRASS CELEBRATION

## JUNE 24 and 25

—Featuring—

* Bill Monroe and the Blue Grass Boys
* Ralph Stanley and the Clinch Mt. Boys
  (Sat. Only)
* Benny Martin & Rudy Lyles
* Hylo Brown
* McCormick Brothers (Sun. Only)

**Plus many more fine bands.**

**HYMN SINGING FROM 9-11
SUNDAY MORNING**

**Camping Facilities Available**

Y ' A L L     C O M E

The first Bean Blossom Bluegrass Festival, held at the Brown County Jamboree, was advertised as the "Big Blue Grass Celebration" in the *Brown County Democrat*, June 22, 1967.

years. The barn wasn't in the best of shape; age and structural damage as the result of a fire gave one such as I pause for thought when the wind blew.

Tuesday afternoon we began barn cleanup. Wednesday we mowed and strung lights for the parking area and continued barn cleanup and repair. . . .

Early Thursday we went to Indianapolis to promote the festival on a morning TV talk show. . . . Before we left the city we packed the bus with folding chairs from a rental company. That evening and the next morning we set up chairs in the barn. . . . The festivities started in the [*sic*] about 6:00 PM Friday evening. Bill had hired several solo acts so the Blue Grass Boys became the house band. Hylo Brown and Red Allen stand out in my memory. . . . Bill Monroe and the solo acts kept the Blue Grass Boys busy. Between sets we were the festival staff. It was a tiring week but I was still excited, I was a budding star (ha). When time for settlement came, one at a time, we were summoned to the "office" near the front entrance. Bill counted out $53.00 and handed it to me. He looked right at

me and said, "I ain't gonna pay you no more'n this cause you ain't in the union."
That was the end of that.[7]

Roland White recalled how unfamiliar the whole experience was for him:

Well, it was just, like, like I say, I had just come from California, I hadn't been at a real down-to-earth bluegrass festival. Anyway there's an old ragged barn. Then suddenly you look around a while later, and all these folks people appeared. There was no rehearsing, or sound check, or anything. Like there was microphones up there, and ol' Silver Spur was there, Denzel Ragsdale, and he had his little sound system. And I remember Bill and Birch were arguing—not arguing, but Bill and Birch would go back and forth about putting speakers outside. Bill felt that there were going to be more people than they could handle, and they could hear the show outside. Which is exactly what happened.

You know, I just do what I'm told. Livin' off the bus, there, and going down to the little restaurant to eat, and then I find myself on Friday afternoon, there, in the ticket booth, taking tickets. Taking money from people; I don't even know if they had tickets, just took the money. I did that for a while. And then, next thing I know, somebody—I can't remember who it was, came over there and says—"Roland, you need to be on stage in about five minutes," and here I am, not dressed for it. You don't go on stage without a coat and hat and all that. "What?" So we run up there, and—Okay, that's right, we stayed in the motel down the highway. Orchard Hill, that's the one. I changed real quick and made it back in time for this because they were running about fifteen to twenty minutes late.[8]

Fortunately, Neil Rosenberg attended the first festival as both a participant-observer scholar and an "insider" musician and perceptive emcee. Rosenberg's tapes of the first festival's shows in the barn document Benny Martin's Saturday shows, on which Neil played banjo. Martin's fiddle rang out that day on his featured selections, including "Bells of St. Mary's," "Wildwood Flower," and "Salty Dog Blues" on both the afternoon and evening shows.

After being introduced by Silver Spur, a familiar Jamboree group, the Moore Brothers, offered a set combining traditional songs ("John Hardy," "Old Joe Clark") with an homage to the first generation of bluegrass ("Baby Blue Eyes," "Teardrops in My Eyes").

Saturday night, Ralph Stanley fronted the Clinch Mountain Boys, with Curley Lambert, mandolin; George Shuffler, guitar; Larry Sparks, lead guitar and vocals; and Curly Ray Cline on fiddle. It was just six months since Carter's death. Seeing Larry Sparks for the first time, Marvin Hedrick was impressed by the young artist's guitar-playing talent. Ralph's show included Stanley Brothers standards like "How Mountain Girls Can Love," "Little Maggie," "Think of What

You've Done," and "Another Night," as well as new pieces like the instrumental "Row Hoe" and the ghost-story song "That Beautiful Woman," performed that night with the song's composer, Gene Duty, singing lead. John Wright, recalling Ralph's evening show at the first Bean Blossom festival, emphasizes that the new bandleader came across not as a "fumbling beginner, but an assured, mature, confident professional."[9] Stanley played the June festival at Bean Blossom through many ensuing decades of the Monroe era, becoming the most frequently appearing artist there other than Monroe himself.[10]

When music-festival audiences share an overnight stay, the parking-lot experience evolves into a campground experience. The collective group of campers establishes a whole new temporary township, a place for musical and social interchange and, over the course of time, a core community of individuals who regard themselves as part of the Bean Blossom family and the festivals as their annual reunions. One key to the success of bluegrass festivals is the creation of this sort of temporary cultural scene, realized anew at every enduring bluegrass festival. The festival scene welcomes newcomers and supports jam sessions that take place at the hearths, campfires, and front porches of the community. In the parking lot, everyone at Bill Monroe's festival is, legally speaking, on Bill Monroe's property, but in the campground, one also picks in places that are the temporary annual property of the camper or RV owner. The expectation that a certain friend or acquaintance always camps in the same place produces shared mental maps and a collectively emergent cultural geography of the park and festival grounds.

Although sporadic parking-lot picking took place for years in Bean Blossom's fields, the festival altered everything. The intensity grew as parking lots were complemented by overnight campers crowded onto the festival grounds for a concentrated bluegrass experience. And in the early festival years at Bean Blossom, the experience was indeed passionate and powerful.

Places to camp at the first festival at Bean Blossom were all "in the rough," lacking running water, electricity, dumping stations, or other modern hookup amenities designed for recreational vehicles, which were then just beginning to come into widespread use. Originally, there was no additional charge for camping; free camping was then commonly offered by promoters of bluegrass festivals on large rural sites, in order to encourage potential audiences. Although the Monroes soon began to assess extra charges for festival campsites, they were slow to upgrade the campground's facilities, so for a long time camping at Bean Blossom meant camping in the rough.

Moreover, the meaning of "rough" at Bean Blossom was evidently a Monrovian one, informed and inspired by Bill and Birch's own rough and "hardscrabble" upbringing on a western Kentucky farm. At Bean Blossom, the Monroes' festival-hosting philosophy centered somehow on the idea that making do with existing facilities, rather than improving them, was the right thing to do. As Bill openly put it, the right way to do anything at Bean Blossom in the way of facilities construction or management was "the way we done it back in Kentucky." At the Brown County Jamboree site in 1967, this philosophy echoed the sanitary inadequacies of Carlton Haney's first festivals: welcoming the festival crowds with only the old, dilapidated concrete-block restroom behind the barn, plus a couple of outhouses. At successive festivals, a modest number of Porta-Potties also appeared. As self-contained RVs became common and grew more comfortable and inviting, festivalgoers at Bean Blossom could better cope with the rough camping style imposed by a lack of modern sanitary facilities at Bean Blossom. But as topics of ironic remembrance, Bean Blossom's chronically inadequate sanitary facilities and the Monroes' old-fashioned aversion to changes have long endured.

In festival campgrounds, an ephemeral community forms for the festival's duration. In the campground, a hearth and a sleeping place are established by everyone from single campers to large families. The precise way in which this is done naturally varies with each camper and depends on the kind of camping gear, vehicle, and other material culture brought to the festival grounds. In making or setting up camp, however, each camper defines a unique personal and social space, a privately invented space within the public space of the festival as a whole. The Monroe-blessed public and temporarily private spaces of the festival campground offered from the start a more comfortable physical setting into which the tradition of parking-lot picking sessions was easily transplanted.

As at Haney's festivals, the range of national and local artists and groups that Monroe presented at the first festival was unprecedented. Emcee duties were carried out by Silver Spur, Roger Smith, and Neil Rosenberg, and Marvin Hedrick and his sons, Jack Cox, Kyle Wells, and many more local musicians and fans were involved in the big June festival right away. Jim Peva's daughters, for example, were sometimes recruited by Birch to take up a collection at the Sunday church service or to help sell tickets at the gate. For both central Indiana boosters and those who came from afar, the festival experience was a heightened one that almost inexorably drew them back in subsequent years.

By 1967, tape recorders' presence at live bluegrass shows was familiar. With precedents set by Marvin Hedrick at Bean Blossom, and by fans and scholars like Pete Kuykendall, Mike Seeger, and Ralph Rinzler at Sunset Park and New River Ranch, recording was openly accepted by Monroe. Although this practice was prohibited by many artists in later years, many festival shows were taped in the early years of bluegrass festivals, sometimes by attendant participant-scholars like Seeger and Neil Rosenberg, but even more often by dedicated fans and students of the music, like Don Hoos, of Evanston, Illinois. Collectively, such live-show recordings offer a closer look at the way the festivals were run and what meaningful things were heard by the first festival audience: for instance, Ralph Stanley's closing words, which not only acknowledged Monroe's importance as the festival's host but also indicated that Bill had already decided to make the "celebration" an annual event.

Only a few hundred people attended the first Bean Blossom bluegrass festival, and Bill made only a modest profit, about seventeen hundred dollars.[11] But Bill Monroe Fan Club members, like other fans in attendance, reported their excitement at meeting stars and virtuosos from each band. Bill's fan club also noted features of the first festival that were quickly repeated and incorporated into the Bean Blossom bluegrass festival tradition: "Even though it was rather warm in the Brown Co. Jamboree hall there were 'Goose Bumps' on a lot of people. After the show Saturday nite Bill suggested a square dance and showed us how that should be done also. Sunday morning brought some of the finest Gospel singing that I have ever heard. Bill opened with 'Wayfaring Stranger' and for some two and one-half hours he and the others took their turns in singing those good old time foot pattin' Gospels."[12]

The Sunday-morning program immediately became a regular feature of the June festival. Other bluegrass festivals also put on Sunday-morning programs of bluegrass gospel music, but the sincerely religious Monroe went beyond them by bringing in real preachers for a church service. Brother Cummings, Monroe's cousin Reverend Wendell Rains, fellow picker and minister Harold Austin, or Pastor Paul Baggett would lead the festivals' Sunday-morning Christian church services, complete with sermon and the uptake of a monetary offering from the audience-congregation. All featured artists were invited to the bluegrass gospel singing before and after the church service, but certain groups, like the Lewis Family, the Sullivan Family, and the Marshall Family, or certain artists, like Don Reno, who were known for their bluegrass gospel performances and compositions, dominated the Sunday-morning stage.

Enoch Sullivan was part of the Alabama-based bluegrass gospel–singing Sullivan Family, who began to play "string band gospel concert" shows with Bill Monroe in the early 1960s. Enoch later described how the Sullivan Family came to be regulars at Monroe's bluegrass festivals. Although Bean Blossom festival advertisements did not list the Sullivan Family until 1973, Margie Sullivan affirmed that the Sullivan Family group actually began to participate regularly by

1968. Though his remembered chronology of events is slightly jumbled, Enoch recalled vividly the special value that Monroe and other participating artists put on the influence of bluegrass gospel performers on the sort of churchgoing family audiences Monroe hoped to attract:

> Mr. Monroe saw from his first bluegrass festival in Bean Blossom, IN in 1966 [*sic*] that there was a spillover from Woodstock [1969] and he wanted to make a distinction between a rock festival and a bluegrass festival. Bluegrass was and is a working man's music—Christian, gospel, and God-fearing. That's how we got the job.
>
> When Mr. Monroe asked me, he said, "I want you to be on my festival and come to Bean Blossom and help me." I remember saying, "Mr. Bill, I don't know how I could help you." I was thinking in terms of music.
>
> He replied, "No, I'm not talking about music, but you can help me that way, too. I've traveled down South with you and doing concerts with you and I realize the fact that the ministers down there and all them church people trust you all. If I advertise that you're going to be at my festival, it'll let people know that God-fearing people come to my festival; the people that go to church every Sunday and read their Bible. People that believe in God will know that we are having a family festival. We're going to have a church service every Sunday and I want you to help me with the hymn singing."[13]

The Sunday-morning gospel sing, as Monroe established it at Bean Blossom, provided a sanctified prologue for the Sunday-afternoon shows: Monroe's own version of Carlton Haney's worshipful "Story of Blue Grass Music," enacted through performances by Monroe and a sequence of former Blue Grass Boys. The line between the sacred and secular worlds at the Bean Blossom June festival was blurry and indistinct. Bean Blossom audiences, characterized aptly by Robert Cantwell, spent all their time at the festival "believing in bluegrass" on both mundane and spiritual levels, embracing the experience in an intense, near-religious frenzy of devotion and focus.[14]

Before the 1967 festival ended, Monroe was planning for 1968. The overflow crowd at the barn convinced him that a bigger performance space was needed. He had his eye on the old outdoor performance platform, last used at a 1959 or 1960 show by Johnny Cash, which was set in a natural amphitheater in the park's overgrown and neglected northern half. Roland White recalled:

> Oh, yeah, that same weekend in '67, we went to walkin' through the park, you know? He [Bill] was out there doing something, so I walked up to him, it was the early morning, and I asked "How you doin' this morning, Bill?" He says "Oh, I'm looking the place over . . . come with me." And so we went walkin'

down through the woods—it was all overgrown with weeds and brush. He says "we had a music park back here one time. I'm gonna go look at it," he says, "I'm thinking we're gonna have to build a new stage, and open up the park again." "Oh, that'd be great! You know, you're gonna do it again, you'll need to do something." So we went back there and looked at it, and the stage had all rotted out and fallen in, you couldn't even step on it, it was just a pile of rotted wood. It was a very small stage, too. I don't think there was a cover on it. If it had, it had fallen down also. There were saplings growing through it and everything. It was just covered—you couldn't even walk through there.[15]

After the 1967 festival, Sunday-afternoon Jamboree shows resumed with the usual mix of local acts, Bryant Wilson and His Kentucky Ramblers playing as the house band, and periodic headliners. Reno and Harrell returned to the Jamboree that summer, as did Ralph Stanley. The last regular show that year saw a return show by Carl Story, with Bryant Wilson, the Brown County Quartet, and Shorty and Juanita. Curiously, Monroe chose to play an additional Jamboree show there in early December, long after the usual season closer.

Once bluegrass festivals began at Bean Blossom, audiences for the Brown County Jamboree's Sunday shows again began to grow. More university students came to the park to see shows in the barn after they first experienced the festivals. Moreover, Bean Blossom began to be thought of increasingly as a focal point for bluegrass musicians. As far back as the early fifties, Roger Smith had moved to central Indiana because he could then plan on interacting musically with Bill Monroe.[16] Later generations of young bluegrass musicians who happened to be growing up in the region would also be drawn to the park's shows, where they not only saw their musical heroes but underwent key experiences as well. At Bean Blossom, the young Hedrick boys, taught by Roger Smith, would be part of a nearby network of such musicians who also came regularly to learn at the "University of Bluegrass." With regular trips to the Jamboree, they grew up under the eye of Bill Monroe and participated behind the scenes at Bean Blossom in jam sessions with a variety of the greatest first- and second-generation bluegrass musicians.

Among these skilled young local musicians was the son of Carlton Duncan, who had played on the Jamboree in the late 1940s. Glen Duncan, later to become a Blue Grass Boy, was born in 1955 and raised in nearby Columbus, Indiana. Carlton Duncan took his son regularly to the Brown County Jamboree from the time he was a toddler; there Glen saw Bill Monroe perform so often that by 1967, he took Monroe's sound for granted. With many musical instruments provided by his parents before he was even ten years old, Glen began "playing out" at square dances before he was a teenager and could play pedal-steel guitar, piano, acoustic guitar, and some rudimentary fiddle. He was "bitten by the banjo bug" after hearing Earl Scruggs. In the fall of 1967, he and his father went to a Jamboree show to see Ralph Stanley, whose recorded version of "Little Maggie" with the Stanley Brothers had impressed the banjo-bedazzled youngster:

> We go over there, and we see his whole show. It was great. They do everything, and right towards the end he does "Little Maggie," and so I'm happy as I can be. So Monroe's getting ready to come on. And my dad said, "Well, you want to stay and see Bill, or what?" It's like, "Oh, I've got to go to school tomorrow, and gosh, we've seen him so many times, let's just go ahead and go."
>
> So we're literally walking out of the old barn, and we're clear back by the concession stand, and knowin' what I know now—Stanley had gone over *so* big, 'cause they'd encored two or three times—that Monroe come right out of the hatch with "Uncle Pen," which he never did. The whole time I played with him, we had a very set show. Now, he would move the banjo numbers and fiddle numbers around, if he was really trying to gouge somebody that he knew was there, but never, ever, did we ever come on with "Uncle Pen" in all those two hundred shows I played with him, or whatever. They come on with "Uncle Pen," so, I mean, we are literally walking out of the place, all the way at the back, and [Kenny] Baker's playing with him. And we're all the way back, where they used to have some bleachers, clear at the back of the place, you remember that? We're back by those bleachers, and they do "Uncle Pen," and I mean, I had never heard anything like—I mean, I literally froze in my tracks, and turned around, and heard them do it. 'Cause he had a great band; it was a great Bill Monroe band. And I had never, ever heard the fiddle played that well in a bluegrass setting. I'd never heard fiddle of that quality, tone, smoothness, precision, and just an elegance and beauty about it that I just had to have it. And then it was like, "Well, can we go watch this?"
>
> So we just go all the way back down, and sit in about the third row, and watched 'em do the whole show. And of course in typical Monroe fashion they probably played ninety minutes, you know, 'cause he's trying to really show 'em, you know, "*I'm* the guy," you know, "Pay no attention to that other band behind the curtain!"
>
> But it changed my life forever; then, from that time forward, I was a fiddle player. It just changed the whole thing. Changed the whole thing. I'm a fiddle player today because of that.[17]

The 1968 season at Bean Blossom opened in late April. At the first show, Monroe introduced a renewed and powerful version of the Blue Grass Boys, with banjoist Vic Jordan joining Kenny Baker and Roland White. Bill and the band returned to central Indiana a week later to play a two-night booking at the

Blue Flame Club in Indianapolis and made more trips to Bean Blossom to begin preparing the park for the second June festival, scheduled for the full three-day weekend of June 21–23, 1968.

The success of the Bean Blossom bluegrass festival was evident not only to Monroe but also to the thinly scattered national population of dedicated fans, the true believers in bluegrass. Nationally, bluegrass fans kept each other informed through long-standing word-of-mouth channels, but after July 1966, they could also rely on the new national fan magazine *Bluegrass Unlimited.*

As fans made plans for the second Bean Blossom festival, Monroe and the Blue Grass Boys began to construct a new outdoor stage. Bill first said they would use double-bitted axes and a two-man crosscut saw for felling trees to make lumber for the stage. When Bill asked who would get on the other end of the saw, the inexperienced Vic Jordan volunteered. Bill's first pull jerked Vic to his knees, to Bill's great amusement.[18] First attempts to truck lumber to the site were thwarted by the steep, muddy ravine separating the southwestern part of the park from the wooded amphitheater area in the north-central part of the property, at the northern end of the murky lake. At Monroe's direction, the Blue Grass Boys hand-carried long boards of heavy native lumber, locally sawn, down through the deep ravine and over to the building site, where they constructed a new outdoor stage facing northwest in a natural wooded amphitheater.

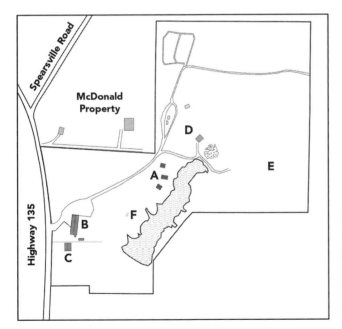

Bill Monroe's Brown County Jamboree Park, ca. 1968. A: Cabins. B: Jamboree barn and restroom. C: Horse barn. D: Outdoor stage-amphi-theater and concessions. E: Hippie Hill.

The design of the 1968 outdoor stage was simple, recalling plain stages built more than a century before for religious camp meetings. The audience saw an elevated stage a little more than thirty feet wide, its floor placed only five feet above ground level, with no footlights or railings obstructing the view. At its front corners, the stage's pitched roof was supported by bark-covered round-log poles. Two symmetrically placed doorway openings at left and right led from the stage itself through a partitioned hallway to the backstage area, where a central staircase divided two "tune-up" rooms and led down to the backstage entrance. Each tune-up room had a large unglazed window opening, lacking any means of closure. A just-adequate electrical circuit was run to the stage by Monroe's friend Calvin Robins, and horn speakers, long preferred by Silver Spur, were hung in the trees shading the amphitheater. As the crowd entered the amphitheater area at the beginning of the 1968 festival, final touches were still being added. Monroe's plan for audience seating closely resembled what Mike Seeger had noted at New River Ranch in the early 1950s.[19] Roland White recalled the scene: "Saturday morning, people were coming in to pick out their seats and camping sites. And we had, probably, ten rows of benches, if that many, and the rest had to be chairs, bring their own chairs. And I dug almost every one of those holes! That's what I was doing that morning, trying to finish up the last row of benches. We were putting in the last few posts, covering 'em up, then putting the planks on, and nailing 'em in there with great big nails. Everything was ready in time for the show."[20]

All music festivals are both public and private events. Monroe's bluegrass festivals provided fans with opportunities to encounter both the approved, controlled, and morally upright events included in the official program and also the informal, uncontrolled, and morally ambiguous or even negative characteristics of festival behavior. These "negative" elements of festivals have always included a certain shared sense that some forms of social misbehavior will be overlooked or tolerated, at least up to a point, because the festival itself defines a "time out of time," during which the social and moral order of normal times is ignored or inverted.[21] Festivals therefore involve people who see one another simultaneously as having the potential to be saints or sinners, as upholders of the society's normal legal and moral order or as temporarily uncontrollable music-party attendees who at any moment (but especially overnight) might be found enhancing their festival experiences with alcohol, drugs, or sex. Even when festival activities did not cross clear legal or moral dividing lines or occur openly, people of varied backgrounds routinely surprised one another with their behavior at the Bean Blossom festivals. Young banjoist Jim Cornell, playing with the Moore Brothers band in the 1970s, recalled his astonishment at the actions of a female fiddle player nicknamed "River Mary," who after jamming with Kenny Baker and others in the campground went back with Jim and several others to a small camper where she partly stripped, changing from a T-shirt to a sweater in their presence.[22] While such displays of partial nudity were never commonplace at Bean Blossom (as they were purported to be at the Woodstock, New York, rock festival), the relaxed standards of appropriateness for festival clothing attracted some criticism.

Many attendees noted the prevalence of drinking. Folklorist and mandolin player Howard Wight Marshall observed in 1972 that the security people at the Bean Blossom festival—either contracted Nashville police officers or Brown County sheriff's deputies—showed remarkable tolerance for possibly illegal displays of drunkenness. Marshall joked that "no matter what you do, they won't arrest you unless you actually throw up on their shoes." The festival offered a setting where tolerance of personal differences—in regional or cultural background, politics, religion, and worldview, as well as in standards of morality and behavior with regard to legal and illegal substance use and abuse—was noted and appreciated. Everyone knew that there were people who drank too much or went out into the far reaches of Bean Blossom's back woods to smoke marijuana or use other recreational drugs of the sixties and seventies. But there was an overall feeling of tolerance, especially at night and especially in the more "private" areas of the campground, as long as those who transgressed legal or moral boundaries did so out of the sight of those who could not tolerate it openly. Some less traveled corners of the campground, especially in the heavily wooded northern section, began to acquire their own names and reputations. Later, Butch Robins would refer to the far northwest corner of the property, where a good deal of drinking and marijuana smoking went on, as "the Amen Corner," and in the next decade a group of hard-partying fans from Tennessee annually established "Camp Rude" on "Rude Dog Hill," also in the sheltered, overgrown north-central part of the park's woods.

The second festival featured not only a new outdoor stage and a longer weekend event but also a larger roster of performers and many more fans. On the 1968 bill were regulars like Monroe and the Sullivan Family, along with other Opry bluegrass stars like Jim & Jesse and the Osborne Brothers. Following longstanding precedents, prominent sidemen were individually named in ads for the 1968 festival; Kenny Baker, Red Allen, Byron Berline, Jim Buchanan, Vic Jordan, James Monroe, and Roland White were thus advertised as "featured" performers, alongside some lesser known or regional names like Neil Rosenberg or radio personalities like WPFB's Paul Mullins and WSM's Grant Turner.

Attendance rose sharply in 1968. Many fans who missed the earlier festivals in Virginia or Bean Blossom were determined to take part in this novel and intensely focused bluegrass experience. Some were part of the massive new wave of converts to bluegrass music who first encountered the bluegrass sound in Arthur Penn's successful film *Bonnie and Clyde.*[23] New festivalgoers drove hundreds or thousands of miles to attend, and everyone at Bean Blossom observed the many different state license plates in the parking lot. Luke Thompson, a mandolinist and mandolin builder, came up from Louisiana and returned every year for a decade, eventually becoming a Bean Blossom emcee. Thompson worked in the late 1970s at Bill's request to tear down the old horse barn south of the Jamboree barn.[24] Thompson also started the first bluegrass festival in Louisiana, booking Monroe as its headliner, and later running his own music park at Folsom, Louisiana.

Although some hard-core bluegrassers had already been to Haney's Fincastle festivals, most who came to Bean Blossom in the late sixties were attending their first bluegrass festival. Not only the audiences but also Monroe, the Blue Grass Boys, and those who worked (formally or informally) on the festival were inventing patterns and traditions that would characterize the Bean Blossom June festival for years to come. For example, the second festival began on Friday with the "Amateur Bluegrass Band Contest," at which Mitchell Land and the Stone Mountain Boys took first place and one hundred dollars in prize money. The Monroes knew from prior experience with the Jamboree and from Haney's "talent contests" that amateur bluegrass music events were a good way to fill the long afternoon hours before the headliners' evening show.

Friday evening a square dance was scheduled at 8:00 p.m. in the old barn. Before the square dance began, something else happened, establishing an annual tradition. Two months later, introducing Loretta Lynn at a Sunday Jamboree show, Bill described it: "We had a jam session here and we had ninety-five in the jam session, everybody playin' bluegrass music. Everybody had learnt from me, or learnt from people that had learnt from me. And we had ninety-five playin,' ninety-four men and one woman was in this jam session, and it was sure wonderful. Started at sunset and wound up around dark."[25] Bill observed that the Sunset Jam gave amateur pickers a welcome chance to play with the professionals, so the Friday-evening "Sunset Jam Session" became a regular feature.

On Saturday, the 1968 festival also added workshop sessions on all the bluegrass lead instruments of that day. There was a fiddle workshop with Kenny Baker, Jim Buchanan, Birch Monroe, Byron Berline, and fiddler-emcee Paul Mullins. The mandolin workshop presented Monroe, Roland White, and Jesse McReynolds, and banjo workshop explanations were handled by Vic Jordan and

Neil Rosenberg. These workshops were conducted after 10:00 a.m. on the new outdoor stage, and although they were nominally an opportunity for students of each bluegrass instrument to learn techniques and approaches from the professionals, they typically turned into miniconcerts, filling the time and entertaining the audience until the afternoon and evening professional concerts began. The real stage shows, emceed by Paul Mullins on Saturday, featured all the big-name bands booked for the second festival: the Osborne Brothers, Ralph Stanley, Jim & Jesse, Mac Wiseman, Red Allen, and finally Monroe's own Blue Grass Boys. On Sunday, Monroe and the Sullivan Family, plus other performers who wanted to participate, provided the gospel-singing core of the morning church service. Sunday afternoon, secular bluegrass shows resumed with emcee Grant Turner and concerts by all the headliners. In keeping with the Haney tradition of retelling at least a part of the "Story of Blue Grass Music," Bill's own 1968 Sunday sets included an appearance by Clyde Moody, one of Bill's first guitar players and singers. Then, slowly, the Sunday audience diminished as campers began to depart for long trips home.

Those who came to the park's shaded amphitheater for the 1968 festival's Sunday-morning "church service" were rewarded by the first significant Bean Blossom involvement of the Sullivan Family, from St. Stephens, Alabama. For this little-traveled bluegrass gospel band from the Deep South, the involvement with Monroe was critical. As a Sullivan-family historian summed it up years later: "Their first step outside of this large regional network of churches and radio programs (and later television) was their appearance at Bill Monroe's Bean Blossom festival in 1968. They caused quite a stir there with their fervent, exhortative music and driving bluegrass backup, and the appearance introduced them to an entirely new audience—the mainstream bluegrass festival goer—they had not played to before."[26]

The June festival was a critical success for most who attended. Filmmaker Stephen Gebhart shot footage of the festival and within a year had produced a twenty-five-minute color 16-mm film titled *Bluegrass at Beanblossom.*"[27] Although this short documentary effort remained essentially uncirculated, Gebhart laid the groundwork for his widely advertised and successful 1993 film, *Bill Monroe: Father of Bluegrass.* Another attendee that year, Bill Grant, of Hugo, Oklahoma, had been invited by Monroe himself and was inspired by what he saw at Bean Blossom to create a bluegrass festival at home: "It was heaven to us. We saw all the bluegrass pickers that we had heard and loved. We decided that we had a similar place at home and there wasn't any bluegrass outings here. There were some fans, but there wasn't any place for them to go. The first year at Hugo, we had 1300–1500 fans at a two-day festival."[28]

Not all were completely content, though. Many noted the shabby, dirty rest-rooms and poorly serviced Porta-Potties, and some who had traveled long distances to attend were also upset by the "no taping allowed" policies of two featured performers. Changes in some of the professionals' musical performance styles were also grounds for discontent. A letter writer to *Bluegrass Unlimited* that fall made his gripes clear: "On the weekend of June 21 I drove a total of 1500 miles to hear bluegrass music—from Raleigh, N.C., to Bean Blossom, Indiana and back. . . . At the Sunday afternoon concert Mac Wiseman could not be recorded (not a word was said and all recorded him on Saturday). Perhaps he was only wanting equal non-time with the Osborne Brothers. At any rate, what he was playing was not bluegrass (even with the Blue Grass Boys backing him up). . . . And the 'new' (read 'soft') bluegrass of the Osborne Brothers with electric bassist Ronnie Reno left a great deal to be desired."[29]

Still, word of the 1968 festival's success spread through the growing national network of bluegrass musicians, and the rest of the 1968 Brown County Jamboree season gave Bill and Birch many opportunities to promote the still-novel annual venture. Just two months later, at a Sunday show, Bill told the audience: "We had our bluegrass festival here, and that always comes off around the twentieth of June, right at the end of the springtime there, and summer gets ready to start. And, uh, we'll be doin' that next year, now, we'll have about, I believe, around four days of it next year. We had three days this past year, didn't we? And we had a wonderful crowd, too, and a wonderful time. . . . And then on Sunday we always have church services here, and the people seem to really enjoy that. They fill the auditorium over there, and we had, really had, a fine bluegrass festival. We're gonna look forward to that this comin' year."[30]

The rest of the 1968 Brown County Jamboree season served up the familiar sequence of weekly country, bluegrass, and novelty acts, always representing both the national context of the Grand Ole Opry and the local music scene as well. Appearing over the weeks following the festival were Carl and Pearl Butler, Loretta Lynn, Jim and Jesse & the Virginia Boys, the Marlin Family (with their famous fiddling father, "Sleepy" Marlin), the Country Travelers, Tommy Cash (younger brother of Johnny), Doug Kershaw, Bill Dudley, Jimmy Wayne and the Country Partners, and 1940s cowboy film star Sunset Carson, who in his later years did a trick-shooting stage act. In mid-July that year, Birch got the Saturday-night "Old Fashioned Square Dance" started again for the season as well.

The closing Sunday Jamboree show that year, on November 10, featured Ralph Stanley and the Clinch Mountain Boys, and Frank "Hylo" Brown also performed, along with Jamboree stalwarts Birch Monroe and Shorty and Juanita. In the modest audience that day were Neil Rosenberg and Norman Carlson, along with several newcomers—including me—whom Neil had invited over for the day following the final sessions of the annual meeting of the American Folklore Society. I was then an undergraduate student at the University of Illinois, and my mentor, Archie Green, had introduced me to Neil previously and urged me to attend the Bloomington AFS meeting that year.

My first impression of the Brown County Jamboree was shaped by Neil's telling me the place was the "country music park" that Monroe owned. I was taken with the interior look of the barn and the close-up view; I sat entranced, seeing deeper into the heart of a musical form I had already loved for nearly a decade. As Norman Carlson had put it so well before, this place's effect was powerful and immediate, astounding me with its rustic look juxtaposed with the commanding musical presences of Monroe and Stanley. By the time I saw them at Bean Blossom, both were artistic heroes of long standing in my personal pantheon. At the Brown County Jamboree, I was on their turf, at Monroe's own place. The manifest power of the music produced by Monroe and Stanley that day was impressive, and I loved the entertaining music and corny humorous patter of Shorty and Juanita. Shorty really worked out with his trick fiddling, accompanied by Juanita's amazing one-chord-per-beat sock-rhythm guitar. Both of them kept up a rapid-fire comedic approach to the audience and to each tune or song. Often their jokes were traditional, and well structured, as when Shorty would remark between numbers, "We can afford to play music because we're really in the iron and steel business—she irons, and I steal!" or, in a feigned forgetful moment, look inside his own coat in order to remember his own name and then announcing that he must be "Robert Hall," or Juanita's yelling out "Derriere!" after several numbers and then explaining that the term was French for "the end."[31] Leaving the Jamboree that evening, I knew I would return, drawn back by the powerful magnetism of the music itself and the esoteric, enigmatic charms of the park and its distinctive hosts.

# 7

## The Festival Becomes
## a Landmark, 1969–71

The 1969 Brown County Jamboree opened in late April, with Bill Monroe sharing the limelight with "Red and Fred," the engaging duo of country comedian and guitarist Fred Smith and mandolinist Red Rector. Red and Fred worked on two key Knoxville, Tennessee, radio and television shows, the *Mid-Day Merry-Go-Round* and Cas Walker's *Farm and Home Hour* television show.

May brought shows by Ernie Ashworth wearing his trademark "Lips" suit to remind fans of his sole hit, "Talk Back Trembling Lips," as well as Martha Carson, Grand Ole Opry guitar wizard Joe Edwards, Jimmie Skinner, and Grandpa Jones and his fiddling wife, Ramona.

The 1969 festival demonstrated lively growth. Returning tent and RV campers discovered a new two-dollar-per-night camping fee. The 1967 festival had offered performances by thirteen advertised artists or bands, but in 1968 the number grew to nineteen, and in 1969 to twenty-eight.[1] Only three bluegrass festivals were held anywhere in 1967, but in 1968 "Bean Blossom" was one of eight, and by 1969 there were at least sixteen competing events.[2] Moreover, the nominal duration of Monroe's festival increased from two days in 1967 to three in 1968 and four in 1969. The band contest was retained in 1969 as a Friday-afternoon event, and the Monroes added a banjo contest for Thursday, with a Gibson RB-100 banjo as first prize. Joseph "Butch" Robins, urged to enter by his father, Calvin, won in 1969.[3]

A lot of devoted first-time attendees returned annually for many subsequent years, not only becoming regulars at the event, but in some cases taking active roles in the festival's production and management. Raymond Huffmaster, a twenty-six-year-old guitarist from Meridian, Mississippi, first attended in 1969. The son of a

BILL MONROE'S
# BLUE GRASS FESTIVAL
## Brown County Jamboree Park
Bean Blossom, Indiana
Highway 135

## JUNE 19-22, 1969
- MIKE SEEGER
- THE COUNTRY GENTLEMEN
- DOC WATSON AND SON MERLE
  SATURDAY ONLY
- MAC WISEMAN
- DOC HOPKINS
- JIM AND JESSE AND THE
  VIRGINIA BOYS

Dozens of other well-known country music
entertainers and performances.

Tickets sold at Jamboree Park

CAMPING FACILITIES $2.00 DAILY

The third Bean Blossom Bluegrass Festival, held at the "Brown County Jamboree Park," as advertised in the *Brown County Democrat*, June 19, 1969.

harmonica player who often played Monroe's tunes around the house, Huffmaster saw Monroe in 1964 and in the next few years learned to play the guitar "out of necessity." He attended in 1969 with a friend from home, Alva Linton, and the two of them set up a tent, played music around the clock, jammed with Eddie Adcock and Charlie Waller, and met young guitar dealer George Gruhn.

The festival's performance scope slowly began to shift. The first two festivals had featured some truly local or regional acts, like the Moore Brothers, Shorty and Juanita Shehan, and Bryant Wilson. Though various separate members of those groups faithfully returned to annual festivals for many years, local bands were increasingly displaced in the advertised festival roster, implying a new national orientation. The year 1969 saw debuts by Jimmy Martin & the Sunny Mountain Boys; Carl Story & the Rambling Mountaineers; Curtis Blackwell, Randall Collins, & the Dixie Bluegrass Boys; Don Reno, Bill Harrell, & the Tennessee Cutups; the Goins Brothers; Wade and Julia Mainer; Doc Watson and his son, Merle; and the Washington, D.C.–based duo of Alice Gerrard and Hazel Dickens. A growing international interest in bluegrass music underlay the appearance of Pete Sayers, founder of England's first bluegrass band in the late 1950s. Sayers moved to Nashville for a five-year period around 1966, so he did not travel any farther than Bill Monroe to get to the festival. The winners of the 1968 band contest, Mitchell Land & the Stone Mountain Boys, returned from Dallas, Texas, to play a featured show on the outdoor stage.

Individual artists appearing in 1969 spanned the rural-urban and north-south spectra. There were venerable country artists, old favorites of Bill Monroe, like Doc Hopkins, Wade and Julia Mainer, and "Fiddlin'" Arthur Smith. New artists appeared as well, with an appeal to northern and urban sensibilities: for instance, New York progressive banjoist Roger Sprung and Monroe's friend fiddler Tex Logan.

The previous fall, after one of their annual "Monroe birthday parties" at Tex Logan's house, Bill had asked Tex, "Why don't you come out to Bean Blossom and cook them beans?"—so in 1969 Tex began a nine-year span as overseer of "Barbecue Bean Day" at the June festivals. At his last appearance there in 1978, he was advertised not only as a fiddler who would perform his own show backed by the Blue Grass Boys, but also as the host of Barbecue Bean Day. This event, usually held on a festival weekday, invited fans to partake in a free meal built around Tex's beans, cooked in a large pot in a shed erected in the front parking lot and served with a garnish of onions and either cornbread or "light bread" purchased by Birch at McDonald's IGA store. The fans, who might have noted Tex scurrying around that morning in a long white "duster" coat, making preparations, would line up outside the bean shed to get a paper plate filled with beans, bread, and onions. Other bluegrass festivals often incorporated such free meals or "potluck" shared-food events that echoed the reciprocal sharing of food familiar to many churchgoing southerners as "dinner on the grounds," and (along with other sorts of food preparation and consumption) was also going on privately in the festivals' campground communities. The offering of a free meal also resonated with the implicit sense that the promoters and fans were participants in a food-based ritual of "southern hospitality."[4]

The year 1969 was when the Woodstock rock festival took place, which in August attracted more than four hundred thousand fans to an upstate New York farm. The notoriety of Woodstock, layered on top of the 1968 "Summer of Love" in San Francisco and growing public protests of the war in Vietnam by the rebellious "youth culture" or "counterculture," helped polarize the American public, seeming to separate older, conservative, rural-oriented constituencies from younger, liberal, urban populations across America. Yet at Bean Blossom, it was clear that fans from these diverse groups and others were drawn together by bluegrass, a fact noted by historians and newspaper writers. Jim Rooney, former performing partner of Bill Keith, characterized the diverse crowd: "college students, bluegrass musicians, rock musicians, country musicians, folklorists, farmers, truck drivers, mechanics, housewives—everyone who has been touched by Bill's music." A perceptive photographer-writer, David DeJean, covering the event for a reflective essay in the Louisville newspaper's weekend feature magazine, noted that bluegrass music had matured from being another kind of hillbilly music into "the people's choice" for both hillbillies and city slickers. In a photo caption, he summarized the event by saying, "'The father of bluegrass music,' Bill Monroe is the founder, director, main attraction."[5]

In the vernacular of the day, the supposedly opposed subcultures at the festival were called "rednecks" and "hippies." At Bean Blossom in the early years, people noticed such diverse groupings, but there was gratitude that during bluegrass festivals, most fans ignored background differences because of their shared love of bluegrass music and the unspoken sense as well that Monroe's festivals at Bean Blossom were potentially fragile events, well worth protecting.

There were intercultural surprises, nonetheless. Many hard-drinking "good old boys" from rural Kentucky found themselves joining in with long-haired university students with bare feet to admire the stage shows and participate in the jam sessions, but friction and shock were almost inevitable. The campground at night was particularly full of people—often the nonplaying friends and family of the committed pickers—drinking, talking, joking, and carrying on at and around the many jam sessions at campground hearths. Sometimes partying got loud and rowdy, but only rarely did it get out of hand, since there was always the anchoring influence of the music itself.

At Bean Blossom in the early festival years, the music was everywhere, and constant, both onstage and in jam sessions. The quietest areas in the campground lay in the undeveloped woods and fields in the park's far-eastern section, north of the lake. Campers who sought a measure of solitude and required no electricity or running water at their campgrounds pitched tents in this upper area. Since a good many of those who first camped in this section were young and long-haired, by 1970 the name "Hippie Hill" was adopted by Monroe and many festival attendees for this part of the park.

Some who encountered the long-haired representatives of a new generation were more positively impressed by their musicianship than they were put off by their appearance. One Oklahoma fan, Royce Campbell, left Bean Blossom with a new opinion after his 1970 picking sessions with some of the new generation, saying, "I was very honored also to have met & played with the so called younger or new generation. You might call them heppies to me but not the term Hippies. Anyone as nice to meet & as dedicated to Bluegrass Music & good showmanship as these people are, have to be 'Hep' & will always be my friends." Monroe voiced similar sentiments in a *Newsweek* article run a few days later, saying, "My hippie fans know when the music is played right."[6]

In early festival years, people continued to sleep in their cars and kept their instruments close by, so the entire parking lot continued to be an acceptable site for jam sessions. Like the developing campground, it was also filled with groups of intensely focused pickers. Some parking-lot or campground jams seemed to be entirely made up of organized bands, who could play in tight synchrony through carefully arranged songs or tunes, but that was the exception. On bluegrass-band contest day, many amateur and semiprofessional groups would warm up and practice behind the outdoor stage, or in nearby groves, or in other odd corners of the park. Fans and friends and other pickers and visitors might wander up to such picking sessions, as they did at the more typical impromptu jam sessions conducted by small groups that included strangers or new acquaintances or others who did not regularly pick together, to observe and listen. At Bean Blossom, a high percentage of the observing, listening fans also thought of themselves as bluegrass pickers, just taking a break from their own music making or, in the case of intimidated beginners, carefully looking for a jam at the right level for their developing skills.

At each annual Bean Blossom festival, the portable camp meeting–like community of festivalgoers formed and re-formed. Coming together for the festival, they re-created a temporary society in which all shared in a kind of voluntary ethnic identity defined by the musical forms and social conventions of bluegrass. This sense was constantly reinforced by Bill Monroe's ubiquitous patriarchal presence at the festivals, moving among those he would sometimes call his "children": "Mingling among them from time to time may be seen a bespectacled figure in a white cowboy hat and a sport jacket, with longish white hair and a wide girth, attending to a variety of tasks: greeting arrivals at the gate, pausing with a group of people to have his picture taken, or striding out to the edge of a field with a group of young roustabouts, all of them skinny as snakes, to sink a few new fenceposts where cars have begun to overflow into a neighboring farm."[7]

Monroe would walk the grounds of the park at Bean Blossom almost continuously when he was not required to be onstage or hosting a workshop. He was sometimes purposeful, remedying problems at the park—fixing fences, running temporary electric or water lines to campers, overseeing small groups of his sidemen or other members of his festival labor pool as they took on the myriad small but essential tasks required each year by the big event. But while he guarded his time and his emotions—he could employ a stony silence and a thousand-yard stare to ignore a pushy reporter's shallow questions—he always made time during festivals to greet his fans, sign autographs, and hand out shiny new quarters to awestruck children. Back in the farther reaches of the parking lot or campground, he would pause in his meandering journey to listen to jam sessions, commenting appreciatively at a well-played break or, on rarer occasions, joining in to show parking-lot pickers the *right* way to play one of his compositions.

Monroe opened the 1970 season at Bean Blossom with Jimmie Skinner as the featured guest, followed by Bill himself with his 1970 band: James on guitar, Rual Yarbrough on banjo, Skip Payne on bass, and Kenny Baker on fiddle. Although that show was advertised in the paper, by 1970 Birch had cut far back on weekly newspaper advertisements. Bill, too, seemed much more focused on his growing involvements with festivals than on the weekly Jamboree.

No other newspaper ads for the Jamboree appeared until after the June festival. Birch relied on the familiar fourteen-by-twenty-two-inch showcards, ordered from Hatch Show Print in Nashville, Tennessee, or from Tribune Press in Earl Park, Indiana. Then he personally drove to surrounding towns and hamlets, where certain stores let him put a poster in the store window or on a bulletin board. In Bloomington, posters would appear in stringed-instrument music stores near the university, like Tom Pickett's Guitar Gallery, and in the windows of an odd collection of grocery stores, gas stations, and farm-supply depots. Birch's system of advertising worked, but only because fans already familiar with the Jamboree had learned to look in the right places for the posters.

As 1970's shows went on, the newspaper advertising record grew increasingly spotty. Some 1970 shows were probably played by an energetic banjo player from Terre Haute named Louie Popejoy. Popejoy was the leader of his band, the Wabash Valley Boys, which included Terre Haute guitarist John Jackson and Ed Whittemore from Paris, Illinois, on mandolin. Popejoy was a singer, songwriter, and multi-instrumentalist who quickly became a regular attendee and performer.

Within a year, Louie was identified as leader of "the regular Sunday house band at the Jamboree." Dedicated to earning a living through his music, Popejoy also went on to teach lessons on banjo, fiddle, and guitar and to play hundreds of educational school-assembly programs, not only in and around Terre Haute and central Indiana but also nationally, with shows eventually presented in more than twenty-five states.

By the Wednesday opening day of the fourth June festival, now five days long, the bluegrass world had completely embraced the idea of large multiday festivals. Such events were popping up all across the country, and their attendance was rapidly increasing. Locally, the impact of Monroe's festivals was noted by the previously oblivious Brown County public, and a crude measure of their success was often reported by news media focusing on impressive attendance figures. For 1970, the Bloomington newspaper stated that Bill Monroe was expecting more than fifteen thousand at Bean Blossom. Planned events included the barbecue bean "lunch" on Wednesday, banjo contest on Thursday, band contest with twenty-four competing bands on Friday, and finally the Friday-evening Sunset Jam Session and square dance. Don Brown & the Ozark Mountain Trio won the 1970 band contest; as a well-known group from Missouri that had briefly had John Hartford as a member, their semiprofessional status provoked grumbling among the amateur competitors. Workshops on the bluegrass instruments were conducted Saturday morning in the barn by Mike Seeger, Roger Smith, Ralph Rinzler, and Jim Rooney, with significant roles played by the Blue Grass Boys, especially banjoist Rual Yarbrough and multi-instrumentalist Joe Stuart. Onstage emcee duties were handled mostly by Jeff Cook and Paul Mullins, assisted by Grant Turner, the "voice of the Grand Ole Opry." On Sunday, the church service and gospel sing were held in the morning, also in the barn, and a final round of concerts by the big headliners on the outdoor stage ended the 1970 festival. Moving throughout the festival was photographer Carl Fleischhauer, whose illuminating photos would help to document this bluegrass festival (and many others).[8]

The 1970 festival featured a long list of bluegrass performers, with shows by Monroe, Ralph Stanley, the Country Gentlemen, Jim and Jesse, Jimmy Martin, Reno & Harrell, and the Sullivan Family and return appearances by Doc Watson, Hylo Brown, Red Allen, Hazel and Alice, Tex Logan, and Nashville-based Englishman Pete Sayers "from London." There was one major new group as well: the Earl Scruggs Revue.

Earl Scruggs broke up with his longtime partner, Lester Flatt, in 1969, and soon formed the Earl Scruggs Revue around his own family, with his sons all taking part and his wife, Louise, continuing (as during most of the Flatt & Scruggs years) to manage the business. The sound of Scruggs's new band was not accepted by most 1970 listeners as bluegrass. Like traditional bluegrass, it was often urgent and loud, but it used drums and electric guitars surrounding Earl's highly amplified rolling banjo and emphasized a repertoire of new popular songs. The Revue did not do pastoral songs based on the nostalgic recall of a simpler bygone life lived in little mountain cabins. The Bloomington newspaper described Scruggs as "acclaimed the fastest banjo picker in the business, [who] developed a style most popularized by 'The Beverly Hillbillies' theme."[9] No one in the audience missed the symbolic import of Monroe's hiring his successful former sideman to play at his bluegrass festival. Monroe's prior legendary hostility to Flatt & Scruggs, once seen as his renegade sidemen who had successfully brought their version of *his* style of country music to the Opry over his objections, did not apply, since the Earl Scruggs Revue's music departed from so many bluegrass norms. Despite the audience's acknowledgment of Earl's artistic greatness and critical historical place in bluegrass music, the Earl Scruggs Revue drew some negative reviews from the tradition-minded audience at Bean Blossom. After this one Bean Blossom festival appearance, the Revue performed for many years at large and successful concerts staged at colleges and large music festivals. They played only once more at Bean Blossom, in the fall of 1981.

Louie Popejoy, on the festival roster in 1971, contributed to the chain of face-to-face encounters that transmit the traditional competence of knowledge and technique identifying individuals as bluegrass musicians. Spencer Sorenson, a musician from Denmark who lived in Urbana, Illinois, for several years, recalled Popejoy helping him with that process: "I think that in order to get better you need to play with those better than yourself, provided, of course, they can turn off their ego and be willing to help. The best example of this that I can think of was a long time ago [at] a jam in Bean Blossom with Louie Popejoy, where yours truly as a beginner made a lot of mistakes. I tried to apologize, but he just smiled and said, 'that's what jams are for,' and we kept on going. I'll never forget that, nor the chords to Blackberry Blossom, which he helped me with."[10] Such instances of mentoring characterized the festivals, making Bean Blossom more than ever the "University of Bluegrass," or at least a learning laboratory for all who played.

The intensity of my own involvement by 1970 was typical of many attendees and was chronicled with colorful exaggeration by a journalist friend, Fritz Plous. In a *Chicago Sun-Times* feature, he wrote:

> The first night at Bean Blossom, Tom Adler didn't sleep at all. When he arrived from Chicago at 1 p.m. Thursday he got out of his car, tuned up his banjo and

immediately joined a pickup band that had hastily formed a few feet from his parking space. In the ensuing 24 hours Adler didn't miss a thing; a 23-year-old graduate student now, Adler has played the banjo for 12 years, and this was what he played it for.

Oblivious to everything about him except the music, Adler played banjo with a succession of fiddlers, mandolin-pickers, guitarists and bass-players from all parts of the United States, usually without bothering to learn his partner's name first. He started on Thursday afternoon with "Fisher's Hornpipe," and when the air got cool and the moon sailed on the clouds like a big mother-of-pearl button he was playing "Little Maggie" and "Flint Hill Special." By 9 a.m. Friday . . . he was still picking his banjo with undiminished rapture and his colleagues were in virtually the same state.[11]

The 1970 festival also drew serious scholarly attendees. Folklorists Archie Green and Judith McCulloh, both from the University of Illinois, were there, as was Ralph Rinzler. McCulloh, whose own dissertation concerned the lyric folk song cluster "In the Pines," tried to use the festival opportunity to learn more about one of the most influential recorded versions of "In the Pines," by Bill Monroe:

> During the mandolin workshop (a.m.) at the Brown County Jamboree—Bluegrass Festival at Bean Blossom, a man asked Bill Monroe about "one of his early records, with Charlie Monroe, 'In The Pines.'" Monroe said that Charlie was not with him on that recording, made in the early 1940s, but Clyde Moody and Cousin Wilbur were.
>
> Later that afternoon Archie [Green] introduced me to Bill Monroe, who was sitting on the steps behind the outdoor stage in the glen. I reminded Bill that Ralph Rinzler had interviewed him about "In The Pines" on my behalf, but he did not appear to remember the evening. His association of the song was with Clayton McMichen. I asked him if he remembered the musicians he had heard sing it over Georgia radio, but got no response. Either he did not remember, or was already tired from the festival, or did not want to get involved in a detailed conversation in the midst of chaos, or whatever.[12]

McCulloh's characterization of her Saturday-afternoon meeting with Monroe "in the midst of chaos" was apt; the fourth June festival, bigger than all the bluegrass festivals that had ever preceded it, was by Saturday night a thrumming mass of fans, pickers, artists, vendors, instrument dealers, and camping families. People were constantly on the go, buying food, drinks, and bluegrass albums at concession stands; checking out concerts at the outdoor stage; and appreciating jam sessions and informal picking parties all over the park.

For many attendees, preparing to camp at the festival and coping with the socially diverse crowd were novel experiences. Bettie Leonard, vice president of the Bill Monroe Fan Club in Murfreesboro, Tennessee, commented on issues of festival preparedness and morality:

> For the first time we carried along a tent this year. Next year we'll know to carry more food. Since the crowd gets bigger every year it is hard to keep enough hamburgers cooking to feed such a crowd. I never thought the day would come that the King of Bluegrass would come up to our camp & say I'm starved. I haven't had a bite of breakfast & all in the world we had to eat was cookies. We didn't even have a cup of coffee. I promise we'll do better next time, Bill.
>
> I hope something can be done about the strong drinks in the park in the future. There are so many children at the festival. I was standing nearby & heard Bill tell a man he shouldn't be drinking such stuff. I felt like saying amen. It's bad enough to see a fellow or a gal walking around drinking, but it's awful when an entertainer comes out on stage so drunk he can't sing his song right. I think he should be called off & sent on his merry way.[13]

After the June festival, the rest of the Brown County Jamboree season seemed a bit anticlimactic to many local bluegrass fans, particularly since the Sunday shows had always been locally known as a place to see country, not bluegrass, entertainment. Bluegrass music was generally ascendant; the first four groups advertised for Jamboree shows after the festival were Louie Popejoy and the Wabash Ramblers, Birch Monroe, the Goins Brothers, and Bill Monroe. Monroe closed out the 1970 year at Bean Blossom on the first of November, about a month after his induction into the Country Music Hall of Fame.

But 1970 also witnessed two very special fall events: the two-day First Annual Old Time Singing Convention with bluegrass and gospel groups in September and the Old Fiddlers' Convention in October. Compared with the successful and nationally visible June festivals, these were much smaller events and much more sparsely attended. As a *Brown County Democrat* reporter noted that fall:

> Last Sunday's crowd was apparently not as large as usual at the Jamboree. Birch Monroe attributed the smaller turnout to the heat.
>
> Popejoy also commented on the size of the crowd. But he wasn't discouraged.
>
> "I've played to smaller audiences than this," he announced from the stage, grinning slyly.
>
> "Why, one time the curtain went up and there was only one man sitting out there," he said. "I told him we were proud to have him and we'd get right on with playing. He said, 'I wish you would, because I'm the janitor, and I gotta sweep.'"[14]

The relationship between Bill and Birch Monroe could be stormy. Birch lived in Indiana year-round, while Bill made trips there only for festival and Jamboree appearances; Bill often seemed to have the upper hand, though.[15] Accounts exist of Bill arguing very seriously with Birch about details of the park's operation. But the leisure moments of long festival days were perfect times for pranks and practical jokes, memorable when they involved the principals. Melvin Goins recalled that in an early-1970s festival, Bill generated a little humor at Birch's expense:

> Bill was always good to play tricks on people. Birch had went down to the store here, where the little restaurant used to be, the little Bean Blossom café, there's a little store stood there. So Birch went down there and bought a dozen doughnuts. And Birch was gonna sell them doughnuts for twenty-five or fifty cents apiece. So Bill knew where Birch had went; he knew he'd went to get them doughnuts.
>
> And he told the woman there, he said, "Make me a good pot of coffee," said, "black and strong." So the woman put Bill on a pot of coffee.
>
> Well, about the time Birch got back, the coffee was done. Well, Birch set the doughnuts down, he was gonna sell 'em, he was markin' down his price. And Bill winked at the woman in the place and said, "Bring on the coffee."
>
> So the lady brought the coffee, so Bill got right in that box of doughnuts. He eat that whole dozen of doughnuts. And drank that coffee.
>
> I'll never forget Birch's remarks. He said, "Bill, I didn't know you liked doughnuts that good."
>
> He said, "Birch, them's powerful doughnuts. Go get us another box!"
>
> Birch said, "Bill, I was gonna *sell* them."
>
> He said, "I needed them worse than you did!"[16]

In 1971, Louie Popejoy officially took over the "house band" position at the Brown County Jamboree, fronting shows put on by headlining artists. Bill Monroe opened the park's Jamboree season in April, and that month featured the return of Lonzo and Oscar. In May, several new bluegrass groups appeared. The famous Lewis Family from Lincolnton, Georgia ("the first family of gospel bluegrass"), made a Bean Blossom debut, as did bands led by former Blue Grass Boys: Rual Yarbrough and the Dixie Men and Bobby Smith and the Boys from Shiloh. There were also country music shows by Jimmie Skinner and by former WLW *Midwestern Hayride* star Charlie Gore. Shorty and Juanita Shehan were on the bill with Charlie Gore in early June, as were Wilma Lee and Stoney Cooper and the Clinch Mountain Clan, all old friends of Bill Monroe.

The 1971 June festival again grew bigger and more complex than all those that had gone before. Even more artists appeared, and the crowd was huge. Two large ads in the county newspaper proclaimed it "the greatest array of Stars ever assembled on one show."[17] The event was scheduled for an unprecedented six days, beginning on Tuesday with "Barbecue Bean Day" and "Bluegrass School," followed by afternoon and evening shows on the outdoor stage. With Wednesday came a new event created by Bill, the "Little Miss Bluegrass Beauty Contest," which drew a few shy teenagers to the outdoor stage, where the winner was selected by popular vote from the audience. She later would receive a $25 prize and a trip to the Grand Ole Opry. By 1971, the festival structure and its traditional orientation were complete in the minds of both the Monroes and the returning fans, so Thursday predictably saw the banjo contest, with a $100 prize for the winner; on Friday came the "big bluegrass band contest," with $575 in prizes, followed by the Sunset Jam and the old-time square dance in the barn.

Bill came up from Tennessee the previous weekend and spent most of Monday at the park working. Frank Overstreet, the lively Indianapolis bluegrass booster, writer, and guitarist for the Bluegrass Blackjacks, envied Monroe's "inexhaustible supply of energy," evident even before the festival began: "Monday I saw him helping to set a fence, then placing a pole in the ground for electric wires, then boarding his bus heading for a TV show in Indianapolis."[18]

Amateur pickers were as deeply involved as ever in round-the-clock parking-lot and campground picking. One newcomer that year was a young banjo player from Iowa named Bob Black, who would become a Blue Grass Boy about three years later. Bean Blossom 1971 was his first bluegrass festival, and he plunged without hesitation into "the midst of chaos" and acquired "a lifelong case of bluegrass fever." Writing about his experiences thirty years later, he recalled the colorful fervor of the Bean Blossom jamming scene: "The number of amateur musicians was astounding, and their excitement was intense and contagious. Bill Monroe's presence had everyone so fired up that they played their music nonstop, day and night, as if possessed by demons."[19]

The audience in 1971 was more diverse than ever, because the festival's reputation had grown and spread. Bob Artis, mandolin player for a western Pennsylvania group, Mac Martin & the Dixie Travelers, heard Bill Monroe boast from the stage that year that "there were people present from every state—Alaska and Hawaii included—and five foreign countries."[20]

If the audience seemed geographically diverse, the stylistic array of artists at the fifth festival was truly stunning. Many stars were, by this time, festival "regulars" whom the fans in the audience expected to see each year: Ralph Stanley, Jim and Jesse, and Don Reno with both his former costar, Red Smiley, and his newer partner, Bill Harrell. Mac Wiseman, Mike Seeger, Tex Logan, Hazel and

Alice, and Doc Watson all returned in 1971, as did gospel bandleader Carl Story with his Rambling Mountaineers.

Fans from Canada and Europe had made their way to Bean Blossom before, but the 1971 festival lineup was, for the first time, truly international in scope. The stage shows included two bands who, unlike "Pete Sayers from London," really had traveled from abroad to attend and perform. The Hamilton County Bluegrass Band from New Zealand featured a female fiddler, Colleen Trenwith. Mike Seeger had helped arrange for the Hamilton County Bluegrass Band to take part, and they performed to great applause on Friday evening's show.

Dick Freeland, founder of Rebel Records, arranged the Bean Blossom debut of the Bluegrass 45, from Kobe, Japan, who played their first shows on Saturday to even greater acclaim. In the afternoon, the Bluegrass 45 delighted the well-versed audience with their version of the Stanley Brothers classic "How Far to Little Rock?" which is an update of the venerable "Arkansas Traveler" dialogue. The Bluegrass 45 did it entirely in Japanese. Their show included some bluegrass standards sung in heavily accented English, leavened with instrumental jazz pieces and a few of their own tunes, sporting names like "Fuji Mountain Breakdown" and "Cherry Blossom Special."

There were also important new American acts, including John Hartford, Cliff Waldron & the New Shades of Grass, and the Bluegrass Alliance. Each of these groups demonstrated significant changes overtaking bluegrass music. Hartford had grown up with traditional bluegrass in the region around his native St. Louis, playing regularly at music parks near there and on radio shows in Missouri and Illinois with the Bray Brothers. Hartford achieved fame and economic success as the composer of "Gentle on My Mind" and a veteran of television's *Glen Campbell Goodtime Hour*, but by 1971 the quirky performer had created a special partnership with former Blue Grass Boy Vassar Clements, flat-picking Dobroist Tut Taylor, and lead guitarist Norman Blake. Bill readily assented when Hartford asked to appear at Bean Blossom, and his 1971 festival show with those other powerful musicians brought to the Bean Blossom audience the memorable and unique "steam-powered aereo-plain" sound.[21] The emcee introduced each musician individually by name, so fans did not necessarily connect Hartford's band that day with his groundbreaking *Aereo-Plain* album.

Several years before his Bean Blossom debut, Cliff Waldron had partnered with banjoist Bill Emerson and, for a time, resonator guitar wizard Mike Auldridge to form a progressive bluegrass band named "New Shades of Grass" and record an eponymous first album. While Emerson and Auldridge did not stay long, Waldron kept up the name and continued presenting popular shows at parks and festivals and especially Washington, D.C.–area clubs like the Red Fox Inn, where, along with the Country Gentlemen and the Seldom Scene, they helped to establish a new modern direction and a vibrant regional bluegrass music scene. Waldron and the New Shades of Grass built their music on customary bluegrass style and instrumentation but used material with contemporary or rock origins, which clearly appealed to newer, younger fans.

The Bluegrass Alliance mesmerized the Bean Blossom audience that year. They had been creating new bluegrass fans ever since guitarist Dan Crary formed the band in Louisville, Kentucky, in 1968. With hot melodic picking by Crary (and later by his replacement, Tony Rice) and the insistent instrumental work of fiddler Lonnie Peerce, banjoist Buddy Spurlock, and bassist Harry Shelor (better known by his stage name, Ebo Walker), the Alliance were young and hip, and they had great onstage energy. They impressed audiences terrifically with their own youth and musicianship, as did later versions of the band. According to nineteen-year-old Virginian Doug Hutchens, attending the festival in 1971 after being hired as a Blue Grass Boy to play bass, Bill Monroe himself did not really like the look or sound of the Bluegrass Alliance, but he perceptively noted the excitement they provoked in audiences and acted on it: "In 1971 Bill hired the Bluegrass Alliance for two days for early in the week and they were very popular so he made a place for them on the weekend, hair and all. If there were ever a phenomena [sic] in Bluegrass, they were it. It didn't really matter that they had long hair and dressed like the young folks. They were reaching for something new and they were accepted and appreciated by older guys in t-shirts and flat top haircuts as well as those who were a part of the rebellion of the youth."[22]

The Alliance at Bean Blossom were led by Lonnie Peerce and featured Tony Rice on guitar, Ebo Walker on bass, and two incredibly talented young long-haired western Kentuckians—Sam Bush and Courtney Johnson—on mandolin and banjo, respectively. The Bluegrass Alliance symbolized the dawn of a new age at the 1971 Bean Blossom festival. They excited the audience with their musicianship and stage presence and also served as an obvious symbol of the changes—not necessarily welcomed by conservative fans of "traditional" bluegrass—that were overtaking the growing world of bluegrass music. Sam Bush later commented, "One of the highlights of my life . . . is how well we did at Bean Blossom in '71. The audience was incredibly responsive and I know it's got to stand out for all five guys in the band at that time."[23]

A year after hosting Earl and his new band at Bean Blossom, Monroe planned to add Lester Flatt with his own new band, the Nashville Grass, to the 1971 program. Before Lester's Sunday-afternoon show, which emcee Ralph Rinzler folded into the "History of Bluegrass" theme of the afternoon, there was much speculation by both fans and the professional bluegrass musicians attending that year, wondering how Lester's presence might play out, given the long-standing and pointedly cold relationship between Flatt and Monroe.

Doug Hutchens later recalled the onstage reunion, preceded by a key meeting in one of the old Rund cabins a few days before the festival:

> I remember one morning at Bean Blossom at the Breakfast table in the little cabin where Bill had cooked breakfast for us. Joe [Stuart] began instigating Bill and Lester doing some tunes together at the festival. Joe said "Chief, I see where Lester is going to be here," Bill said "Yeah, that was some of James's doings." Joe said "Don't you think it is about time to bury the hatchet?" Bill didn't say anything for a long time then said. "I heard they used to talk about me pretty bad." Joe said "you know when I was working with them they'd always listen to your show and the only thing I ever heard them say was, 'It sounds like the bass player's pushing a little.'" That was all that was said until the Sunday of the festival when Lester and Bill walked out on stage and sung "Little Cabin Home on the Hill."[24]

Flatt's music after the Flatt and Scruggs breakup was undeniably acoustic "bluegrass," so—unlike the amplified Earl Scruggs Revue—Flatt's musical offerings were greeted enthusiastically every time he played at Bean Blossom. There were eight more June Bean Blossom festivals until Lester's death in 1979, and he and a slowly changing set of Nashville Grass sidemen returned every year. In 1971, Bill greeted Lester on stage with a handshake and four words: "Welcome to Bean Blossom." The public end to a legendary feud on the outdoor stage at Bean Blossom was a watershed moment for Bean Blossom and for bluegrass.

November 1971 brought one more Monroe innovation to the old music park: a three-day mini bluegrass festival with a modest number of "name" acts: Monroe, Stanley, the Goins Brothers, and James Monroe with his new band, the Midnight Ramblers. The weekend event built on the precedents of earlier special shows marking the end of the Jamboree season. Several times before, Birch had staged such shows at the end of the year, featuring fiddlers' contests or singing conventions like the ones held in 1970. But this new 1971 event, staged over a whole weekend, laid the foundation for a second Bean Blossom bluegrass festival that would eventually take place every autumn.

Brown County Jamboree tent. The photo was taken September 29, 1941—the day following the first grand-opening show—by Frank M. Hohenberger. (Courtesy of The Lilly Library, Indiana University, Bloomington, Indiana)

Guy Smith, emcee, amid a group of unidentified Brown County Jamboree entertainers inside the tent, 1941. (Courtesy of Guylia Bunge)

The Hickory Ranch Ramblers, performing inside the tent: Cecil, Maurice, and Owen Duckett and their cousin Orville Duckett. (Courtesy of Maurice Duckett)

Francis Rund, first owner of the Brown County Jamboree, ca. 1944. (Courtesy of Lettie Mae "Sandy" Rund)

Denzel "Spurts" or "Silver Spur" Ragsdale and his 1941 Chevrolet Suburban sound truck—his "ballyhoo car"—parked by the Brown County Jamboree barn, ca. 1945. (Courtesy of Loren Parker)

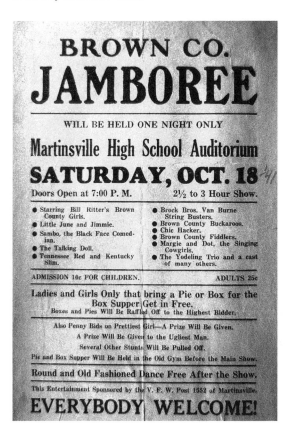

# BROWN CO.
# JAMBOREE

### WILL BE HELD ONE NIGHT ONLY

## Martinsville High School Auditorium

# SATURDAY, OCT. 18

Doors Open at 7:00 P. M.          2½ to 3 Hour Show.

- Starring Bill Ritter's Brown County Girls.
- Little June and Jimmie.
- Sambo, the Black Face Comedian.
- The Talking Doll.
- Tennessee Red and Kentucky Slim.

- Brock Bros. Van Burne String Busters.
- Brown County Buckaroos.
- Chic Hacker.
- Brown County Fiddlers.
- Margie and Dot, the Singing Cowgirls.
- The Yodeling Trio and a cast of many others.

ADMISSION 10c FOR CHILDREN.          ADULTS 25c

### Ladies and Girls Only that bring a Pie or Box for the Box Supper Get in Free.
Boxes and Pies Will Be Raffled Off to the Highest Bidder.

Also Penny Bids on Prettiest Girl—A Prize Will Be Given.
A Prize Will Be Given to the Ugliest Man.
Several Other Stunts Will Be Pulled Off.
Pie and Box Supper Will Be Held in the Old Gym Before the Main Show.

### Round and Old Fashioned Dance Free After the Show.

This Entertainment Sponsored by the V. F. W. Post 1552 of Martinsville.

# EVERYBODY WELCOME!

Brown County Jamboree promotional flier for Martinsville, Indiana, show, October 18, 1941.

Brown County Jamboree and WFBM Indianapolis "bus," ca. 1946. (Courtesy of Jack McDonald and Jim Peva)

Promotional Brown County Jamboree car, a 1947 Kaiser-Frazer ordered by Jamboree manager Kenneth Rund. (Photo provided by Lettie Mae "Sandy" Rund)

Brown County Jamboree
advertisement in the
*Brown County Democrat*,
October 20, 1955.

Kyle Wells, Red Cravens, Birch Monroe, and Jerry Waller posed in front of the
Brown County Jamboree barn, ca. 1958. (Courtesy of Harley Bray)

The Stanley Brothers and the Clinch Mountain Boys performing an outdoor show on the dance platform, July 20, 1958. (Courtesy of Harley Bray)

# BILL MONROE'S
# BROWN COUNTY JAMBOREE

### BEANBLOSSOM, IND.

## Sunday, September 15

### 2 SHOWS 3 & 8 P.M.

## Local Talent Hootenanny at 6 p.m.

*Stars from Grand Ole Opry*

## COUSIN JODY and DEL WOOD

**Local Bluegrass artist
ROGER SMITH, VERN McQUEEN AND
THE BROWN COUNTY BOYS**

**BLUEGRASS AND FOLK MUSIC HEADQUARTERS IN INDIANA
DANCING EVERY SAT. — 8 - 12 P.M.**

Brown County Jamboree advertisement in *Brown County Democrat*, September 12, 1963. The folk-music connection was emphasized with a "local talent hootenanny" and the slogan "Bluegrass and Folk Music Headquarters in Indiana."

Brown County Jamboree advertisement in the *Brown County Democrat*, June 4, 1964. Along with a temporary change in management at the Brown County Jamboree came this reminder of the Saturday-night dances, with an appeal to both the "square-dancing" and the "rock an' roll" fans.

Jam session in the parking lot, 1969. This striking photo by journalist David DeJean captures the spontaneous excitement of a great jam session. Most of the participants were unknown amateur pickers, but the smiling fiddler at the center is Art Stamper, a well-known Kentucky native whose long career included professional stints with the Sauceman Brothers, the Stanley Brothers, the Osborne Brothers, Bill Clifton, Larry Sparks, Bill Monroe, Ralph Stanley, and the Goins Brothers. (Photo by David DeJean)

Denzel "Silver Spur" Ragsdale in his sound truck at the fourth Bean Blossom Bluegrass Festival, 1970. He mounted similar horn speakers in the trees around the outdoor stage to provide sound for the first few festivals. (Photo by Tom Ewing)

Large 1971 poster from Hatch Show Print (Nashville, Tennessee), advertising the fifth June Bean Blossom Bluegrass Festival.

# BILL MONROE'S
## 5th ANNUAL
# BLUEGRASS FESTIVAL

# JUNE 15-20
## BROWN COUNTY JAMBOREE PARK
### BEAN BLOSSOM, INDIANA
#### 40 Miles South of Indianapolis, Highway 135

Bill Monroe & Blue Grass Boys
Lester Flatt & Nashville Grass
Jim & Jesse and Virginia Boys
Country Gentlemen
Doc Watson
Don Reno · Red Smiley · Bill Harrell and the Tennessee Cut-ups
Jimmy Martin & Sunny Mt. Boys
Mac Wiseman
Carl Story & Ramblin' Mountaineers
Ralph Stanley & Clinch Mountain Boys
James Monroe & Midnight Ramblers

Hamilton Co. Bluegrass Band
from Australia, New Zeland
Cliff Waldron & New Shades of Grass
Mike Seeger
Louis Popejoy & Wabash Valley Boys
Goins Brothers
Tex Logan
Bluegrass Alliance
Rual Yarborough & Dixiemen
SPECIAL GUEST

# JOHN HARTFORD

## SUNDAY . . . THE STORY OF
# BILL MONROE & BLUEGRASS MUSIC

Bill Monroe and Lester Flatt shake hands, "burying the hatchet" and ending the decades-long "bluegrass cold war," as Ralph Rinzler looks on, June 20, 1971. (Photo by Mike Seeger)

Bill Monroe directing "the roll call of nine fiddlers" onstage for the festival's finale, 1972.

Birch Monroe onstage in the barn, backed by the Newgrass Revival: Courtney Johnson, Sam Bush, Ebo Walker, Curtis Burch (not visible), August 6, 1972.

Birch Monroe's car parked in front of the "Bean Shack" built for Tex Logan in 1973. Logan prepared and helped serve the free "Barbecue Bean Day" meals offered to festivalgoers between 1969 and 1979.

Birch Monroe overseeing the construction of new rustic tables and benches for artists to display their records and tapes, 1973.

Bill Monroe and his Blue Grass Boys (Kenny Baker, Butch Robins, Randy Davis, and Wayne Lewis), on the outdoor stage at Bean Blossom, 1974.

Behind the outdoor stage, 1973. The stage's central staircase leading to the "tune-up rooms" and the stage is visible at the far right. Audiences sat amid a sheltering grove of trees in the festival's early years.

Carl Butler—Grand Ole Opry artist, songwriter, guitarist, and former Blue Grass Boy—performing onstage in the "old barn," 1977.

In 1992 this new outdoor stage replaced the older one built in 1968. In the process, numerous trees were removed, and the proscenium was moved back, to enlarge the seating area for audiences. The "Back Home Again In Indiana" sign in this photo was a temporary replacement.

The Bill Monroe Bluegrass Hall of Fame and Museum, built in 1992 on the approximate site of the "old barn" razed in 1986.

As part of the 1992 construction, a re-created version of "Uncle Pen's Cabin" was set up adjacent to the Bill Monroe Hall of Fame and Museum.

The last official name of the music park during Bill Monroe's life, seen in this 1996 photo, recognized the partnership of Bill and his son, James, and acknowledged the centrality of festivals to the park's functions.

Dwight Dillman renamed the park in 1998 to memorialize Bill Monroe. Dillman's large sign at the park entrance continued to proclaim the "Home of the Brown County Jamboree," even though no regular Sunday-afternoon shows had been held for decades when the "For Sale" sign went up in 2007.

# 8

# The Festival's Golden Age, 1972–82

By 1971, Monroe's festival archetype was complete. His June festival became a prototype for bluegrass festivals everywhere and became a model Monroe seemed driven to follow thereafter, not only at new festivals but at Bean Blossom itself. The June festival grew in size and stayed perennially profitable, but its evolution as a new sort of business ended once the key elements had been invented or discovered.

Although Monroe accepted change as it overtakes music constantly being re-created in performance, he did not always favor change in running the festival, often preferring to do things in a deliberately old-fashioned way, "like we did it back in Kentucky."[1] Monroe's management and promotional sensibilities, effective or not, were always his own. He stood at the center: host, owner, and principal architect of the festival at his music park.

Each June brought signs of increasing attendance: larger numbers of out-of-state license plates reported, more foreign countries providing artists and fans. Music festivals, and especially bluegrass festivals, seemed to be happening everywhere. By many measures, Bill's Bean Blossom festival was at the top of the list of the 180 bluegrass festivals held nationally in 1971.[2] The six days of the 1971 festival grew to eight days in 1972 and nine in 1973 and 1974, with the event beginning on a Saturday and ending more than a week later on Sunday. Between 1974 and 1987, most of Monroe's June bluegrass festivals were more than a week long.[3] With near-constant growth, the staging of the June festival quickly became an established annual ritual of work for Monroe personally, as well as a Brown County tradition with local and regional economic impact.[4] "Bean Blossom"—-metonymic shorthand for the festival—rapidly became a bluegrass music institution.

Monroe soon began to copy his own model. In August 1971, Bill inaugurated the "First Annual Bill Monroe Kentucky Bluegrass Festival" in Ashland, Kentucky (presenting, among others, the Bluegrass Alliance),[5] and that spin-off event was closely followed by "Bill Monroe's Dixie Bluegrass Festival," at Chatom, Alabama; "Bill Monroe and Ralph Stanley's 1st Annual Delaware Bluegrass and Old Time Music Festival"; "Bill Monroe and Lester Flatt's Mississippi Delta BG Festival" at Runnellstown, Mississippi; and dozens of others.

Bluegrass festivals catalyzed further expansion of the national fan base. Festivals offered artists and promoters a new circuit of regular jobs for professional bands. The festivals provided new cultural scenes, centered on jamming, for fans and amateur pickers. In festival jams, pickers developed their musical chops and learned about jam-session etiquette. With low ticket prices and easy personal transportation, no wonder the bluegrass festivals blossomed.

One consequence of festivals' rapid growth was a gradual lessening of Bean Blossom's uniqueness. Other demands on Bill Monroe's time diminished his management of the Bean Blossom festival. His stewardship of the park, always mediated through Birch in his absence, became routine. He still loved the park's terrain and was pleased that the place kept Birch occupied with seasonal Sunday Jamboree shows and Saturday-night dances. But Bill did not have to make many changes, once he knew how to successfully market and stage the festival. In the early 1970s, it was all working, and growing audiences found their way to Bean Blossom.

Bill's best marketing technique was his own access to audiences. He proudly plugged the festival on Grand Ole Opry shows and at concert appearances, exhorting receptive audiences, "Now come to see us at Bean Blossom, we have a festival there every June. And it runs from Friday to the following Sunday, come see us!"

At the sixth June festival in 1972, all the critical components were in place. One element was local advertising and support by Brown County businesses. The *Brown County Democrat* ran a large spread welcoming everyone to "Brown County—Home of Bill Monroe's Bluegrass Festival," running under a banner headline: "Welcome to Beautiful Downtown Bean Blossom in Scenic Brown County." The lighthearted reference to the "beautiful downtown" of tiny Bean Blossom was founded on an earlier local in-joke: Carl Brummett's wrecker truck once bore a painted door identifying it as the "Beautiful Downtown Bean Blossom Wrecker Service." Around 1972, Jack McDonald began to offer a line of colorful T-shirts at his grocery, the local IGA, featuring the motto: "Beautiful Downtown Bean Blossom."[6] Hundreds of these shirts would eventually be sold to visiting bluegrass fans and taken home or shipped to locales from Boston to Tokyo. The newspaper also ran a map of the festival, indicating restrooms, concessions, the Jamboree barn, the outdoor stage, and the campground areas.

The 1972 lineup of performers was strong on the first Sunday, with Bill Monroe, James Monroe, Birch Monroe, Wilma Lee and Stoney Cooper, and Louie Popejoy on that day's four-dollar ticket. Monday the price dropped to two dollars as the hours of professional shows dropped, and then the advertised entertainment value and ticket prices both increased as the week progressed. Most of the same groups performed on Monday, before and after the proffered "free ham-and-bean dinner." Tuesday repeated Monday's stage program, minus Wilma Lee and Stoney. On Wednesday, some entertainers became judges for the Little Miss Bluegrass Queen contest, and shows that followed featured Tex Logan, the Goins Brothers, and Larry Sparks and the Lonesome Ramblers. Thursday, for a three-dollar ticket, fans took in the amateur banjo contest, and then a new set of major entertainers who joined those already present. Professional acts on the more significant second weekend included Ralph Stanley, Jimmy Martin, the Jones Brothers & the Log Cabin Boys, Randall Collins & Curtis Blackwell, the IInd Generation, the Bluegrass Tarheels, and the McCormick Brothers. The second Friday was event filled, with the amateur bluegrass band contest, then an afternoon show, the Sunset Jam, the old-fashioned square dance in the barn, and another evening show at the outdoor stage. On Saturday, the biggest day of the festival (and the most expensive at six dollars), the last of the big-name acts joined in: Lester Flatt, Jim and Jesse, Don Reno and Bill Harrell, Cliff Waldron and the New Shades of Grass, Bill Clifton, Buck White and the Down Home Folks, and the Calton Family.

Jim McReynolds observed that the 1972 attendance was virtually double that of the previous year, and a newspaper article published at year's end, recalling the events of the festival, noted an anticipated attendance of twenty thousand for the final Sunday.[7] That day, there was hymn singing by the name entertainers beginning at 9:00 a.m. and then an outdoor church service at 11:00. The final outdoor concert began at 1:00 p.m., and around 4:00 p.m., toward the end of Monroe's final segment, he happily presented an onstage "special event" that he had begun to build years before in the "Story of Bluegrass," now staged as the "Annual Old-Time Fiddlers Reunion." Under Bill's supervision, nine fiddlers, accompanied by the Blue Grass Boys, played several separate tunes and medleys. The fiddling was more bluegrass than old-time, since the artists were all sidemen in the headlining bluegrass bands. For the first Fiddlers' Reunion, Monroe had drafted Kenny Baker, Howdy Forrester, Tex Logan, and Curly Ray Cline. At the last moment, Paul Warren, Buck Ryan, Art Stamper, Vernon Derrick, and Jim Brock were added. Baker kicked off a series of well-known fiddle tunes, including "Back Up and Push," "Soldier's Joy," "Sally Goodin," and "Katy Hill," spreading around the breaks in succession on each tune. The audience loved it.

After the nine fiddlers' show, Bill closed the festival with his own version of the Rinzler- and Haney-inspired "Story of Bluegrass," appearing in a rough chronology with a series of other artists, not all actually former Blue Grass Boys. In 1972, the "Story" included Lester Flatt, Don Reno, Carl Story, Jimmy Martin, James Monroe, banjoist Earl Snead, Ralph Stanley, Melvin and Ray Goins, Bill Harrell, Jim and Jesse, Eddie Adcock, and Hubert Davis.

Bill acquired another F-5 mandolin during the 1972 festival from a widow, whose husband had requested that, after his death, her first offering of his prized Lloyd Loar Gibson mandolin for sale would be to Monroe. She brought the instrument to the festival; Monroe bought it. Right away, he showed off the new mandolin to Jack Lawrence, Kenny Baker, and others who were jamming before the Friday-night square dance. Later, Bill usually kept this second Loar in the "Get Up John" tuning or used it when his primary instrument was returned to Gibson for repairs.[8]

The national influence of Bean Blossom kept developing throughout the early 1970s, not only through reporting in *Bluegrass Unlimited* but even more through the example it gave others. Three years earlier, the Bean Blossom torch had been carried to Oklahoma by Bill Grant. In 1972, Dick Tyner, an avid California banjo player, talked with Bill Monroe about his hope to stage a real bluegrass festival in Southern California. Encouraged by their Bean Blossom meeting, Tyner moved forward and inaugurated the Golden West Bluegrass Festival in October 1973.[9]

Bean Blossom during the festival was effectively the epicenter of the as yet unorganized bluegrass music industry. A few active fans distributed literature and bumper stickers at Bean Blossom in 1972 to advocate the creation of a Bluegrass Music Association. This particular effort did not succeed, but its goals were seen by many bluegrass artists and promoters as sincere and important and were recalled more than a decade later when similar plans were attempted again by others, and again failed. These were signals of a desire for a viable trade association, which would be finally met with the creation of the International Bluegrass Music Association (IBMA) in late 1985.[10]

A slick newsstand magazine, *Country Music,* began publication in 1972; its second issue featured essays by journalist John Filiatreau and bluegrass guitarist, singer, and author Jim Rooney chronicling the big festival. Filiatreau emphasized the huge crowd, its regional and educational heterogeneity, the muddy campground, and the unceasing parking-lot picking. He discussed at length the impact of a group of professional "Young Turks," namely, Eddie Adcock and the IInd Generation, whose music he felt was admired despite being "subversive" or "anti-bluegrass." The article describes Adcock's band doing humorous onstage sketches: playing their instruments behind their backs or doing a slow-motion "78-rpm record played at 33-rpm," morphing into a blazing breakdown. Fili-atreau claimed that he had discerned "a common look of sadness in the faces of such old bluegrass prophets as Bill Monroe, Lester Flatt and Ralph Stanley, as if they're paying tribute to a passing order."[11]

Jim Rooney's write-up of the 1972 festival, in the wake of his 1971 book, *Bossmen: Bill Monroe and Muddy Waters,* was understandably focused on its central figure. Rooney's "sketches" presented Monroe at key times and places during the festival: wearing an impeccable suit and greeting pickers and fans at the Sunset Jam; at the Friday-night square dance in the barn, with Mike Seeger calling, Tex Logan fiddling, and both Buck White and Monroe himself taking part in the dancing; playing his newly purchased Lloyd Loar mandolin all night; and leading powerful instrumentals and songs on his own part of the Sunday program, accompanied by Blue Grass Boys Kenny Baker, Jack Hicks, Joe Stuart, and Monroe Fields. Rooney quoted Tex Logan on the diverse "cross-section" of the crowd and on the effect of Monroe's vitality and impressive musical presence on all the fans and attendees. Bill's attachment to the park and to his matured festival's features also emerged in Rooney's perceptive description of the Sunday-morning service, when Bill talked about the park, the lake, and the importance of supporting that year's preacher, Brother Cummings from Nashville, Tennessee, with a good collection offering. Rooney described the wistful late-Sunday aspect of the festival, as the crowd slowly thinned out. He noted how Bill would walk people to the gate, reminding them that no one else did the Sunday-morning services at their festivals and asking people in his habitual way to "come see me in Nashville, at the Grand Ole Opry."[12]

The park got busy again later in the year. In October, the Brown County Republican Central Committee held a "Bean Supper and Rally" at the Jamboree Barn. This was among the last nonmusical events staged in the Jamboree barn, for the 1970 construction of Nashville, Indiana's Seasons Lodge and Conference Center meant that Brown County finally had a modern large-meeting alternative to the old barn.

October also brought the Jamboree's "6th Annual Old Time Fiddlers' Contest," preceding a Sunday show featuring Renfro Valley star Claude Sweet. The "6th Annual" name was misleading, since several fiddle contests were held in the

Rund-owned park in the 1940s and two in the Monroe era: an unnumbered October 1970 event and the "4th Annual," in 1971, one year before the "6th Annual."

Several milestone events occurred that fall. First came a special September Jamboree show in honor of the 1972 centennial of Nashville, Indiana. This celebratory performance featured, "for the first time together," three members of Nashville, Tennessee's Country Music Hall of Fame: Ernest Tubb, Roy Acuff, and Bill Monroe. Bill, inducted into the Hall of Fame in 1970, was proud of his elite status and of the idea of a "Hall of Fame Show." The big autumn Hall of Fame Show was presented annually in 1972, 1973, and 1974. Its name lasted even longer, though with an altered meaning, in association with a series of annual fall festivals established in 1977.

Another 1972 highlight was a three-day November "closing-of-the-season" minifestival, built around the prior year's participants plus the Bluegrass Alliance. In the early seventies, these late-fall minifestivals continued to be held without much fanfare. There was a two-day event in 1973, a single day show in 1974, and three days again in 1975. No event was advertised for the autumn of 1976, but the three-day 1977 "Final Show" event began a regular series as a fall festival.

Rising sales of albums by festival artists impressed the management of early-seventies bluegrass record labels. MCA Records, which had inherited Monroe as a major artist in their 1962 purchase of the Decca label, reacted by recording a live double-LP album at the June 1973 festival. The recording involved most major artists playing the festival that year. A sound crew hung microphones in the trees shading the amphitheater area, and audience applause and shouts, prompted by a stage director and a flashing red light, were edited into the final mix.[13] The twenty-seven-track double album had an exciting live-show sound, with energetic cuts by Monroe, Jim & Jesse, Jimmy Martin, James Monroe, Lester Flatt, and more. For two instrumentals in the finale, Monroe upped the ante with *twelve* bluegrass fiddlers. Monroe himself led the whole assembly in one of his gospel favorites, "Swing Low, Sweet Chariot." The album, with its Woodstock-inspired cover art featuring birds, butterflies, and a frog, was released to great acclaim on November 1. *Bean Blossom* (MCA 2-8002) became a top-selling album, enduring for months on 1974's country charts. Monroe's most successful LP, it helped spread awareness of the music park and Monroe's annual festivals to huge new audiences.[14] Many would eventually make the trek to Bean Blossom to see for themselves. A second live album, *Bean Blossom '79* (MCA-3209) was released in 1980; it helped sustain the impression that Bean Blossom remained a thriving festival park, but it was a less ambitious and smaller-scale production. In the dawning age of disco, it impacted fewer potential fans than the 1973 release.

Each year, the Bean Blossom festival witnessed a return of the family of local and diehard national bluegrass followers, joined annually throughout the 1970s and 1980s by new cohorts of fans. Part of the attraction was the strong core group of first-generation bluegrass artists at the heart of each of the festivals. A bluegrass pilgrim attending Bill's main festival anytime in the 1970s or early 1980s was virtually guaranteed to see the core Bean Blossom acts: Bill Monroe, Ralph Stanley, Birch Monroe, James Monroe, the Sullivan Family, and Jim & Jesse. A secondary core included others who also repeated for years at a time: Lester Flatt and the Nashville Grass;[15] Carl Story and the Rambling Mountaineers; Don Reno, Bill Harrell, & the Tennessee Cutups; the Osborne Brothers; and Wilma Lee and Stoney Cooper & the Clinch Mountain Clan.[16] Even more were "semiregulars," like Larry Sparks & the Lonesome Ramblers, the Goins Brothers, Jimmy Martin and the Sunny Mountain Boys, the Indianapolis-based Bluegrass Blackjacks, Bobby Smith & the Boys from Shiloh, the Lewis Family, the McLain Family Band, Hubert Davis & the Season Travelers, A. L. Wood & the Smokey Ridge Boys, Lillimae & the Dixie Gospelaires, and from California, High Country, led by Monroe-style mandolinist Butch Waller.

Monroe's influence on the artistic direction of groups who played his Bean Blossom festivals was considerable. He'd take stern, direct action if he felt a band presented inappropriate music. Jim Moss, a California fiddler who first came to Bean Blossom in 1973 and documented many late-night jam sessions by Kenny Baker and Bob Black, recalled the sudden departure of the McLain Family Band from the outdoor stage in the mid-1970s after Monroe suddenly fired them for being "too vaudeville" in their approach.[17] Raymond W. McLain later remembered that the contretemps occurred around 1975; the McLains were surprised at Monroe's abrupt criticism, for they were "going over pretty well," and Bill had always been very supportive. Bill told them the problem was "too much western swing" in their sound.[18]

"Tradition" was enforced in many ways at Bean Blossom—sometimes selectively. Bands using electric basses could not compete in the annual June festival band contest, though professional bands like Jim and Jesse and the Osborne Brothers featured electric bass in their stage shows without question whenever they chose.

Bill exercised tight control over his band and even over the festival audience when necessary to enforce his own ethics relating to work and his morality relating to play. Jim Peva witnessed Bill firing two Blue Grass Boys quite suddenly for sleeping late the day after the festival and not helping pick up trash. Raymond Huffmaster, managing the festival in 1979, saw Monroe "stopping the music on

Sunday when them little hippie girls tried to dance to the Gospel Music. He would not allow it, although I'm sure he enjoyed watching them on Saturday."[19]

Succeeding June festivals in the 1970s brought new groups to the park. Bean Blossom was still *the* place to be for fans of traditional bluegrass music in the Midwest and the Upper South, despite hundreds of festivals competing for fans and pickers across the country. Other festivals' offerings revealed evolving interpretations of the genre. The Telluride Bluegrass Festival offered Colorado audiences "progressive bluegrass" as defined by the Newgrass Revival. This stellar group formed in 1972 when Sam Bush, Courtney Johnson, Curtis Burch, and Ebo Walker all left Lonnie Peerce's Bluegrass Alliance. Just like the Bluegrass Alliance, the earlier Front Porch String Band, and later groups like Hot Rize or the Seldom Scene, the Newgrass Revival performed music from a wide range of popular sources, mining rock and roll, reggae, country, and pop music for new material. Telluride was a receptive venue for nontraditional bands that were aware of the roots of their music, yet happy to experiment; they saw themselves constituting new branches still connected to the metaphorical tree of bluegrass history.

At Monroe's Bean Blossom, the roots of bluegrass in old-time and country music were acknowledged and feted, and progressive branches of the music were often thought unacceptable. In 1974, pondering the style of the still-new Seldom Scene, reviewer Robert Cantwell reported their repertoire made him uneasy when he considered whether they were a bluegrass band at all. His explanation was grounded in the widely shared idea that Monroe's music park represented the very idea of tradition in bluegrass: "I suspect that 'Hail To The Redskins' won't be played much at Bean Blossom next year."[20] The Seldom Scene did not play at Bean Blossom until 1991.

In June 1974, U.S. senator from Indiana Birch Bayh read a proclamation from the governor, officially naming one of the festival days "Bill Monroe Day in Indiana." Bayh delighted the crowd by singing "Back Home Again in Indiana," the 1917 Tin Pan Alley composition that Bean Blossom audiences recognize, at least by name, from the sign above the proscenium of the 1968 outdoor stage.

Hazel Smith, a country music writer and friend of Bill's from Nashville, brought her fourteen- and seventeen-year-old sons, Terry and Billy, to the 1974 festival for their first time there, along with two other young men, fiddler J. B. Prince and banjoist Alan O'Bryant. They all shared a tent, and the young musicians, who would go on to extended and successful professional musical careers, performed as "Blue Haze."[21] They returned to Bean Blossom many times, individually or as sidemen and principals in other groups.

The 1974 band contest introduced the Bluegrass Martians, a jug band–flavored ensemble from Wisconsin. They were quickly eliminated in the contest, but two years later they returned as the Piper Road Spring Band and subsequently played Bean Blossom festivals through the late seventies. Fiddler "Big Al" Byla said years later that they were amazed at the help and encouragement they got from Bill Monroe and others, especially Tex Logan,[22] who appreciated their enthusiasm and the rousing effect their music had on fans.

Another impressive new group was Betty Fisher and the Dixie Bluegrass Band, which guitarist Fisher formed in 1972 with Bill's encouragement. Sometime before 1970, Fisher planned to form an all-girl bluegrass band, but Bill Monroe advised her against it, saying, "The kind of girls you would want are the kind of girls who would leave home and you just don't need that." So Fisher's band at Bean Blossom that year had three male players: Marvin Tuck on mandolin, Tommy Jackson on banjo, and George Gillis on fiddle. There was also a young woman playing bass: Murphy Hicks, who had originally answered Fisher's newspaper ad for female players. Murphy had learned to play bass in order to play in the band, but later, after leaving Fisher's band, she changed over to banjo, figuring she'd get more attention on that instrument. Later, following her marriage to mandolinist Red Henry, Murphy Henry matured as a performer. She went on to become, first, an innovative banjo teacher using her nationally known nontablature system, the "Murphy Method," and, later, a prolific writer, researcher, and forthright advocate for women in bluegrass.[23]

There, too, were former Blue Grass Boys. One was Clyde Moody, "the Hillbilly Waltz King." Moody had pioneered with Bill's Blue Grass Boys in the early 1940s, replacing Cleo Davis. Another former Blue Grass Boy, banjoist Hubert Davis, brought his family band, the Season Travelers, to play on the show that year. So did guitarist Bobby Smith, who appeared with his band, "The Boys from Shiloh," all wearing gray Confederate Civil War uniforms.

The 1974 Brown County Jamboree's newspaper advertisements grew ever spottier, as Birch relied increasingly on fourteen-by-twenty-two-inch posters, distributed on Birch's regular circuit. In September, Birch put up posters for the third (and last) of the original autumn "Hall of Fame" shows featuring Monroe, Roy Acuff, and Ernest Tubb.

A month later, a Brown County Jamboree poster announced another impending show: the Old Fiddlers Contest (with "large cash prizes"), plus Bryant Wilson & His Kentucky Ramblers, Birch Monroe, a door-prize drawing at 4:00 p.m., and Tom Atler & His Band.[24]

In the spring of 1975, just three early-season shows were advertised: an April opener with Larry Sparks, an appearance in May by the Blades of Grass, and in early June, a typical Sunday show opened by the Pigeon Hill String Ticklers and headlined by the venerable McCormick Brothers from Tennessee, bluegrass recording stars since their first release in 1954.

The 1975 June festival—the ninth—was erroneously advertised in *Bluegrass Unlimited* as the "Eighth Annual," though the next month's ad corrected the error. Both stated that the festivals were being run from "Monroe Festival Headquarters" in Nashville, Tennessee. The listing of featured performers and festival events in each ad was perfunctory; perhaps it seemed sufficient to simply remind the national bluegrass audience that the June festival was happening again.

By the third or fourth June festival, Bill Monroe started bringing a team of his horses or mules from Tennessee to Bean Blossom, where he might work them with a horse-drawn mower before the festival. He would keep them at the park during the festivals, stabled in the old horse barn that stood just across the fence line south of the Jamboree barn, bringing them out to entertain festival visitors. In 1975, Bill asked fifteen-year-old Terry Smith to drive Monroe's truck to Bean Blossom from Tennessee, bringing Bill's wagon and midget mules. Hazel Smith recalled the entertaining use Bill planned for the mules, for Monroe had carefully instructed Terry and Monroe's old Goodlettsville neighbor Archie Martin:

> "Now listen, when I sing 'Muleskinner Blues,' I want you all to come down through here with the little mules and the wagon." So he's up there singing, and they come around the whole thing, you know, they *circled* the whole park area down there. They went around one way, back behind the stage, and up the other side. He said, "Terry Smith and my friend Archie Martin, they gonna come down here with my little mules, and he's gonna be drivin'," and I'm gonna sing 'Muleskinner Blues.'" It worked great. Well, they went back, Terry cleaned the mules up, got 'em some water, give 'em some hay. Bill never mentioned anything about them doing it but one time. And Bill does the second show, he starts that same routine again. So Terry jumps up, and he *runs* up there, hitches up the little mules, and just as he starts down across the hill, and they get down to the bottom right there at the stage, Bill is now singing "Old, Old House," just staring at Terry! He'll never forget that as long as he lives, 'cause they had *really* messed up.[25]

Bill brought draft animals and wagons to Bean Blossom for many years and often paused for photographs as he happily drove through the park, giving wagon rides to children and friends.[26] His luminous smile, normally a rare sight, is common in such photos, and at Bean Blossom in the mid-1970s Bill Monroe was almost always a happy man, enjoying "his best days on earth."[27]

In 1975 the newest sensation at Bean Blossom was the Marshall Family, who had burst onto the bluegrass scene only a year before, at Ralph Stanley's festival. Their brilliant bluegrass gospel performances captivated the crowd.

A young Iowa banjo player named Bob Black, who played old fiddle tunes "note-for-note" in the melodic style, had joined Monroe in September 1974. In 1975, Black experienced his first festival as a Blue Grass Boy and quickly realized that the park, the event, and the growing family of regular fans were "Bill's pride and joy." Black took special pleasure that year in the Friday-evening Sunset Jam and the ensuing "dance show" in the barn. He observed that nearly no one danced, but Bill occasionally broke into a "Kentucky backstep" alone onstage or found a willing female partner to lead through some basic square-dance figures.

Monroe required Black to do the menial prefestival labor then expected of most Blue Grass Boys: repairing concession stands, helping put up the speakers at the outdoor stage, setting out trash barrels, helping Birch build benches and narrow tables for artists to display their wares, and so forth. Black's least-favorite duty was being the "ticket man" who rousted out campers early in the morning to check if they actually held tickets good for the dawning day.[28]

In 1976, the beginning of the nation's bicentennial year was formally observed on July 4, but the music festival scene (and other public events of all types) had already moved into a temporarily heightened state of excitement. Californian Dick Tyner organized the Golden West Bean Blossom Caravan that spring, placing an ad in the March *Bluegrass Unlimited* that recognized the preeminence of Bean Blossom:

ATTENTION WESTERN U.S. BLUEGRASSERS! Want to attend the WORLD'S LARGEST and most popular bluegrass festival? It's happening this year at Bean Blossom, Indiana, June 16–20. That's the "Biggie" conducted by Bill Monroe each year and it's truly the most spectacular bluegrass event on earth. There'll be 5 days and nights of down home bluegrass by the world's finest, along with workshops, contests, a bean bake and a sunset jam session hosted by Bill Monroe plus countless other exciting features you'll never forget. You'll have the opportunity to jam with such notables as Kenny Baker, members of Ralph Stanley's band and spectacular groups from all over the globe.

The coordinators of this caravan have often heard people say they would love to attend this festival but they dread the long trip alone (approx. 2200 miles from L.A.) so . . . the answer was obvious, and here's your chance! [We] are accepting memberships for the caravan which will depart June 11 from a location to be announced later.[29]

For such efforts, continuing after Tyner's founding of the first California bluegrass festival, some would later call him the "Father of Southern California Bluegrass."

Many attending the tenth June festival in 1976 joined in the usual frenzied off-stage scene. A hot young fiddler, Stuart Duncan, bought a fine "red fiddle" from Kenny Baker that year; he had greatly impressed Baker and went on to build his own professional career with his powerful and sensitive playing.

The audience appreciated several groups who had never appeared before at Bean Blossom, though most of the "new" artists had enjoyed substantial prior careers, and some had appeared previously at Bean Blossom in other bands. The Bluegrass Martians returned from Wisconsin in their new configuration as the Piper Road Spring Band. Harold Austin, former sideman for Carl Story, appeared with his own gospel group, First National Bluegrass. Bluegrass pioneer Carl Sauceman was there; he had recorded several influential cuts with his brother, "J. P.," for Rich-R-Tone Records in the 1940s as the Sauceman Brothers. Those recordings involved notable sidemen and Blue Grass Boys Joe Stuart and Clarence "Tater" Tate.

Another act that summer was Lillie Mae and the Dixie Gospelaires, from Ohio, a bluegrass gospel group that coalesced in 1959 around the guitar and vocals of Lillie Mae Whitaker and her mandolin-playing husband, Charlie Whitaker. Lillie Mae and Charlie met Bill Monroe repeatedly over a long period of time, and in the early 1970s the Dixie Gospelaires booked through the Monroe Talent Agency. At a bluegrass festival in Ottawa, Ohio, Bill told Lillie Mae that he especially loved their quartet gospel singing. Concerning promotion, he said only, "I'll see what I can do," but he soon booked them at Bean Blossom.

Harold Austin and Lillie Mae and their groups appeared both on their own and at the Sunday-morning church service, taking part in Bill's "Bluegrass Choir." Several months later, Dixie Gospelaire member Wayne Lewis, originally from Sandy Hook, Kentucky, became Bill Monroe's newest lead guitarist. He held the job for the next full decade, serving the longest tenure of any guitar-playing Blue Grass Boy. Lewis was a seasoned bluegrass musician, but he soon discovered, like other Blue Grass Boys, that the time he spent with Bill Monroe would be profoundly educational: "When I came to work with Bill, I was thirty-one or thirty-two years old. And I had been playing music since I was eleven years old. Started working clubs when I was fourteen, and I thought, 'There ain't *nothing* that I don't know about the bluegrass music,' because I had studied under Reno and Smiley, Jimmy Martin, Lester 'n' Earl, and Mac Wiseman. And I really thought that I knew it all. But when I came to work for that old man, it was just like going back to school."[30]

Arguably the most important "new" major artist that year was J. D. Crowe and the New South. Crowe had achieved national fame in bluegrass circles for his work with Jimmy Martin between 1956 and 1961. He later organized the Kentucky Mountain Boys, who had backed Red Allen at Bean Blossom in 1970. Around 1971, the key Kentucky Mountain Boys departed, and Crowe organized a new group: J. D. Crowe and the New South. Their eponymous 1975 debut album (Rounder 0044) helped establish Rounder Records as a source for outstanding contemporary bluegrass.

Crowe and the New South melded the traditional timbres of the bluegrass sound with a progressive repertoire that drew from rock, country, and popular music. At the heart of it all, as with the Kentucky Mountain Boys, was J. D.'s own exquisitely timed, inventive, and compelling banjo picking. The New South that came to Bean Blossom in 1976 on a rising wave of popularity and influence included several of the hottest young instrumentalists and vocalists around: brilliant guitarist and lead singer Tony Rice, mandolin and fiddle player and tenor singer Ricky Skaggs, and Jerry Douglas on the resophonic slide guitar, then commonly called a "Dobro."

Bluegrass music and Bean Blossom captured a good deal of national publicity in 1976, even as local advertising, other than posters, became scarce. *Bluegrass Unlimited* published a "Bluegrass '76" edition, listing nine bluegrass festivals happening in Indiana that summer, with the entire Bean Blossom schedule stapled into the centerfold. *Pickin'* observed in its "Parking Lot Pickers" column that the third-place winner at the band contest was "New Jersey's Millstone Valley Boys, with Tom Adler [not this author] substituting on banjo."[31] In stark contrast to the ample press given the June festival in advertisements, letters, and articles, only a single Sunday Jamboree show was noted in the *Brown County Democrat* that year: a Monroe show in mid-September.

The 1977 June festival began with tragedy. En route to Bean Blossom from Nashville in a camper van, James Monroe was asleep in the back, and his bass player, Tommy Franks, was driving. Near Elizabethtown, Kentucky, Franks apparently fell asleep. In the ensuing horrendous collision with a semitruck, he was killed, and James Monroe was bruised and shaken up.

As James recovered, the festival went on. The groups debuting that year included many experienced musicians, some of them friends or acquaintances of Bill's. Clyde Bowling, a Kentuckian raised near Loretta Lynn's family home in

Butcher Holler, came with his Southern Bluegrass Boys. Two acts had deep roots in country music: the Down State Ramblers, from Effingham, Illinois, and the Jimmie Skinner show, featuring the Berea-born country singer and songwriter who sang in a honky-tonk-influenced style. Skinner wrote many songs that found their way into the bluegrass canon; "Doin' My Time," "You Don't Know My Mind," "Don't Give Your Heart to a Rambler," and others were covered by Flatt and Scruggs, Jimmy Martin, the Osborne Brothers, and dozens of other bluegrass groups. By the time he played Bean Blossom in 1977, Skinner's instrumental sound had become less country and more bluegrass, and the Monroe Talent Agency was handling his bookings.

Returning to the 1977 festival stage, too, was Wilma Lee Cooper. After the death of fiddler Stoney Cooper in March of that year, Wilma Lee became the leader of the Clinch Mountain Clan. She and her group were absent for three years, but she resumed playing Bill's festival in 1981 and continued her long streak as one of the regular core performers through 1988.

In November, the multiday Jamboree closing shows that had begun as early as 1971 and sputtered along after that resumed. A large poster advertised the "Final Show of 1977" for three days, beginning November 4. The show was built mostly around Bill and the Blue Grass Boys and James Monroe with his Midnight Ramblers, but the poster singled out three of the bands' sidemen (Kenny Baker, Alan O'Bryant, and James Bryant) in a familiar attempt to make the event seem larger. Brother Birch Monroe was there, and a young band from Tennessee, Knoxville Newgrass. Former Blue Grass Boy Doug Hutchens brought his Kentucky group, the Phuzz Street Knucklebusters. The poster announced that the "Gospel Ramblers" would play on Sunday; that inclusion of a special Sunday program implied that the event was more a minifestival than a routine Sunday closing-of-the-park show. This weekend show was not called a "festival" and was not really the season's last show, either, since Hutchens and the Knucklebusters put on a final Sunday show two weeks later.

Between 1978 and 1981, no Jamboree ads appeared in the *Brown County Democrat*. Sunday shows and Saturday-night dances continued at the old Jamboree barn, but Birch had finally turned exclusively to his posters for advertising. Bill still played frequent shows there, and Monroe's shows were usually well attended because of the high level of interest among Indiana college students and those who had learned about the Jamboree through the festivals.

The June 1978 festival opened on Saturday afternoon with sets by Jimmie Skinner, Don Reno, Birch Monroe, James Monroe, and Bill Monroe. The week proceeded in the now traditional fashion: Monday was Tex Logan's Barbecue Bean

Day beginning at midday near the Bean Shack, then the "Little Miss Bluegrass Beauty Contest" for fourteen- to eighteen-year-old girls, at the outdoor stage. Tuesday came the banjo contest and Wednesday the band contest, which the printed program warned could not be held unless at least five bands signed up. Next came shows by new groups. High Country, from California, was there for the first time. There were also sets by Bill Harrell, now leading his own band, and a local group, the Brocks. Thursday featured afternoon and evening shows led off by Clyde Bowling and Louie Popejoy, climaxing with Bill Monroe and the Blue Grass Boys. On Friday, bigger-name bands would be added, like Del McCoury and the Dixie Pals and Lester Flatt and the Nashville Grass, featuring young mandolinist Marty Stuart. A Danish bluegrass group called Blackberry performed, and as usual, many featured artists joined Bill Monroe to lead amateur pickers in the Sunset Jam. On the final weekend, headline groups included Ralph Stanley, the Osborne Brothers, and the Country Gentlemen, who delighted the audience with a skit in which they each wound up playing simultaneously on both their own and another bandmate's instrument. Sunday-morning services and gospel music shows with perennials like the Sullivan Family and Ralph Stanley helping Monroe would inevitably move the devoted crowd. Bill Monroe Fan Club member Bettie Leonard described that year's Sunday gospel singing as central to the connection she felt with others at the festival: "Nobody can sing a gospel song like Bill and the Bluegrass [sic] Boys and I feel so close to God out there under all those trees. I can't help but wonder if next year, all of those we love will be back for another festival."[32]

In September 1978, the multiday fall festival returned, having grown from 1977's three-day November "final show" to a four-day event, scheduled two full months earlier. The on-again, off-again series of fall events began for the first time to be advertised in national fanzines as "Bill Monroe's 2nd Annual Autumn Festival." This numbering sequence—begun in error, since multiday autumn bluegrass events had been taking place since at least 1971—continued. Obvious numbering errors happened several times over. The well-advertised numbering scheme that began in 1978 continued more or less correctly until 1986, when the fall festival was canceled for two years in a row for "park remodeling." Another new numbering sequence appeared in 1994, with ads for the "20th Annual Hall of Fame and Uncle Pen Day Festival," implying that the first fall festival must have taken place in 1975. The "Hall of Fame" part of the fall festival's name also demonstrated an altered meaning, for while the 1970s Hall of Fame fall shows featured Monroe, Acuff, and Tubb (all members of Nashville's Country Music Hall of Fame), in the 1990s and beyond, the Hall of Fame fall event signaled the induction of a new artist into Bill Monroe's Hall of Fame. The 1994 autumn festival invoked the name of Bill Monroe's legendary Uncle Pen and the Hall of Fame and permanently established the current fall-festival numbering scheme.

The thirteenth June festival, in 1979, mostly reprised familiar core Bean Blossom groups. A few new groups were on the first weekend and early weekday shows: the Lawsons, the Meyers Brothers, and High Country, returning from California. The most memorable of the new groups was the Dry Branch Fire Squad, led by mandolin player Ron Thomason. The band aroused the audience with their heartfelt traditional bluegrass gospel singing and Thomason's droll, satiric emceeing style. The band contest was won by four teenage musicians from Ohio playing together as Young Blades of Bluegrass; they returned three months later for the "3rd Annual" fall Bean Blossom bluegrass festival.

A unique perspective on the 1979 June festival was that of Mississippian Raymond Huffmaster, who came back that year not only as a fan, singer, and first-rate jam-session guitar player but also to help manage and "work the park" for his friend Bill Monroe at the festival. Huffmaster spent a good deal of time with Monroe, who told him at that time how he had purchased the park and the Brown County Jamboree twenty-eight years before. Huffmaster was in a great position to observe both the business and the social aspects of the festival that year and was already a seasoned bluegrass music veteran who knew what was typical and what was not. He saw the entrance into the park of a relatively new band, the Boys from Indiana, who had been making a big splash in bluegrass circles since their formation in late 1974. That year they attended Bean Blossom as fans, since they had not yet achieved a booking on the festival show. Huffmaster watched as their blue bus marked "Boys from Indiana" pulled into the festival grounds with only a single person on board—the driver—who paid for one ticket. Once the bus was parked, a large tarp on top unfolded to reveal the rest of the band. Many fans were continuing to try to sneak into the festival, but Huffmaster and his helpers "beat the bushes" for ticketless attendees as in prior years, and in 1979 sold thirty-six hundred dollars' worth of tickets to fence hoppers.

Huffmaster also noted the huge crowd that year and observed that many new campground pickers did not really understand the etiquette of impromptu jam sessions, or the delicate balance of instruments and voices that could be destroyed if too many pickers tried to join in and take part. His memorable take on this problem was quoted nationally several months after the festival: "It's like getting a big bowl of corn flakes ready, putting the milk and sugar on and then having forty guys with spoons show up!"[33]

July brought another new event to the Bean Blossom calendar. The Indiana Folk Festival was a three-day show, not bound by the same commitment to tradition as the June festival. The artists clearly represented a newgrass wave: Sam Bush, Courtney Johnson, the Newgrass Revival, Norman Blake, and John Hartford. Yet the roster also had old-time fiddler Birch Monroe, country-guitar wizard Merle Travis, and the musical guitar and mandolin team of Bill Clifton and Red Rector, both long veterans of the traditional bluegrass music industry. This "folk festival" was not nearly as well attended as the big one in June, but it marked a surprisingly tardy Monroe effort to use the park's music-festival facilities for more than two weekends a year.

The three-day fall festival in mid-September brought back the three Monroe acts (Bill, Birch, and James) and others from the core. The contest-winning Young Blades of Grass returned for a show. Several groups were new to the venue. Appalachian Grass (led by Vernon McIntyre Jr., son of Earl Taylor's legendary sideman, Vernon "Boatwhistle" McIntyre) played, as did comedian-musician Harold Morrison & Smokin' Bluegrass.

The dominant popular group at Bean Blossom that fall was the Bluegrass Cardinals. The Cardinals formed in California in 1974 around the family talents of banjoist Don Parmley and his guitar-playing son, David. With glorious harmony singing and great vocal arrangements topping off superb instrumental skills, the Bluegrass Cardinals took the bluegrass world by storm after moving to Virginia in 1976. Their 1979 fall appearance was the first of many at Bean Blossom over the next fifteen years.

The big news that fall weekend was the reappearance of Earl Scruggs, returning with the Earl Scruggs Revue. As in 1970, the music played by Earl and his boys was far from the traditional bluegrass sound, but a magical moment for many fans was Earl's Saturday appearance onstage with Bill. A contributor to Bill's fan-club newsletter described the reunion: "The one thing I can say that everyone enjoyed the most was when his second banjo player played with Bill and that was Earl Scruggs. Earl said that he had waited all summer for the special moment. As Earl was getting ready to leave the stage, he had tears in his eyes."[34]

The year 1980 was a difficult and controversial time for the Monroes and for Bean Blossom. James ventured into the hospitality business that year in Nashville, opening a nightclub in his own name near Vanderbilt University, but the club closed after only three weeks of operation.[35] Another problem was sixty-nine-year-old Bill's declining health. After collapsing in pain in February, he was diagnosed with colon cancer and soon underwent surgery. Yet by June, he was ready once again to host his famous festival.

While Bill was healing from surgery, Birch followed the previous year's Indiana Folk Festival with another new event, a rock music festival in early May called the Rain or Shine Jam. Attendee Dave Underwood, from nearby Morgantown, observed in a letter to the local newspaper that the rock-show fans were as well behaved, friendly, and good-natured as the bluegrass crowds, although obviously younger. The musicians were all well received and enjoyed having Birch play with some of them onstage, and the event was undoubtedly good for business in the area. Although there had been "rock" and "twist music" shows on the Sunday-evening Jamboree almost a decade before, this was the first rock-music festival program at the park. Underwood asserted that rock festivals *can* happen without disaster and said he looked forward to the next rock-music show as well as the traditional entertainment.[36] But the "Rain or Shine Jam" was never repeated, perhaps because Birch's health and energy were also slowly declining.

The 1980 June festival returned with the traditional groups constituting Bean Blossom's festival core. Several new groups debuted as well that year, including Lawrence Lane & the Kentucky Grass and North Carolina's Raymond Fairchild, "King of the Smoky Mountain Banjo Players." Fairchild was a later addition to the core Bean Blossom festival performers, returning periodically throughout the eighties and into the early nineties, sometimes backed by the Crowe brothers, Josh and Wayne, or by Fairchild's sidemen, the Maggie Valley Boys.

The bluegrass band contest in 1980 was won by a pickup group of players who had met the day before while jamming at the festival. The group included Kentucky mandolinist Tommy Hill, Cincinnati guitarist Wayne Leason, and a new resident of Lexington, Kentucky, on banjo.[37]

The 1980 June festival brought problems. Previously, Monroe had awarded a security contract to either the Nashville Police Department or the Brown County Sheriff's Department, depending on which group could provide the security service at a lower price. For most of the 1970s, the Nashville police provided the service, and in 1979 Monroe paid them fifty-nine hundred dollars. Through a series of misunderstandings and miscommunications about price, the 1980 contract negotiations provoked a rift between Nashville town marshal Ron Wayt and Brown County sheriff Rex Kritzer. When Wayt heard that Kritzer had taken the security job away from him for forty-five hundred dollars, he approached Monroe and offered to do it for thirty-six hundred dollars. Monroe accepted that deal, and Wayt's men began working the festival on Sunday afternoon. Kritzer promptly issued a letter to his officers, banning them from working independently at the festival or being found in uniform at the festival. Wayt took that to mean that if he or one of his men needed assistance, the Brown County Sheriff's Department would not respond. However, there were in fact several calls for assistance from

Monroe or his management to the county Sheriff's Department, and that office responded when the calls came.[38]

A larger controversy erupted while the festival was still under way, when the weekly newspaper published—on the same day as an article detailing the festival security problems—four front-page photos of festivalgoers lounging about on reclining chairs or on the ground, apparently passed out, with many beer cans and bottles around them. The largest photo offered a nice view of the outdoor stage, but foregrounded an unconscious man, sprawled asleep on the ground. The negative portrayal of the festival was a surprise, since the newspaper had previously seemed supportive of events at Bean Blossom. Perhaps the newspaper's new negative take on Monroe's festival was a response to Birch's discontinuation, almost two years previously, of most local newspaper advertising for the Sunday Jamboree shows. For the next two months, heated letters from fans to the *Brown County Democrat*'s editor questioned his choice of photos, noting that the negative newspaper coverage was both unwarranted and in stark contrast to the positive Bean Blossom press on regional television and radio. Bluegrass devotees from distant states joined local readers in complaining, pointing out that Monroe brought a lot of bluegrass music fans into Brown County as tourists and urging that he and the festival be celebrated for that success, not smeared and vilified. One Oklahoma writer, Betty Scott, angrily observed that she and others usually purchased hundreds of dollars' worth of gifts for friends when they visited Nashville but would do so no more. She also explained that there is "no person nicer than Bill Monroe." Her evidence: When a tornado hit the 1980 festival on Thursday, her camper was nearly ripped in half. Monroe and his crew had the festival cleaned up within ninety minutes, and he gave Scott and her family his own motel room, lent them his pickup truck, and took them out for every meal. People parked near them offered shelter, food, and clothing; all pitched in and were "more like family than strangers." No one stole anything from the Scotts' ripped-open and insecure (but fully stocked) camper.[39]

In 1981, the Monroes tried again to develop a new entertainment site, but of a very different nature than a music-festival park. In April, they opened a restaurant and museum in Nashville, Tennessee, the Monroe Manor Steakhouse and Lounge. But the location on Dickerson Road was too remote from Nashville's busy downtown, and the enterprise soon failed. The idea of a museum housing Bill's memorabilia, however, would soon be resurrected.[40]

The June festival in 1981 was one of four presented that summer by Monroe Festival Headquarters. New Monroe festivals were staged at Rosine, Kentucky (at Monroe's "Musicland Park"); at Crossroads Country Music Park in Kings Mountain, North Carolina; and at Bill Monroe's West Tennessee Bluegrass Festival, in Waynesboro, Tennessee. The new festivals took some of the focus off Bean Blossom, where the lineup featured the well-worn and mostly familiar core list of performers. New on the 1981 June show were Doyle Lawson, leading his powerful new band Quicksilver; the Boys from Indiana, with the talents of the Holt family and Harley Gabbard; a young Louisville group called New Horizon; and the Wildwood Pickers, an all-female band formed in Downer's Grove, Illinois, in 1976 by "Darlin' Cory" Koskela with daughters and friends. Bill seemed especially fond of the Wildwood Pickers, who returned each June for six years.

Each succeeding festival brought memorable events, with Bill typically at the focal point. The previous winter, on a sleepless, freezing night, Bill composed his haunting tune "My Last Days on Earth." When he recorded the tune in February, he had just been diagnosed with colon cancer and surely was confronting his own mortality. The mandolin's plaintive melody, rendered in an unusual lowered D-minor "cross-tuning," was set to a distinctive overdubbed aural background comprising a vocal chorus, an orchestral section of violins and cellos, and evocative sounds of oceanic winds and seagulls. At the June festival, the MCA album with the new composition was still days away from official release, but Bill felt the Bean Blossom fans ought to have a preview. Glen Duncan remembered, "They just had given him a mix of it, you know. He said 'You gotta hear this. This is the most powerful thing I've ever heard in my life.' And he said, 'There's a bunch of fiddles a-playing on it. And, now, they told me, 'cause they did that after I had gone, and they said that when all them people was a-playing, that there wasn't a dry eye among 'em. Now, it's really powerful, and it tells the story of a man as he goes on up through his years,' and all that, and stood there and held a cassette recorder up there in the mike."

The moment was emotionally magical, for Monroe and for hundreds in the audience. Raymond Huffmaster was transfixed by the experience, recalling it vividly more than twenty-five years later: "It had been raining all day and was still really dark and cloudy and Monroe had this feller to play the tape through a mic, telling everybody 'Now you all listen really close.' The boy starts the tape, Monroe is standing off to the right end of the stage . . . when the tune starts . . . the sun breaks out and shines JUST on Monroe through all those trees that used to be up there. It was a moment I'll never forget and don't want to."[41]

Unfortunately, the mundane realities of life and work often interrupted Monroe's moments of musical magic. A month after the June festival, the State Board of Health conducted an inspection of the park, evaluating it for possible problems. Several needed improvements were demanded, including elimination of the routine discharge of wastewater on the ground, installation of new water-heating controls and equipment for concessions, and the addition of a sanitary dumping station and more water hydrants. The State Board of Health gave Monroe until September 1 to make the improvements, and some upgrades were evidently carried out. In mid-November, Carl Brummett appeared before the Nashville town board to request a new water line and one-and-a-half-inch water meter to supply the property with more water, noting his concern that the Board of Health might shut down the entire Bean Blossom and Jamboree operation.

As these issues were in play, the shows went on. Bill Monroe's fifth Autumn Bluegrass Festival, held September 17–20, 1981, was much more heavily advertised than previous fall festivals, with a large Hatch Show Print poster announcing the lineup. Earl Scruggs returned with the Earl Scruggs Revue, and there were also appearances by James Monroe, Birch Monroe, Carl Story, Don Reno, the Lost Kentuckians, and the Boys from Indiana. A ticket for the whole four-day event cost twenty-nine dollars.

Birch had turned eighty in May 1981, and though some had jokingly called him "Mr. Slow Motion" decades before, it was increasingly clear that he was slowing down even more, and perhaps even tiring of his work at the Jamboree. He did what he could at Bean Blossom but returned to western Kentucky to live with a friend as his health worsened. When Birch passed away on May 15, 1982, the Sunday shows continued for a short time, but the Jamboree's end was near.

A month later, the 1982 June festival was held June 11–20. Appearing for the first time were Joe Val and the New England Bluegrass Boys, displaying for the Bean Blossom crowd Val's soaring tenor voice and Boston accent and his worshipful Monroe-inspired approach to hard-driving bluegrass. Festivalgoers loved Joe Val, enjoyed the usual core groups, crowded around the stage to see Earl, and picked and partied all night in the campground as usual. Yet that year, they really began to understand, without always saying so, that the park, and perhaps also the festival, had reached a turning point with Birch's death.

On the day of Birch's funeral at Rosine, Bill Monroe expressed his disappointment to Jim Peva about the scanty attendance at the latest Sunday Jamboree show featuring Lonnie Glosson and Wayne Raney. Although no one specifically announced the end of the Brown County Jamboree, the inescapable fact was slowly accepted. Sunday shows in the barn ceased entirely for three months after the Glosson-Raney debacle; then, after forty-one years, the long run of the Jamboree sputtered to a stop. In the fall of 1982, a Jamboree show in September presented the groups Rising Sun, Bluegrass of the 80s, and Diana Gilaspy & the Misfits.

In early November, the barn was rented again for a nonmusical local event, a Christmas toy sale and auction by local merchants. On November 21, Bill and the Blue Grass Boys put on the last regular Jamboree show, opened by the group High Cross Road. One more such late-season Brown County Jamboree show by Bill Monroe occurred on the first Sunday in November 1985, but predictable seasons of Brown County Jamboree shows ended after 1982.

After that, Bill's Nashville-based management team at Monroe Festival Headquarters usually staged only two big bluegrass festivals a year, in June and September. From Nashville, they simply could not manage the promotion of weekly Sunday shows at Monroe's rural and increasingly outdated music park more than two hundred miles away.

Thus, Birch's death marked the start of a more widely perceived change in Bean Blossom's reputation. Sensed slowly by some longtime fans over more than a decade as "a decline," it was less obvious to the new Bean Blossom converts who kept arriving each year. Once "Uncle Birch" was gone, regular fans felt that the most heady, exciting early days of the park and the huge June festival belonged to a bygone era. Birch had played so many key roles in his three-plus decades at Bean Blossom—as old-time fiddler, singer, manager, promoter, organizer, maintenance man, emcee, and the principal subject of so many local or wide-ranging fan stories regarding his appearance, his exaggerated old-time sense of thrift, and his attempts to make a modest concessionaire's profit from Jamboree and festival events—that his absence meant not only the end of the weekly Jamboree but also a meaningful change for the festival faithful. No longer would there be even a nod to the old-time fiddling tradition in the midst of Monroe's sets with the Blue Grass Boys at Bean Blossom, for Birch was gone. Regulars at Bean Blossom all felt as if they had lost a quirky, irreplaceable uncle of their own. Throughout subsequent festivals, the core groups kept performing, thrilling new musicians came along, and magical moments still happened, but the festivals would never again be the same.

# 9

# Festival People and Lore

In the earliest festival years, many attendees slept in simple tents, or on the ground next to their cars. The camping experience played a part in forming the shared sense of community that eventually coalesced as an annually recurring cultural scene at Monroe's festival music park.

At a festival park, a cultural space is mapped onto the physical site. Concurrently, time itself, at a bluegrass music festival, is suspended as one moves between encounters with transcendent moments of live musicianship. At Bean Blossom, such moments came often. Pickers and heartfelt fans came back reliably, addicted to the timbres of bluegrass instruments and voices. The value of all the music making at Bean Blossom (onstage and off-) to the annual community was incalculable. From 1968 on, music was being played everywhere on the June festival's grounds, nearly all the time, onstage and off-. Fans, campers, pickers, and literal or figurative family members saw and heard, sometimes up close, all sorts of serendipitous bluegrass music-making moments: jam sessions near a campfire, planned but unscripted workshops onstage where the stars responded to questions, informal one-on-one lessons proceeding quietly behind a parked car—as quietly as two banjoists or two fiddlers can be while thus engaged. There were spontaneous rehearsal sessions by contest bands or aspiring unknowns, overmanned nighttime "monster jams" with four or five guitar players, two or more banjoists, and often a crowd of happily lubricated onlookers or fringe pickers. Such musical moments and hundreds more complemented Monroe's planned program of organized shows by the great exemplars of the bluegrass style, as he saw it.

Large bluegrass festivals like Bean Blossom quickly became scenes for the sale or trading of musical instruments, especially rare and valuable models: Martin dreadnought guitars, Gibson Mastertone banjos, and Gibson F-5 mandolins. George Gruhn, who later became a major Nashville, Tennessee–based dealer in stringed instruments, attended all the early Bean Blossom festivals to buy, sell, and trade. A local old-time fiddler, fiddle dealer, and collector, Bob Alcorn was also a regular sight, often hovering around the open trunk of his old car, from which he would slowly produce an amazing variety of old fiddles for Kenny Baker, Alison Krauss, or anyone else to play, critique, or buy. Many instruments changed hands at Bean Blossom; probably more old instruments were sold than new ones bought from the tent-covered concession-stand booths of manufacturers like Gibson, Martin, Liberty, or Stelling.

Every June at Bean Blossom, attendees renewed annual acquaintances and enjoyed meeting and picking with people who, through recurring encounters, sometimes became friends. It seemed as if everybody at Bean Blossom picked. All participants shared the campground space and constructed mental maps, learning the layout of campsites and checking out focal campground and parking-lot places where great jam sessions repeatedly happened. Great professional musicians could be heard and seen onstage, backstage, offstage around the Jamboree barn and outdoor stage-amphitheater. After the stage show was over, pickers formed up into late-night jam sessions. Jams could break out anywhere, under a convenient tent flap or tarp, out by the side of the road under a convenient utility light, or between a set of cars and trucks arranged just so in the parking lot. Jams also happened often beneath RV awnings or around the welcoming campfires at certain campsites, where odds were good that the camper was himself—later on, increasingly, herself—a picker.

The multiple dimensions of experience of a June Bean Blossom festival almost overwhelmed one's senses and provided lifetimes of memories for many. Guitarist Jack Lawrence, later a regular accompanist for Doc Watson, recalled high points from 1972 more than thirty years later: "I went up from Louisville with Sam Bush and his first wife, Kathy. I remember Birch Monroe opening our tent flap at 6:30 AM to check our tickets. I had just left the Bluegrass Alliance and Sam and I were there as spectators. I was in a jam session with Kenny Baker and Tex Logan when Bill Monroe walked up to show off the Loar he'd just bought. The guitar with the Kay emblem on the headstock was a '46 Herringbone. It belonged to my dear, late friend Calvin Robins, Butch's dad. I played that guitar many times when I was a kid. Calvin wasn't afraid of thieves, he just thought it was funny. Beanblossom '72 was about as much fun as a 19 year old could have."[1]

All who came for more than a year or two joined the growing nucleus of a Bean Blossom festival superfamily of fans, who looked forward to returning each year not only for the concerts and jam sessions but also for the renewal of repeated social recognitions that turned over time into real friendships. Although the festival's attendance was always too large to ever constitute a single social network, it provided a renewable context for many smaller groups of friends, families, or acquaintances to socially jell into a loosely structured portable community, tolerant of complete strangers but ready to make friends. Some members of the community reinforced their associations when they met at other bluegrass festivals or concerts, but all looked forward to a Bean Blossom homecoming around Father's Day weekend in June.

The first five or six festivals seemed to be dominated by unmarried men who arrived alone or in small groups. But the idea of a bluegrass festival campground as a good location for *family* camping grew quickly, both because of promotion and because of the festival's social precedents as established at prior generations of rural country music parks. Family-friendly sensibilities at Bean Blossom and other festivals helped slowly increase the presence of women in bluegrass. A brief surge of rare problems with drugs, motorcycles, alcohol, or other issues in the early days of festivals led to a huge response by bluegrass promoters, who by the late seventies inevitably emphasized that their events happened in family-friendly and secure parks.

Jim Peva and his family always made the forty-two-mile trip from his home in Plainfield, Indiana, to his "festival home" at Bean Blossom. There Jim and Ailene would set up the family campsite with an ever-burning fireplace, welcoming benches and chairs, and a bounty of tasty food that the Pevas would generously share with visitors to their campsite, new or old. With Jim as principal public host, the Peva family established their site as a magnet for new Bean Blossom visitors. International fans from Japan and Europe were always invited to eat and share in the cooking. The Pevas served up special meals at their campsite along the west boundary fence of the park, behind the public concessions on "Concession Row." For 1970s fans from Japan, where beef in any form was then expensive and extraordinary fare, hamburgers cooked on a tripod-hung grill over the Pevas' fire were a special annual treat.[2] Jimmy Martin and others staged evening fish fries or country "game" breakfasts with biscuits and gravy and squirrel or rabbit provided by the host or other avid hunters.

At home in his Bean Blossom camp, Jim Peva would meet and greet friends from the greater Indianapolis region, like guitarists Paul Cox and Bud Freedman.

They would talk, share meals, stay up listening to stage concerts, host or take part in jam sessions, and tell and retell their own festival stories, spinning a web of social bonding ever more tightly.

Stories told at Bean Blossom campsites covered a wide range of topics. As Butch Robins changed banjo strings among a sociable group hanging out under the awning at Frank Neat's RV, he and the others recalled the lives and activities of favorite bluegrass artists, always including Bill Monroe; techniques of playing, caring for, or enhancing instruments; remembrances of spectacular jam sessions at this and other festivals; tales of unique characters and oddballs among festival attendees; accounts of jokes and pranks played by (or on) musicians; memorable sayings and stories of past and future events and happenings at the park and in the bluegrass world beyond it; and much more.

The Bean Blossom festival family's sense of being part of a periodically re-created community grew over time, not only by sharing such camaraderie, food, drink, and more at one another's campground spots at the festivals—especially at the places where great campground music regularly occurred in the 1970s, like Doc and Hazel Wards' campsite just north of the power line—but also by the impressions they annually formed and shared about the festival itself and, most important, by their own stories, built from their memories and a shared universe of experience. In recounting the history of the park, stories told by festivalgoers are significant because their recall and re-creation highlight the campground experience. To the extent that stories told are actually about this park and *this* festival, the history of Bean Blossom festivals and the Brown County Jamboree is melded into a mutually networked experience of the festival, carried around continuously in individual memories as well as in photo albums and scrapbooks. The "best" experiences are often finally realized as stories that can be told and retold.

In the formative festival years, regulars experienced the festival's best and worst aspects. For Bud Freedman, as for many other less creative souls, the "worst" may have been the primitive and often filthy bathroom facilities at the park. Around 1971, Freedman improvised a simple song to express his fellow festival attendees' shared sense of revulsion; it was "The Six-Day Bean Blossom Blues," transcribed here from a performance at Peva's camp involving Freedman, Cox, and several Japanese fans and pickers:

> I got those Bean Blossom six-day blues,
> I got those Bean Blossom six-day blues.
> Because the shithouse I refuse to use.

Well, your Momma's a honey-dipper, and your Daddy's
    doin' time, [spoken: "yes, he is!"]
Yeah, your Momma's a honey-dipper, and your Daddy's
    doin' time,
Your sister's in the Port-O-Let, doin' the dishes
    for a dime.

I got those six-day Bean Blossom Blues,
I got those Bean Blossom, six-day blues,
Because the shithouse I refuse to use.

[spoken: "Paul Cox on the six-string Martin guitar, ladies and gentlemen . . .
    Miss Yuki on the five-string Gibson . . . Take a break, mama! . . . How do
    you say *shit* in Japanese?"]

Water boy . . . Bring that bucket 'round, yeah, yeah,
If you don't like your job, take your shit in town.
Yodel-ay-hee, hee hee, hee hee hee.

Got those Bean blossom, seven-day blues
I got those Bean Blossom seven-day blues,
Because the shithouse, I refuse to use.

I got the nine-day Bean Blossom blues
I got the nine-day Bean Blossom blues
Because the crappers, I refuse to lose.

Constipation ain't no big thing
Constipation ain't no big thing
But after nine days, your head begins to ring.[3]

In later years, Freedman improvised additional verses. After 1973, he changed the title and chorus to "Nine-Day Bean Blossom Blues," reflecting the festival's increased length. Bud did not attend every annual June festival as Peva did, but whenever he did return, he and Paul Cox and others could still easily recall or re-create the song, and they were still occasionally performing it for their mutual amusement more than thirty years later. The singing of it, and remembrance of the reasons for its composition, had become for this particular branch of the Bean Blossom "family" a funny and treasured part of their own Bean Blossom tradition.

A similar item, shared by the same group, is Jim Peva's oft-repeated funny tale about loudly emptying his small RV's sewage-holding tank into a pit under the men's side of an old festival outhouse, very, very early one morning; the sudden thunderous sound scared a female user of the outhouse's other side into screaming, "Oh, my God!" and running out of the building.[4]

Regulars retold such Bean Blossom narratives, or through their own exploits spawned new ones. Morris Barnett, born in Kentucky in 1941, shared in this process. Barnett was raised on the south side of Indianapolis in a musical family; his father was a good harmonica player who also could play in an archaic guitar style, and Morris's uncles and grandparents played guitars and fiddles. Each year in Indianapolis, the Barnetts had a family reunion with homemade music. Sometimes they also attended the "Kentucky Reunion," a musically rich annual Garfield Park event for transplanted Kentucky "briars." Barnett listened to country radio as a child and liked a good deal of what he heard, particularly the bluegrass material.

In 1958, after getting his driver's license, Barnett drove to Bean Blossom for the first time, bringing a date to the Brown County Jamboree. He returned often in the next few prefestival years, enjoying shows by Lonzo and Oscar, Kitty Wells, and especially the bluegrass sound of the Stanley Brothers' final show in 1966. At the Jamboree's Sunday shows, he enjoyed the warm-up act of Shorty and Juanita, whose presence meant to him that "you'd get to hear a little bluegrass along with the country show."[5]

Barnett became completely hooked on Bean Blossom festivals: "That really impressed me, having three or four, five bands, in one place, in one show. I loved the whole idea of having all those bluegrass bands together. It beat our family reunion all to heck!" He saw problems, too: slow service and limited selection at the barn's concession stand, Birch's "buying a quarter pound of cheese at a time to make cheeseburgers," and Bill's failure as a merchandiser, since during the late '50s and early '60s he did not have even his own albums available for sale when Morris wanted to buy them at his Jamboree shows.

After 1968, Barnett joined the annual Bean Blossom June festival "family." He missed the 1967 festival entirely due to a lack of advertising: "They never done any radio or newspaper advertising, stuff like that. I understand they *did* do some advertising at Columbus radio, but I never listened to Columbus radio much then." To his great annoyance, he heard about the 1967 festival weeks afterward, and he learned of the 1968 festival only by chance when he encountered Birch and some helpers "out on highway 50, between Seymour and Brownstown, nailing up festival fliers on telephone poles." After 1968, Barnett missed just one of the "Father's Day Festivals," as he called them; he was absent only in 1980, after he had suffered a terrible shoulder injury. He remained upset about that for years, saying: "I'll still never forgive my wife and kids for not hiring an ambulance to bring me up here in 1980!"

Rambling through the campground areas north of the high-voltage power line in the early 1970s, Barnett noticed overgrown conditions at the property's far north end, where the woods and fields were most distant from the barn and the outdoor stage: "I walked into the woods there where there was nothing back there, not even the power line [separating the north woods from the rest of the park property]. This was all growed up back here, they called it Hippie Heaven. It was chigger city, too, I mean them bushes, and—You couldn't walk through there without getting a big batch of chiggers, but—For some reason it didn't bother them, they'd pitch their tent back in there, I mean, it was like a jungle." Eventually, Barnett and others took serious steps to improve the overgrown northern wooded campground area, working on things they felt the Monroes neglected, because "the way the festival worked, for a lot of years, you paid your money at the gate, and [then] you was on your own!"[6]

In the early festival years, young long-haired attendees were regularly disparaged by others as "hippies." Some long-haired young participants were also excellent musicians who made positive impressions on their older and more conservative counterparts in the park. One agreeable hippie who regularly spent time in the far fields on the east and north end of the park was a tall, skinny Indiana University student named Robert M. Hannemann. Hannemann was born near Oklahoma City, but his parents had moved to Chicago and then Indianapolis when he was a youngster, making periodic trips to Brown County in the fifties to visit friends with a cabin on Railroad Road, just a mile west of Bean Blossom. Young Robert, who had started his own 78-rpm record collection in the early 1950s with Bill Haley's "Rock around the Clock," developed a broad interest in music of all sorts. He enjoyed the big-band sounds of Glenn Miller and Woody Herman that his parents liked but listened increasingly in the mid- to late fifties to country and bluegrass, as well as rock and other popular music. Hannemann was already a Monroe fan, old enough to drive, and already grown to his impressive adult height of six foot seven when he attended the first Monroe festival: "In 1967 my folks said, 'There's a bluegrass festival in Bean Blossom.' I guess it was in the paper or something. And I said, 'I got to go to that, I *got* to go to that!' And I went there—'course I got arrested, for DWI [laughs]. I was partying with Frank Overstreet and the Bluegrass Blackjacks. And they watched me, as soon as I left the park. I had this old Bronco, and I had floored it, and was getting rubber. And of course Wayne Branham—deputy in charge of security at the first festival—put the disco lights on me. And I went to jail."[7]

Despite the rough start to his festival experiences, Hannemann returned for the June festivals each year after that. In 1969, he became much more directly involved: "The first time I saw Bill up close I actually went to work for him. I think it was '69, I believe. I was driving around Brown County, and I had noticed there was some cars here, right before the festival. And I pulled in here, right where we are now, and Bill was in there [the barn]—had bib overalls on—and Kenny Baker and Joe Stuart. They were all moving lumber around. And James had a pair of blue jeans that were—like tie-dyed blue jeans. And I asked Mr. Monroe—it was the first time I ever actually got to talk to him—and I said 'Mr. Monroe, will you need any help on your festival?' and he says 'Sure, I could use some help parking cars.' And I ended up working in the ticket booth, taking money."

Hannemann parked cars, sold tickets, and more. At Birch's request, he took out a supply of posters to nail up throughout the area. He also brought a group of his long-haired student friends ("'course, we were all pretty much hippies back then") over from Bloomington to help with general festival work. At the end of the festival, Hannemann got another surprise. He had never discussed payment with Monroe before committing to work for him, and when the 1969 festival was over, Monroe summoned him: "I'll never forget, I was flabbergasted—the end of the festival came around, he was paying everyone. Paid the people who worked for me, who I brought over here, he paid them some money, and then he paid me—six hundred bucks! I couldn't believe it! I about had a heart attack!"

Hannemann worked for Monroe through the early festival years. After graduating from Indiana University in 1972, he spent the summer traveling with Monroe on the bus with the Blue Grass Boys. He helped on the road, doing many of the same tasks at other festivals that he had helped with at Bean Blossom, especially setting up Monroe's table to sell his records, tapes, and eight-tracks. He talked a lot with Bill and Kenny Baker and noticed Bill sometimes sitting in the front of the bus at night, playing his mandolin and toying with new melodies and tunes. Hannemann took due note of Bill's womanizing on the road, saying, "There was *always* a woman on the bus. Women liked Bill because he was the classic southern gentleman. He had that look about him, and that demeanor."

Sometimes Hannemann's work at the park was supervised by Butch Robins's father, Calvin. Calvin Robins was a good friend of Monroe's and an avid guitar-player with a wry sense of humor; at Bean Blossom, he jammed with a "Kay" label stuck on the peghead of his prized Martin "herringbone" guitar. He was also a skilled electrician: "Calvin Robins, one of the electricians, Butch Robins' daddy, he's the one who gave me the name 'Lightning.' Well, I used to have to help Calvin do the wiring, string wiring around here. Boy, Calvin could cuss up a blue streak, too, man, he was a character! I guess they redid it every year. There was always problems. It was never right until after Dwight [Dillman] bought it [in 1998]. They put the cheapest stuff they could in."

Working for Calvin Robins, Lightning Hannemann discovered that the electrical infrastructure of the park, barely adequate to supply the park's southern end where the barn stood, was nearly nonexistent in the expanded and growing northern campground areas. Each year, temporary electrical lines would be deployed from the main circuits, which themselves were fitfully extended into the campground over the early festival years on new power poles, which always seemed to be installed as the festival was actually proceeding. Temporary power wires, laid on the ground or jury-rigged in the campground trees, terminated in a few central locations within the campground area, usually in a single small stake with one or two outlet boxes attached. The exploding campground attendance each year meant that increasing numbers of campers plugged their own long heavy-duty extension cords into these inadequate sources. That, in turn, led to brownouts, blown fuses, and tripped circuit breakers in the campground, particularly if someone decided in the summer's heat to run an RV air-conditioner, a hair dryer, or any other high-wattage device on the overstressed circuit. After the festival each year, the unburied temporary wiring would be taken up, so there was a yearly need for the services of capable electricians, like former Jamboree performer "Cowboy Jack" Cox, or Calvin Robins, and their temporary crews of hired help, including Lightning.

Hannemann sported several more nicknames in addition to "Lightning" during his years at Bean Blossom. In the early years, many attendees noticed him; he stood out for his striking height, long-haired and mustachioed "hippie" look, and loping gait as he busily moved around the park working with Birch and Bill. Many heard him being called "B. C.," short for "Brown County." Another nickname—"King of the Hippies"—was conferred by Bill:

> The years I brought my friends here from Indiana University, they were all hippies too, you know, freaks. We smoked a lot of dope, did a lot of acid. Bill came up—I was supposed to set up his record table and stuff for him. He came up on Hippie Hill . . . and he tapped me on the shoulder, and I turned around, I had a bottle of Jack Daniels in one hand and a big doobie in the other. He went ballistic. He said, "All these hippies are your friends, you're the King of the Hippies!" He was kind of angry with me for being drunk. I thought he would throw me out, but then—I wasn't really wasted. I was pretty coherent. And he lit into me pretty good about having to set an example, and if I'm going to be part of his organization, having to live the clean, straight life. So I went back down and set up his record table and stuff.

Helping Birch Monroe with the concession stands in the barn and along Concession Row on the road west of the park amphitheater, B. C. discovered Birch's legendary habit of extreme thrift: "Birch sent me to the McDonald's IGA to get cheese for his cheeseburgers, and then he'd take these squares of cheese and quarter 'em. And put one quarter of one square of cheese on a hamburger. And one time we had 60-watt bulbs in there, and he went ballistic, wanted us to get 40-watts! That man was so tight, he could squeeze a dime until it turned into a quarter."

B. C.'s accounts of Birch's legendary stinginess were based on real experiences, but such stories grew, recirculated, and spread constantly among the community of fans and pickers during these early festivals, demonstrating the minor variations characterizing oral tradition. Jack Cox told how Birch went to Carl Brummett's grocery store to buy cheese for the concession stand, and after being told that only a single package of eight individually wrapped cheese slices was available, Birch said, "That's fine, that'll make thirty-two cheeseburgers." Since Jack Cox's death, Jim Peva and others have kept that story very much alive. Morris Barnett recounted a variant of the "cheeseburger" story, specifying the store as McDonald's IGA. Bob Black remembered Birch shopping at the IGA for a single package of hot dog buns to feed the festival crowd and also instructing the concession cook to "cut holes in the center of the meat patties so they could make and sell more burgers."[8] Jack Cox also recalled the tale of Birch and the 60-watt bulbs but said it referred to the lights he himself had put up at the park's entrance along Highway 135. Andrea Roberts, who grew up in central Indiana and came to Bean Blossom each year, recalled Birch's removing lightbulbs from the stage after shows "to be sure they wouldn't be stolen overnight."[9] Talmadge Law, who played many Jamboree and festival shows with his family band, the Bluegrass Sounds, often accompanied Birch when he went out to the concrete-block restroom by the barn after shows to remove and store the single rolls of toilet paper he had placed there prior to the show.

Various Blue Grass Boys have told in public "storytelling" workshops how working with Birch was always an exercise in frustration, since he hated to spend money on new tools or materials for improvements. Wayne Lewis recalled contending with Birch's decision to use a broken roll of worn-out roofing paper to fix the leaking barn roof and how Birch believed that most new construction should be inaugurated by pulling the nails from old lumber and straightening them one at a time for reuse. In this respect, according to Bill's close friend Hazel Smith, Birch was just like Bill: "Bill wasn't anybody to go buy something new. He would straighten nails, reuse nails, and reuse boards and planks, rather than get new pieces of lumber, he would use old lumber to fix things. And that's just the way he was. That's the way he was raised up in Kentucky, and he just continued on that all through his life, you know."[10]

Birch tried to save money on every sort of supply for the festival. He posted a sign in the outhouse east of the Jamboree barn, at the edge of the woods near the lake, asking users of that facility to limit themselves to *one* square of toilet paper. Photographer MaryE Yeomans, like Hazel Smith, remembers both actual events and stories told by others about "frugal Birch Monroe going down to Jack McDonald's IGA market, just off the festival grounds, for a four-roll pack of toilet paper to serve a few thousand campers."[11] Hazel Smith's son Billy provided yet another version: "They had run out of toilet tissue up there. You probably remember that, but it's like the whole place had, I don't know, it's like two male and two female toilets there, and twenty-five or thirty thousand people there. And they'd run out. And they run—needed hot dog buns. So Bill said, 'Here, you gotta take some money, Birch, and go get some stuff, we're running out, you gotta go get some things!' So when Birch returned, he had two eight-roll packs of hot dog buns and one four-roll pack of toilet tissue, for thirty thousand people!"

Sooner or later, regular festival attendees noticed Birch selling small items for some extra profit. His merchandise was varied, whether it was the box of "for sale" donuts that Bill consumed in jest or the abandoned lawn chairs he fixed up to resell. In 1972, when the festival was very large and successful, Birch hawked small plastic letter openers, with a ruler molded along one side and the legend "Souvenir of Bill Monroe's World Famous Bluegrass Festival 1972" in raised letters on the handle. In 1973, he sold the leftover 1972 souvenirs, as Paul Birch discovered:

> I remember seeing [Birch] up near the stage during an afternoon show with a big handful of festival souvenirs. I immediately recognized them as these white six-inch plastic ruler/letter openers with embossed lettering advertising the 1972 festival I'd first attended. I'm pretty sure I'd bought one or two back then, and probably from Birch. At any rate, Birch wasn't quite ready to hawk these rulers. Instead he was occupied with scraping off the "1972" with a pocket knife (that's SO Monroe . . . <g>) so that they wouldn't seem out-of-date to his customers. This part I'm not sure about, but I think I asked him how much he wanted for one, and he told me that the already-scraped ones would be a dollar. I told him I'd rather have the original 1972 version if he didn't mind and he let several of them go for 50 cents apiece. In retrospect, I appreciate his honesty in cutting the price on what I guess he considered the inferior product.[12]

Birch's habit of thrift extended to every part of his life. Kenny Baker recalled Birch's taking a "girlfriend" down to the Lavender House restaurant, located just outside the park entrance, where he ordered one chicken dinner—with two plates.

Stories about Bill Monroe were central. Many of these provided snapshot glimpses of his unique personality and his musical or moral sensibilities. Kenny Baker told of Bill's ability to resolve serious disputes among festivalgoers, if they involved him in his role as owner and manager. Baker said, "A guy from Louisiana came up, with his family—wife and two kids—and set up their campsite." The couple sought out Bill Monroe, saying they were offended by the presence of a racially mixed couple at the festival. When they confronted Monroe about the "problem" and demanded to know what he was going to do about it, he told them, in Baker's presence, "They got as much right here as you have," and the offended family immediately left. So Bill, in Baker's words, laudably "traded out four tickets to keep two."

Stories about Bill, Birch, and other Bean Blossom characters came from the observations of those around them at the park. The stories, retold in variable forms, quickly moved, as such stories always do, out of the control of individual tellers to become part of a floating set of oral traditions that make up, in part, the folklore of Bean Blossom. The nearly palpable sense of tradition that has developed at Bean Blossom feeds back into the thoughts and actions of the returning portable community of annual festivalgoers.

Fans often discussed Monroe's running of the Bean Blossom festival itself. Some noted how the Monroes and their festival managers regulated tradition at Bean Blossom, always ensuring that at the June festival, only "traditional bluegrass" would prevail. The desire to protect tradition meant slow turnover in the festival lineup and also a kind of bias: new bands, especially "progressive" or "newgrass" bands, did not seem to get booked very often. Monroe's predilection for "traditional" bands was interpreted by fans as his personal rejection of the young "long-haired" players, especially those who brought what Monroe thought of as "rock and roll" into his music. For a time, Monroe would not book the Newgrass Revival at Bean Blossom, believing their look and their music would offend his local tradition-minded supporters in Brown County. They never did play the June festival but played the Jamboree several times. Hazel Smith recalled, "Birch was supposed to be runnin' Bean Blossom, and Bill had told him, 'Don't you have no rock and roll up there!' Well, he'd slipped around and had Newgrass Revival, and didn't tell Bill, and Bill found out about it and got on him about it. Then—Birch had booked a rock and roll show at Bean Blossom. Then—I was privy to Bill gettin' on Birch about it—and Birch denied it at first! Bill said 'I *know* you did,' and they were arguin' about it. Bill said, 'I want *clean* music up there, I don't want that rock and roll stuff with all that long hair! My people up there, they won't want to come if they know that kind of stuff's being played!'"[13]

Bill could be flexible if he felt it served his business interests, as when he suddenly extended the Bluegrass Alliance's dates at the 1971 festival. Doug Hutchens saw Monroe's 1970s actions toward young long-haired musicians and fans differently, in light of his own Bean Blossom experience:

> Bill was pretty much down on most young people at that point. But let's explore
> that a second and take a short trip back to those thrilling days of yesteryear in
> the later days of the "hippie" movement. Bill didn't particularly like the hair
> and the appearance but the thing he would not tolerate was being dirty and in
> many cases some of the young campers were downright nasty. He didn't agree
> with the drinking and dope but the thing that would get his temper up the most
> was when one or two would come in the gate and pay and go set up a camp site
> and four others would slip over through the woods and come through the back
> way. I spent many a morning with Kenny Baker, Rual Yarbrough, Calvin Robins,
> Joe Stuart, and Silverspurs doing what we called "beating the bushes" to check
> tickets for that day. It was a never ending problem, with substantial numbers
> trying to slip in the far campground just past the power line camping area.[14]

Ticket and camping costs were themselves a subject for talk and, for some, motivation to take subversive action. Some fans tried to attend the festivals without paying for tickets. James Monroe bragged to a friend that more people used to *sneak* into Bean Blossom than the number who *paid* to get in at other festivals. There were near-legendary stories of fans cheating on ticket purchases. Bean Blossom regular Jack Derry remembered "when a guy and his buddy cut their ticket in half at BB and each stuck his half in his hat. The security people were fooled and the perps thought it was a great joke."[15] Moreover, after the adhesive-backed fabric tickets of the first three or four festivals gave way to simple, inexpensive cardboard tickets, counterfeits were produced by many enterprising fans. The counterfeiting problem worsened after the festival grew to a week or more and an authentic "combination" ticket could cost the buyer one hundred dollars. Louisville-based old-time banjo player Harry Bickel remembered that one year, the expensive combination ticket Birch sold consisted only of a white index card with the words "Bluegrass Music" stamped on it with a rubber stamp. Bickel and friends quickly bought their own stack of index cards, had a rubber stamp made up, and distributed tickets to friends.[16]

Many other expressive forms, including paintings and quilts made of T-shirts, preserve and reflect Bean Blossom's bluegrass heritage. But songs and tunes dominate and can be re-created in jam sessions; they have evoked the park and its Brown County setting since 1955, when Bill first recorded "Brown County Breakdown." More followed, such as Kenny Baker's "Festival Waltz," Louie Popejoy's

1978 album *Bean Blossom,* and James Moss's "Midnight in Bean Blossom." The old barn inspired Bill Monroe's song "The Old Brown County Jamboree Barn," and the park and its festival are at the heart of James Monroe's 1997 recording of Damon Black's "Bean Blossom Memories."

Nascent songs sometimes are expressed first as poetic lyrics. One year after the old barn's demolition, Bernard Lee penned a nostalgic poem or song illustrating the barn's persistent grip on his memories:

### "THE OLD BROWN COUNTY JAMBOREE BARN"

We wander back to the hills of Brown County,
There with our friends, we've spent many happy days,
Playing bluegrass music into the night around our campfires,
Enjoying our way of life, all the way.

Chorus:
We still play bluegrass music by the campfires,
Some friends are no longer around;
And there is something missing,
The old barn was burned to the ground.

Remembering the old barn,
When shows were held on Sunday afternoons;
Selling tickets for Brother Birch Monroe,
Then on stage, before my fiddle was in tune.

Brother Birch would open his shows with, Hi friends and neighbors
On his fiddle play "Coming Down From Boston" and "Florida Blues";
Then, on with "Tennessee Wagoner,"
You wanted to dance out of your shoes.

The barn was filled with music and laughter,
Food served from the kitchen with a special treat;
Some days out in the chilly rain with a buck-saw,
Brother Birch gathered wood for inside heat.

The Bluegrass Boys bus pulls into Bean Blossom,
Bertha would say, "Oh, there's my brother Bill";
As Monroe strolled through the old barn,
His sister's heart was gladdened and thrilled.

So the old barn is gone forever,
Campfires still glow just as bright;
Bluegrass music flows through the backwoods,
Into the wee hours of the night.

# Bill and James Monroe's Festival Park, 1983–97

Birch Monroe's death brought resonating memories of his former presence at the June and fall festivals. Fans' fading memories of "Uncle Birch" fed a dawning sense that times had changed and that the festivals' early excitement and intensity had waned a bit.

More changes came from new demands on Bill Monroe's time, because of his many appearances, honors, and new endeavors. He was honored and lionized around the country, receiving a National Heritage Fellowship in 1982 and being ever more widely recognized, nationally and internationally, as the founder of "a legitimate American art form."[1] The 1980s witnessed a rise in the count of bluegrass festivals, so Monroe the artist enjoyed increased opportunities to play profitable shows. But for Monroe the promoter, success meant less focus on Bean Blossom.

During the 1983 June festival, Bill's workers began building a new bathhouse and restroom facility in the northern wooded campground. But Indiana's Administrative Building Council stepped in on June 16, issuing a building-code violation, for Bill had neglected to file any plans with the state prior to construction. A relatively minor infraction, this case apparently ended with a delayed filing of plans by Monroe. The completed building, with toilets installed by Kenny Baker, had been built without the formality of a required septic-system "percolation test." When a belated test proved the septic capacity inadequate, local authorities ordered the Monroes to remove all plumbing and fixtures.[2] The building's empty shell remained as a campground shelter for rainy-day jam sessions, a "pickin' parlor" in the woods. The incident may have refocused the county government's scrutiny on the Jamboree grounds and its management.

The seventeenth annual June festival in 1983 reprised most of the core group of familiar performers. Joe Val and the New England Bluegrass Band returned for a second and final time that year, and A. L. Wood, who for the prior decade had been a regular with his band the Smokey Ridge Boys, did not return. Debuting artists included the Carl Tipton Show, Country Gazette, the Good Ole Persons, Curly Seckler and the Nashville Grass, Canada's Dixie Flyers, the team of Josh Graves and Joe Stuart, and Pete Corum and the Red River Band.

Many "new" groups at Bean Blossom were already known to Monroe and his management from years of prior encounters on the road. Acts like Country Gazette included experienced bluegrass performers already familiar with the park; Alan Munde had played the first couple of Bean Blossom festivals with the Stone Mountain Boys and returned later with Jimmy Martin. Other fresh groups, like the Dixie Flyers, had earned fame and prestige in bluegrass music circles and had personally encountered Bill Monroe before being booked. The Dixie Flyers formed in 1974 and had begun to attract great attention in Canada by 1977, when they won the Annual Gold Award for promoting bluegrass in Canada at that nation's biggest and longest-running festival, Bluegrass Canada, held in Carlisle, Ontario. After repeatedly trying to sound out Bill Monroe at Carlisle about getting booked at Bean Blossom, the Flyers finally found a way. Several years later, guitarist Bert Baumbach recalled the scene: "Bill Monroe had been up to Carlisle. We'd met him before and left off albums. We said 'Do you ever have Canadian bands down there?' He said, 'Well, I'm kind of looking at getting a Canadian band down there.' We took that as a hint and got on the phone. We finally got it."[3] At the 1983 festival, the Dixie Flyers—the first Canadian band to play Bean Blossom—were surprised at the warm reception by the "truest-blooded American bluegrassers" there.

The fall festival in 1983 was again smaller and more open to new groups than the June festivals were. Adding to the regular core, the fall festival brought in J. D. Crowe and the New South, the Doug Dillard Band, Clyde Moody, Bobby Smith and the Boys from Shiloh, Steve Crockett and the Log Cabin Boys, the Pathfinders, the Lost Kentuckians, and the Wildwood Pickers. New that year was country and gospel singer Dee Dee Prestige (known later as Diana Christian or Butterfly Rose Christian), who met Bill Monroe in Tennessee in 1981 and befriended him, accompanying him to Israel in 1983.

Advertising for the fall festival was minimal, perhaps because once again, Bill's attention was focused elsewhere. Through his successes of the seventies, he had, according to many credible observers' accounts, amassed a good deal of money. By October 1983, Bill was moving ahead with plans to spend some of it on another new venture: the creation in Nashville, Tennessee, of the Bill Monroe Bluegrass Hall of Fame and Museum. He formed a corporation with his son, James, and they bought four acres of land on Nashville's Music Valley Drive, about a mile from Opryland. The remodeled and expanded building on the site incorporated three main features: the Bluegrass Hall of Fame, a museum of Monroe's own memorabilia and that of other contributing country music artists, and a record and souvenir shop. When the Bluegrass Hall of Fame and Museum opened in 1984, *Bluegrass Unlimited* reported that it included "a Bill Monroe Room, a Hall-of-Fame Room, the Blue Grass Boys' Wall, a gift and record shop and a Walkway of Stars."[4] Plans were announced for a bronze statue of Bill to be erected on "Bluegrass Hill," behind the museum, near an area where the Monroes hoped to have live performances on weekends. The initial Hall of Fame featured ten member groups, all chosen by Bill and collectively representing most of the first bluegrass generation: Bill Monroe, Lester Flatt, Mac Wiseman, Earl Scruggs, Carter and Ralph Stanley, Carl Story, Don Reno and Red Smiley, Sonny and Bobby Osborne, Jim and Jesse McReynolds, and the Country Gentlemen. Manager Jim Bessire predicted a bright future at the June 4, 1984, grand-opening ceremony and was already thinking about plans for future expansion. Bessire and the Monroes had big hopes for the museum's growth and dreamed of its destiny as a focal point for growing legions of bluegrass music fans.[5]

Within two brief years, the Bluegrass Hall of Fame dream began to fade. The site was just too far from the action near the Opry and was concealed from casual tourists by an uninviting and poorly signed access route. Lacking a strong performance venue to draw active bluegrass fans, the Bill Monroe Museum and Hall of Fame lured few visitors, and in the summer of 1986 it closed its Nashville location. It soon reopened at a less pricey, but even less visible, site, at Music Village USA in Hendersonville, Tennessee, but it failed at that location as well. Eventually, Bill would move it to Bean Blossom.

The 1984 festival season saw more diversity in both the musical offerings at Bean Blossom and Monroe's own promotional efforts around the country. But the eighteenth annual June festival, scaled back to five days, continued focusing on familiar festival events, identified succinctly in the *Bluegrass Unlimited* ads as "Bean Day," "Band Contest," "Little Miss Bluegrass Contest," and "Sunset Jam & Square Dance." The local paper published a complete schedule of events sponsored by six local merchants in support of the "internationally famous 18th Annual Bean Blossom Bluegrass Jamboree." The businesses, recognizing the festivals' positive economic effects, were Brown County Real Estate, Michael's

Motel (where Monroe had often been a guest), McDonald's IGA, the Lavender House Restaurant, the Village Real Estate Company, and the Bean Blossom Inn.

The groups performing that year were all Bean Blossom veterans. Dee Dee Prestige appeared on Friday and Saturday along with a familiar roster of stars: Bill Monroe, James Monroe, Jim & Jesse, Bobby Smith, the Lost Kentuckians, and the Wildwood Pickers. On Saturday, clogger Jackie Christian joined Bill onstage for exhibition dancing as the Blue Grass Boys played spirited instrumentals.

The June festival was often the scene of important transitions in band membership. In 1984, Bill's bass player, Mark Hembree of Wisconsin, repeatedly announced the availability of the new album (*Snakes Alive!*) by a band he was working with on the side, the Dreadful Snakes. Hembree had teamed up in 1983 with Bela Fleck, Jerry Douglas, Pat Enright, and Roland White to create this informal group to play local Nashville shows when they were not on the road with their regular groups. Their album, which included Monroe's own "Brown County Breakdown" and other traditional and venerable bluegrass pieces, was released early in 1984. After the June festival and nearly five years as a Blue Grass Boy, Hembree left Monroe to help found the Nashville Bluegrass Band. His leaving cleared the way for another big change: Clarence "Tater" Tate, who had been a Blue Grass Boy for eight months during the lean times in 1956, rejoined Monroe as the new bass player. Tate fiddled at Bean Blossom that year for Wilma Lee Cooper's Clinch Mountain Clan, but he was pleased to work once more for his former boss, enduring a chronic shoulder injury that made fiddling painful. For the next decade, Tate would perform most frequently with Bill on bass, though he played fiddle again occasionally after Kenny Baker's sudden final departure from the band in October 1984. Tate, nominally the bass player, would happily join in on a twin-fiddle number or two when another fiddler was present.

Bean Blossom continued to bring out the best in Monroe as he performed for his fans. Not all performances for fans were onstage; bass player and talent agent Mike Drudge observed Bill at the June 1984 festival in a situation that symbolized to Drudge both Monroe's humanity and the special access fans enjoyed to traditional bluegrass artists: "As I entered the festival area, there stood Bill Monroe with veteran sideman Wayne Lewis singing the chorus of 'Blue-eyed Darling' to a crippled child laying in the back seat of her parent's car. She was unable to attend the festival because of her physical condition. I would hate to see bluegrass lose this type of 'personal touch' if it were to become massively popular and commercialized."[6]

In July 1984, Bill inaugurated a reciprocal arrangement with country music star George Jones, who had opened his own music park in Colmesniel, Texas.

Bill, James, Wilma Lee Cooper, Mac Wiseman, Dee Dee Prestige, Lonzo and Oscar, and the Newgrass Revival all did shows at the three-day "First Annual Bill Monroe Texas Bluegrass Festival," held at Jones's park. Then, in August, Monroe hosted a new Bean Blossom festival, the "First Annual George Jones Country and Bluegrass Music Celebration." This weekend event presented Monroe and Jones, as well as other country and bluegrass acts. On the country music side, there were performances by Mel McDaniel and Oklahoma Wind, Little Jimmy Dickens and the Country Boys, and the Leona Williams Show, which highlighted the singing and songwriting of Williams, who had recorded her own song "Best Friends" as a duet with Jones that year. Bluegrass music was represented only by Bill's Blue Grass Boys and James's Midnight Ramblers. The festivals were not huge successes, and (despite the optimistic "First Annual" in their names) they never recurred.

The 1984 fall festival, advertised as "Bill Monroe's Autumn Bluegrass & Country Festival," was not publicized as the eighth of the numbered series of fall festivals that were supposed to have begun in 1977. Despite the name, it was mostly bluegrass; eleven of the twelve headlining artists were prominent bluegrassers. The Johnson Mountain Boys, who had formed in 1978 and rapidly achieved nationwide fame for their neotraditional style, played Bean Blossom for the first time. Country music was represented by the popular southern gospel star Wendy Bagwell and the Sunliters, who had previously appeared there just once, on a Jamboree show in 1973.

Although the seventy-three-year-old Bill Monroe was professionally perturbed by the precipitous fall departure of Kenny Baker, whom he had often called "the greatest fiddler in bluegrass music," he forged on with new Blue Grass Boys and the power of his own considerable artistic momentum. He rejected proposed hillbilly costuming for his "Uncle Pen" role in Ricky Skaggs's music video "Country Boy at Heart" but was delighted by the popularity of the video in the summer of 1985.[7] His personal life moved on as well. In the spring, he married a woman he had known for years and to whom he had initially proposed in 1980, Della Streeter. After proving his intentions to remain faithful to her, Bill and Della signed a prenuptial agreement waiving Streeter's rights to Bill's property if a divorce should occur. They married on April 24, less than a year after the death of Bill's first wife, Carolyn Minnie Brown, from whom he had been divorced since 1960.

Another positive event came on May 11, when Monroe was awarded an honorary doctor of letters degree by the University of Kentucky. The honorary doctorate was originally planned to have been conferred at the 1984 graduation ceremonies, but Monroe could not make it on that date.

Invigorated by such affirming events, Bill again planned a big ten-day festival at Bean Blossom for June 1985. In addition to the 1980s core of regular Bean Blossom performers—Bill, Ralph Stanley, the Osborne Brothers, the Country Gentlemen, Jimmy Martin, J. D. Crowe, Larry Sparks, Bobby Smith, the Lewis Family, the Goins Brothers, the Sullivan Family, and the Boys from Indiana—there were appearances by California-based bands High Country and the Good Ole Persons. Also featured were the group Bluegrass of the '80s, the well-known local family band Talmadge Law and the Bluegrass Sounds, and several other groups that were either newly organized or new to Bean Blossom: the Detroit Bluegrass Band, led by Dana Cupp Jr.; the New Coon Creek Girls; Redwing; Paul Mullins and the Traditional Grass; the Reno Brothers; and the Virginia Squires.

One of Bill Monroe's most celebrated attributes, his incredible musical inventiveness, had not lessened with his advancing years. Former Blue Grass Boys often recall the moments of invention and the odd circumstances that seemed to inspire Bill. He would explore his mandolin's well-worn fingerboard as he traveled late at night on long bus rides or come up with new melodies at odd solitary moments in his busy life on the road, seemingly moved by some sight or sound or place-name that stirred his own thoughts of older generations' music, the "ancient tones" he spoke of learning from his own childhood musical idols like Uncle Pen Vandiver and Arnold Shultz. These inspired Monrovian moments of musical discovery and creativity sometimes happened right at the park, "in the midst of chaos," at Bean Blossom. Fiddler Glen Duncan, who grew up in Columbus and became a Blue Grass Boy in 1985 after leaving a very successful country group, the Kendalls, played a key role in naming one Monroe tune born in just such a creative moment. It happened after the June festival's Friday-night Sunset Jam in 1985, just before Duncan and the other Blue Grass Boys were to join Monroe in the barn to play the traditional Friday-night festival square dance:

> So we go in the barn, and Bill's fooling around, playing this tune in B. And, uh, [mimicking Monroe's voice], "This is a new number I just wrote." "Yeah, is that right?" "Yeah."
>
> And so he's playing it, and asks, "What should we call it?" I said, "Well, we ought to call it 'The Old Brown County Barn.'" And he said—kind of shook his head, you know—and didn't say anything for a while. Then he played a little more and said, "How 'bout if we call it 'The Old Brown County *Jamboree* Barn'?"
>
> "That'd be a great title!" [laughs]. That was his—he put "Jamboree" in there, but that—'cause we're standing in there, and I'm thinkin,' "Hey, man, you know, this is the reason I play the fiddle; this is the reason I'm playing with Bill Monroe today: it's the old Brown County barn."[8]

Attending the June festival in 1985 was Sue Galbraith, a banjo and guitar player from upstate New York who came with most of the members of her band, Dempsey Station. Nearly overwhelmed by the wonderful first experiences in "bluegrass land," Sue later realized that the New Yorkers spent their first two years at the Bean Blossom festival "kind of hanging out and learning the ropes of surviving for ten days at a festival."[9] For Sue and the others, including her guitar-playing sister Kathy, learning the ropes included plenty of jamming in the woods at the park's north end or on Hippie Hill. Within two years, Sue and most of her band members had become a regular part of the Bean Blossom family of participants, and their regular involvement led to many onstage appearances there in subsequent years.

Another newcomer at the fall 1985 festival was Rattlesnake Annie (Rosan Gallimore McGowan), an eclectic singer-guitarist who had developed her own singular style out of her Tennessee upbringing and her association with such blues artists as Ma Rainey, Lightnin' Hopkins, and country stars such as Floyd Tillman and Willie Nelson. She had met Monroe on the 1982 Wembley European Country Music Tour and found common ground in their mutual love of blues: "We were somewhere in Germany, it was 2am in the hotel bar. My husband Max and I were visiting with our guests from Czechoslovakia. I had my guitar at our table and was singing blues when suddenly Bill Monroe appeared at our table and joined me with his mandolin. He was pickin' single note blues, what a mean and lonesome sound! From that moment on we were blues friends."

Later, Rattlesnake and her husband would visit Bill at home whenever they came to Nashville. When she phoned him, she'd say, "Hey, Bill, this is Rattlesnake," and he'd invariably reply, "You wouldn't bite a feller, would you?" Invited personally by Bill to play Bean Blossom's 1985 fall festival, Rattlesnake appeared there onstage during several evening shows, playing to warm, open, and responsive audiences. At a late-night jam session, Monroe again demonstrated his ability to play blues mandolin: "All the musicians who were on the show that night, had gathered in a circle in the barn for a jam. Each player took their turn and the other musicians joined in. I played a blues song and Bill appeared out of nowhere, right behind my chair and poured his blues out directly into my ears. I turned my head around towards him and he looked like a giant, his hand and mandolin were at my eye level. It was one of the most profound moments in my musical life."[10]

Rattlesnake invited Bill to record "Blue Moon of Kentucky" with her, and he played mandolin backup on her 1992 studio CD, *Crossroads*. One of their live 1985 Bean Blossom performances together was the blues classic "Trouble in Mind," which also appeared as a cut on Rattlesnake's 2002 CD, *Southern Discomfort*. Accompanied only by her own guitar and Monroe's mandolin, the performance was a radical departure from the traditional bluegrass sounds at Bean Blossom and a further indicator of Monroe's deeply ingrained sense that his own musicianship could never be limited by categories like "bluegrass" or "country music."

The run-down old barn, which had not featured regular Brown County Jamboree Sunday shows after mid-1982, remained in use for occasional special music events, particularly private college-student parties, which were still said to be taking place at the Bean Blossom Jamboree. Beginning around 1985, W. M. Bentley began managing such events. Bentley had moved into Brown County not long before. A week after an October 1985 event degenerated into a drunken brawl, Bentley wrote to the *Brown County Democrat* to express Bill's "thanks to the Brown County Sheriff's Department and the State Police for the great job they all did keeping a group of college students under control during the party they had at the Jamboree grounds at Bean Blossom Friday night. They kept things from developing into a large riot."[11] While Bentley's nominal mid-1980s role as Bean Blossom Jamboree manager did not last long, he continued a long association with the park through Bill and James and their eventual successor, Dwight Dillman.

November brought another calamity for Monroe: someone broke into his log house north of Nashville and employed a fireplace poker to inflict terrible damage to his beloved July 9, 1923, Lloyd Loar F-5 Gibson mandolin (serial number 73987) and the other vintage Loar he had purchased at Bean Blossom.[12] The act shocked Monroe, his family, and the entire bluegrass music world, as it not only put his favorite instrument out of commission but also seemed to validate rumors concerning anonymous enemies of Bill's. Was it an old girlfriend who felt wronged by his marriage to Della, or perhaps some musical rival? No credible answers resulted from the police investigation, leaving Bill and his immediate associates deeply anxious for his safety. The Grand Ole Opry provided him with extra security guards backstage, and rumors at Bean Blossom said that even at the festival in his own park, he was being protected by private bodyguards.

Things seemed to look up the next year. By the spring of 1986, Gibson's brilliant craftsman Charlie Derrington had painstakingly sorted out the splintered pieces of the two instruments and rebuilt them. Monroe resumed performing with his signature instrument and marveled along with the fans that its legendary tone had been restored along with its appearance.

At the twentieth annual June festival—again a ten-day event—Bill performed and presented nineteen other acts, most of them very familiar. The new groups included only the Whites—mandolinist Buck White and his daughters, Sharon and Cheryl, who had actually performed there several times during the 1970s as Buck White and the Downhome Folks—and the Sanders Family, who had then operated their annual bluegrass festival at McAlester, Oklahoma, for a decade. The 1986 festival event was generally successful, though attendance seemed slightly diminished. Some familiar food vendors and concessionaires, like T-shirt City, had abandoned annual ventures at Bean Blossom because of Birch and Bill's demands for ever-higher fees, but new food and souvenir concessions replaced them. In 1986, a T-shirt vendor from Illinois offered a shirt proclaiming, "If you lead a good life, say your prayers, go to church and listen to bluegrass music, when you die, you'll go to Bean Blossom, Indiana."

A couple of months after the big June event, a two-line note in *Bluegrass Unlimited* informed the fans, "The 10th Annual Bean Blossom Autumn Bluegrass Festival will not be held as scheduled September 19–21. The Brown County Jamboree Park will be closed for renovation." But "renovation" was not really in the works. After the 1986 festival season, the Monroes decided to tear down the venerable old barn. According to James Monroe, the Brown County authorities insisted, asserting that the barn had become structurally unsafe: "It just got to the—it burned once, and they replaced some of the wood, but after a while—in fact, when we had to have it taken down—the county said that, you know, 'You gonna have to take this down. It's dangerous for the folks to be up under there.' And my father wasn't happy to hear about it at all. But, uh, he had to take that down, and that's what really started it."[13]

However, according to fan gossip, Bill had been approached that summer by a preacher who proposed that the barn be torn down and replaced by a new building to be used for both musical and religious services. Morris Barnett recalled, "Rumor was that some southern evangelist convinced Bill to tear it down, 'cause he was gonna build a nice restaurant and a concert hall and all this other stuff. And after they tore down and burnt the barn, they found out the guy didn't have any money."[14]

The rumors of a "southern evangelist" might have been based on the fact that Bill's friend Bob Chapman, a mandolin-playing preacher and retired locksmith from Mer Rouge, Louisiana, traveled with his wife, Gloria, to Bean Blossom that October to demolish the barn for Bill. Chapman, born in Kermit, West Virginia, had been a Monroe fan and follower from his childhood days and had installed a safe in Bill's bus. By his own account, he also volunteered to help build Bill's Nashville Hall of Fame. But rumor is a slippery thing; Chapman later remembered the involvement of *another* preacher, a Methodist who was "helping with Bill's paperwork," when the decision to raze the barn was made. Before the barn was razed, the Chapmans met with Bill, James, and the preacher to discuss plans for the building, which was indeed in poor condition, with a visibly sagging roof. Chapman first proposed that he simply reinforce the "historical" structure with steel I-beams, but when that idea was rejected by the others, he agreed to personally raze the barn. Plans were also discussed to replace the show barn with a modern steel building—perhaps the unidentified preacher's suggestion?—but nothing would be erected on the barn's site for six years. In late October, the newspaper tersely broke the news to the public in a two-line note: "Barn's Days Numbered: The old barn that housed many a performance at Bill Monroe's Brown County Jamboree grounds at Bean Blossom is being torn down. According to Gloria Chapman, the plan is to build a new auditorium at the jamboree to house future performances."[15]

The destruction of the barn was accomplished around the third week of October 1986. Chapman disassembled the structure, saving as much lumber as possible for later shipment to Bill's farm north of Nashville. According to Bernard Lee, a bulldozer operator had to repeatedly attack the building before it would fall; if so, this would seem to challenge the claim by unnamed Brown County officials that the structure was unsound. Eventually, the old building yielded, and once Chapman sent the salvageable lumber off to Nashville, Bill and James and the Chapmans set the ruins afire.

Neither the Chapmans nor the Monroes seemed to take into account the barn's emotional value to fans. Many Bean Blossom regulars would later remember and mourn the barn and its hidden treasures, like the wall boards in the backstage "warm-up" rooms that had been signed over the years by hundreds of memorable country and bluegrass artists who had played there, from Lulu Belle and Scotty to Mac Wiseman, from Jack Cox to the Rising Sun Band. A few of the barn's memorable components, like the eight iron potbellied stoves, were salvaged or "liberated" by faithful locals like Bernard Lee. Some of the least-damaged weathered boards were also saved by Lee and a few others. But most of the structure disappeared into a heap of ashes. After Frank Overstreet visited the site in November, to confirm rumors he had heard that the barn was gone, he wrote of the momentous change in an illustrated article in *Bluegrass Unlimited*, "Ashes of Bean Blossom."[16]

There were more changes: in 1987, Della began divorce proceedings against Bill for "irreconcilable differences," possibly based on Monroe's ongoing womanizing as a road musician. Yet his professional career continued with few letups. The 1987 June Bean Blossom festival offered ten days of shows put on by the sixteen groups named in advance ads, plus the usual special events: the banjo, band, and beauty contests; Bean Day; the Sunset Jam; and the Sunday-morning gospel sing and service. But attendance was again somewhat sparse, and there were lapses in management and planning. Because nothing had been rebuilt on the razed barn's site, festival workers erected a large open-sided tent on the barn's roadside site to shelter special events, workshops, and jam sessions. The ephemeral structure faintly echoed, for some older Bean Blossom residents, the presence of the original Brown County Jamboree "circus tent" on the same spot forty-five years before.

More planning and management gaps appeared as the festival got under way. Sue Galbraith, again making the trek from Buffalo, New York, with her band-mates in the group Dempsey Station, recalled years later how the sloppy festival planning worked out well for them:

> Somehow in '87 we had one of those very special adventures because of the way things ran at the Monroe park that year. Seems that the schedule had not really been solidified for the week—Yep, they were taking peoples' money at the gate, and those folks were setting up their chairs in front of the stage but the insiders who had been there a few days knew that they didn't have anybody booked for Monday, and not much for Tuesday and the schedule would fatten up by the second weekend. Blake Williams [Monroe's banjo player] had put the call out from the stage that first Saturday that "If anyone had a band and were there at the park that they could come see him and maybe get some stage time that evening." Well, we thought we'd give it a shot. They had the evening show up under the tent where the old barn had stood. We went over our tunes in the mule shed out back and was all ready to be called up, when they said that they didn't need us after all for that evening. Oh well, we thought, we tried.

But by Sunday afternoon, Galbraith and many other parking-lot pickers were called to perform. The four emergent "bands" entertained on the outdoor stage and continued to fill in over the next few festival weekdays as well. Many of the fill-in participants are well known to this day in Bean Blossom:

> We had been asked to back up Clarence and Armolee Green for a show (it was the first time I ever had to play banjo in such keys as they sang in—scary not having things "worked out" ahead of time). We also went up as Dempsey Sta-tion—Craig Kellas on Mandolin, Greg Garing on fiddle, Kathy Galbraith on guitar, me on banjo and [Dave] "Hägar" [Nelson] (the cookie man) on bass. Then me and Kathy and Greg, Jill Schneider on second guitar, Sonya Yoder on mandolin and Jim Schmaltz on bass was a third group and heading up the 4th group for Monday was Joe Stuart and the other group of young pickers from the woods. Well, the week played out like a tall tale that nobody would really

believe. Most of us from the Dempsey bunch, with the three bands we were all part of, played 27 shows on that stage that week, but the guy who was working the hardest to entertain the folks was Joe and his group of pickers. He'd sing and pick lead, while directing his band of what came next and who was supposed to do it. He was on that stage so much with them that at one point when we came out, Greg Garing introduced us as the "Joe Stuart Relief Band," which got a big laugh—we even signed the stage as such!

While Galbraith's animated account reveals the poor oversight of the 1987 festival, it also shows the deep bonds developed by many regular festival attendees. Most of the fans who attend a ten-day bluegrass festival are also pickers, and over the years Sue and her Buffalo bandmates had befriended many members of the Bean Blossom "festival family." Jim Schmaltz's campsite in the north woods, where many of them may have originally met, had from the midseventies been a place where high-quality festival jams were known to take place often and enthusiastically. Burly, bearded Dave "Hägar" Nelson of Milwaukee, Wisconsin, was already then well known to both professional and amateur bluegrassers as the "cookie man" because of his invention of giant chocolate-chip cookies ("Hägar's Half-Pounders"), which he would pass out to appreciative artists and friends at many festivals. Longtime Blue Grass Boy Joe Stuart, though in failing health, rallied to the cause and energetically kept things running. Sue Galbraith's evocative account of their role in the 1987 June festival went on to reveal the core of emotions and sensations that working at Bean Blossom produced:

> We learned a lot about the ways of bluegrass that week—working up tunes, making friends, feeling like you are really a part of what's going on, putting on the stage show, sweating, like wringing wet while doing the set—had a whole new appreciation of bluegrass men in suits. How sometimes the MC would sneak to the doorway and egg the audience on to cheer some. You could catch him out of the corner of your eye doing it—then as the week went on, if the audience did that we'd whip a look back to the door but he wasn't there—we were earning what we got! How kind the audience was, even if they were used to hearing what you did each day—they'd still come to the stage—even in the rain (show goes on rain or shine—no refunds!) so we'd have somebody listening to all the bands, and had nice things to say when we were done, even started making requests of our songs, and that unbelievably strange but wonderful feeling to wander down backstage in the morning to check out the day's schedule that was stapled to the tree and find out that we were going to be playing that day along with Bill Monroe, Ralph, the Whites, Ricky Skaggs, the Osbornes, and Joe Stuart! It was quite an adventure for a little band from New York on vacation in bluegrass land.[17]

Joe Stuart, the multi-instrumentalist who had once played the "Sparkplug" comedy role for Monroe and at one time or another played every instrument (including as a fill-in on mandolin) as a Blue Grass Boy, was also loved and respected by another person who helped out at Bean Blossom that summer: Cotton Ginnee, a Texas fiddler, who played on festival shows that June with Joe, Wayne Lewis, and Bill Monroe.[18] Ginnee helped manage the cobbled-together stage shows that year and spent a good deal of time with performer Armolee Green as they sold tickets from the old ticket booth trucked in by Jim Peva more than twenty years before. Ginnee and the many others who enjoyed Joe Stuart's larger-than-life presence were distressed by his bout with cancer. The constant headaches he endured throughout the big festival were symptoms of the brain tumor that resulted in his death that fall.

No fall festival was held in 1987; as in 1986, when the "10th Annual Autumn Bluegrass Festival" was canceled for "park renovation," a small advertisement in September's *Bluegrass Unlimited* informed distant fans that the "12th Annual" autumn event, again curiously misnumbered, was also canceled. This disappointment foreshadowed a greater threat: in April 1988, a small ad revealed the worst: "Bill Monroe's Brown County Jamboree Park and Annual Bean Blossom Bluegrass Festival are For Sale. Park consists of 53 acres with 7 acre lake, amphitheatre, stage and campsites with city water and electrical hook-ups. For Further information call 615–868–3333 / SERIOUS INQUIRIES ONLY / Bill Monroe's 22nd Annual Bluegrass Festival will be presented this year as usual—Come Join Us!"[19]

James Monroe explained the decision to sell the park to a *Brown County Democrat* reporter as a consequence of Bill's "trying to cut back on his busy schedule" and because "the family has been working on other projects, like the Bill Monroe Museum and Monroe's Bluegrass Country, a dinner club and show place near the Grand Ole Opry in Nashville, Tennessee." The announcement of the final four-day June festival brought a large crowd of fans to the park to see, once again, the familiar core acts and a few "new" groups like the Wayne Lewis Band and Freddie Sanders. A retrospective two-page *Bluegrass Unlimited* article two months later noted the melancholy mood that pervaded the "last" festival. Not only were fans saddened by the prospect, but also Bill Monroe himself spoke from the stage about not wanting to see the old park close. He wished that someone would buy or rent the property to continue holding festivals there. Longtime attendees Bill Stedman and Kevin Doyle gave Bill a plaque to express their appreciation of Bill's having spent so many Father's Day weekends entertaining fans at Bean Blossom. The plaque was made from wood rescued from the old barn by William Bernard Lee. Monroe ended his last show with "I'm on My Way Back to the Old Home."[20]

That fall, an ardent fan complained of *Bluegrass Unlimited*'s inadequate coverage of the last festival, given its historical importance; his summary stated, "It was the epitome of a bluegrass festival. No place can match its mystique."[21]

But in January 1989, ads ran in *Bluegrass Unlimited* for three successive months announcing a reprieve: "Bill Monroe has changed his mind. There will be Bean Blossom festivals in 1989." Perhaps Monroe simply gave in to his own desire to carry on at the deep-rooted park. His interest may also have been heightened by his imminent career milestone: fifty years of performing on the Grand Ole Opry. Whatever Monroe's reasons, the fans and Bean Blossom community of regulars were delighted. When they returned in June for the twenty-third festival, they found a full lineup of artists booked for the four-day event. In addition to the core artists, banjoist Bob Black, a Blue Grass Boy from 1974 to 1976, returned in 1989 with Groundspeed, a German bluegrass band he had joined about six months before. In his 2005 memoir, he noted that there lingered an unspoken, generalized fear that Monroe would *still* sell the park, but the audience was almost palpably relieved when Bill came onstage to say he "had just made the decision to continue the festival." Bill was again happy to be the host at Bean Blossom; Black was impressed and moved to see his former "bossman" out "riding around the festival grounds on a beautiful white Appaloosa horse named Speck . . . waving his hat to the audience and stopping every few feet while people snapped photographs."[22]

By 1990, the number of June festival attendees at Bean Blossom had visibly improved. The twenty-fourth festival brought new fans into the Bean Blossom experience even as it delighted most regulars in most respects. Nine-year-old fiddler and multi-instrument prodigy Michael Cleveland attended Bean Blossom with his grandparents, and there he not only met Bill but also got to play "Katy Hill" with him at the Sunset Jam. A radiant Emmylou Harris performed with her group, the Angel Band, on the prominent Saturday-night show, where she praised Monroe as the patriarch of bluegrass music and told the fans how much he had influenced and inspired her. That June, there were again great shows by familiar Bean Blossom groups such as Jim and Jesse, Ralph Stanley, the Osborne Brothers, Mac Wiseman, the Sullivan Family, the Boys from Indiana, the Goins Brothers, Paul Mullins & Traditional Grass, the Bluegrass Cardinals, and Bill Harrell & the Virginians. Minnesota native Dee Dee Prestige again appeared as Diana Christian, and clogger Jackie Christian was on the show again too, dancing with Bill as the Blue Grass Boys played. A new headliner in 1990 was Charlie Sizemore, fronting his own band, but he had played the park before as lead vocalist for Ralph Stanley. Wayne Lewis, again heading his own band on several shows, also managed the festival. Lewis generally succeeded managing the festivals through the early

1990s because of diligent planning and long familiarity with the site, the event, and Monroe's preferred ways of doing things. Moving everywhere throughout the festival landscape that year was veteran filmmaker Stephen Gebhart. He had collected footage at Bean Blossom in 1969, but now he began a two-year stint of filming, focused on Monroe, that would culminate in his 1993 Original Cinema video release, *Bill Monroe: Father of Bluegrass*. Gebhart and his crew covered several Bean Blossom festivals in 1990 and 1991, creating some remarkable aural and visual documents of Monroe, the band, and the park during this era.[23]

Wayne and Sue Lewis again managed "Bill Monroe's Autumn Bluegrass Festival" that year. The three-day 1990 fall festival, always less constrained in its roster of artists than the traditional June event, brought in the Country Gentlemen, Raymond Fairchild, the Reno Brothers, Dana Cupp and the Detroit Bluegrass Band, and the Skyline Bluegrass Express, and of course it featured Bill and the Blue Grass Boys all three days. Lewis also hired the Eddie Adcock Band to perform and inaugurated an arrangement whereby Adcock would provide and operate sound-reinforcement systems for Bean Blossom's festivals for the next decade. A new group on the fall program, from Akron, Ohio, was Larry Efaw and the Bluegrass Mountaineers, a Stanley-style band with a lot of comic presence. They had been playing regionally since the early 1960s, led originally by Larry's father, Edward.

Despite demonstrable novelties in the lineup, some longtime fans kept voicing their slowly growing disenchantment, based not only on the slow-to-change core lineup but also on the Bean Blossom "traditions" of limited and ill-maintained sanitary facilities and rudimentary campground amenities showing little improvement. Despite urgings from fans and occasionally the State Department of Health, the Monroes had made only modest upgrades to the park's grounds, even when they seemed cash rich from the huge festival gates of the early 1970s. Although sanitary facilities were somewhat improved by 1990, the faithful who returned to the "Mecca of bluegrass" had become less forgiving of such lapses, which they inevitably compared to the staging and management of other, newer, bluegrass festivals.[24]

For many, the annual reappearance of the same core groups for the Bean Blossom stage program slowly made the whole enterprise less attractive. The booking of performers is always subject to the ever-changing demands of other groups' performance schedules, but it made good sense to Monroe and the festival staff that the repeated booking of Bean Blossom festival headliners—especially those like Ralph Stanley or the Sullivan Family, who put on their own annual bluegrass festivals—meant a reciprocal relationship, with regular work for both Monroe and themselves at each other's festivals.

Reliance on the core group of bluegrass performers was originally a point of pride with Monroe and those who ran the Bean Blossom festivals in his name. The Monroes made it clear through their rules and the emphasis that emcees provided that they were trying to achieve Bill's idea of "traditional" bluegrass at this site. So, with the exception of a few festival headliners like Jim & Jesse or the Osborne Brothers, who as "professionals" could get away with it, electric basses and other plugged-in instruments were forbidden at Bean Blossom.

The 1980s brought a seemingly endless supply of new festivals. This manner of promoting music in combination with an outdoor camping experience was increasingly seen to be cheap to put on and potentially lucrative. In the early festival years, a promoter could book nearly every nationally known bluegrass act for the duration of his festival. But by the 1980s, that pattern was changing. More festivals meant many more local and regional amateur and semiprofessional bands sharing the stages with the big nationally known stars, who were increasingly booked at the festival for only a single day at a time. While the professional bands became more able to economically sustain themselves by playing more festivals, the new scheduling inevitably reduced the chances for their socializing with regular festivalgoers. Thus, the headiest experiences fans typically raved about at early bluegrass festivals—playing offstage or at jam sessions with their musical heroes—became rare.

In 1989 and 1990, according to Morris Barnett, "Wayne Lewis ran the festival. He cleaned the place up and everything." The musical campground experience at Bean Blossom in the late 1980s was still very strong, if not as frenzied and intense as it had been in the first five years. The Bean Blossom jamming scene was still very much alive. Barnett noted that "Huffmaster's jam [at the Wards' camp] just got so big, you had to stand in line to do any jamming, you know." Motivated also by Dan Jones's request for a better spot where they could jam together, Barnett decided that it was time to tackle conditions in the still-overgrown north end of the campground:

> The next year, I brought a chain saw, and a Weedeater, and a rake, and all kinds of stuff, and started cleaning brush and started burning stumps out back there. It was all growed up back there, and if you wanted something cleaned out, you done it yourself. Back there in the same place, the lot where I normally camp in, along the fence, oh, it was all growed up in brush. And it was thick with stumps in there. Everybody was runnin' over stumps, you know, you couldn't get hardly many campers, and everybody was denting their cars and trucks up. . . . So I learnt that you could take a trench around a stump, get a fire started, and—I mentioned to Jim Schmaltz later, I said, "Why didn't we do that twenty years

ago?" When people started a campfire, just start it around a stump. You know, you didn't have to trench around it. You know, just burn that stump.

Wayne Lewis, seeing Barnett preparing to burn a large stump, decided to bring Bill Monroe around to see this unauthorized activity for himself: "Bill came up with a stern look that said, 'What the heck are you doing?' I said, 'When I leave here Monday, this stuff'll be gone.' He got the biggest, widest smile on his face, and he thought, 'Man that's neat!' That's the way to get rid of stumps, you know. I ended up burning five or six stumps out of that one lot. And Bill thought that was a neat idea."[25]

Bill's enthusiasm for the park seemed high in 1991, though the four days of the June festival seemed almost routine. Management of the festival took a backseat to concerns over Bill's cardiac health and the planning going on behind the scenes for the fall festival that would coincide with Bill's eightieth birthday. The June festival succeeded by following the customary template, with the seasoned core roster of familiar artists and groups. In early August, Bill underwent coronary bypass surgery in Nashville. He was still recuperating but clearly looking ahead when he took part later that summer, remotely, in a nationally broadcast live event at Wolf Trap Farm called *Ricky Skaggs's Pickin' Party*. During the show, Skaggs took Bill's spot in front of the Blue Grass Boys, then fielded an orchestrated live phone call from Bill Monroe, heard by the audience through the sound system, in which a convalescent-voiced Bill first gave him permission to play the show with his band, and then added, "Be sure to tell the folks to come to [the] festival in Bean Blossom, Indiana."[26]

The fall festival was called "Bill Monroe's 80th Birthday Celebration and the Autumn Bluegrass & Country Music Festival." Bluegrass acts, led as always by Bill, were drawn from a mostly familiar but pared-down list that included the Osborne Brothers, James Monroe, Larry Sparks, the Sullivan Family, Bobby Smith and the Boys from Shiloh, and the Reno Brothers. A new all-female bluegrass group, Petticoat Junction, made their Bean Blossom debut. But there was also a significant country music contingent, with notable artists like Emmylou Harris, Johnny Paycheck, Jim Ed Brown, and the Kentucky Head Hunters, who had recorded Monroe's "Walk Softly on This Heart of Mine" on their hit debut album in 1989. Gebhart continued filming throughout the eightieth-birthday festival and commented on Monroe's vitality: "He amazed me. I went to wish him a happy birthday. It was in the mid-nineties that day. He played that afternoon. He had been onstage for a birthday celebration and was meeting and greeting people. He played again at eleven and then gave autographs. After everyone had left he went with his son and grandson down to one of the food stands and got a meal that had been prepared for them. It was poignant—this living legend being the last guy to leave the place."[27]

Close on the heels of September's birthday festival, Bill and James began to relocate Bill's struggling Bill Monroe Museum and Bluegrass Hall of Fame from Nashville, Tennessee, to their park at Bean Blossom. To the consternation of Ohio County, Kentucky, newspaper writers, the Monroes moved the remains of Uncle Pen's cabin from the outskirts of Rosine, Kentucky, to the site in Bean Blossom for later reassembly.

The Uncle Pen cabin was just part of the new plan for construction at the music park. Almost on top of the footprint that the old barn had occupied from 1942 to 1986, the Monroes began in early 1992 to erect a steel building to house the Bill Monroe Museum. Placed with its columned gable end facing the highway, the new building enclosed not only exhibit space but also a room for Bill Monroe's Hall of Fame, some office spaces, and two gift and souvenir shops. "Uncle Pen's Cabin" was re-created in a fenced enclosure just south of the new building. Although most of the cabin was a reconstructed replica, visitors could still appreciate the intimate setting of the tiny one-room log cabin in which Bill had "bached" with his beloved uncle after the deaths of his parents. The new museum building was nearly complete when the June 1992 festival began.

An even more dramatic change in 1992 was the replacement of the 1968 outdoor stage. The new outdoor stage more than doubled the size of the old one and offered heated and air-conditioned lounge and dressing rooms for artists. The new proscenium was set about twenty feet behind the plane of the old one, enlarging the amphitheater's seating space, and a regrading of the site offered parking for performers' buses and vans right behind the stage. Although most performers welcomed the improved facility, some disgruntled fans noted that the new stage's low front railing partially obscured the audience's view of performers.[28]

James Monroe's role in the management of the music park at Bean Blossom slowly expanded, paralleling his increasing influence in Bill's business decisions. He had worked closely with Bill in the 1980s when they created their ventures in Nashville, Tennessee, and played a growing role as facilities at the park changed in 1992.

By early 1993, James Monroe's mounting authority was made evident with the renaming of the park as Bill and James Monroe's Festival Park and Campground. Other changes came along as well; advertising for the music park listed not just the two regular bluegrass festivals in June and September but four new ones, heavily weighted with country and gospel music artists, as well. The summer of six festivals began with a small three-day festival in May, with country artists John

Conley and Janie Fricke appearing along with Bill Monroe, James Monroe, and Eddie Adcock. The big June festival lasted four days, and brought in not only bluegrass stalwarts like the Monroes, Ralph Stanley, the Goins Brothers, Jim and Jesse, and the Sullivan Family but also Doc Watson, Alison Krauss, and a country music trio, the McCarters—three East Tennessee sisters who were nationally successful country artists for a decade beginning in the mid-1980s. Hard on the heels of the mid-June bluegrass festival came another country music event, five days long, in early July, with Bill and James Monroe alternating onstage with Jack Greene, Stonewall Jackson, Gene Watson, Faron Young, and Del Reeves. A similar mixed-genre minifestival took place in August, with Bill, James, and Eddie Adcock presenting bluegrass sounds and shows by B. J. Thomas, T. Graham Brown, Asleep at the Wheel, and Mel McDaniel presenting a modern pop, country, and western approach. The fall bluegrass festival spanned four days early in the month, running from Friday through *Monday;* the roster of artists seemed familiar, with the Monroes and Adcock joined by Jim and Jesse, Mac Wiseman, the Country Gentlemen, Paul Mullins, Dallas Smith (Bobby Smith's brother, who took over the Boys from Shiloh band after Bobby's death), Ricky Skaggs, the Lewis Family, the Sullivan Family, Del McCoury, the Boys from Indiana, and J. D. Crowe. A final fall festival, held on a Saturday and Sunday in late September, focused on bluegrass and southern gospel music. Its bluegrass artists ranged from Bill and James Monroe through the Whites, the Sullivan Family, and the gospel-oriented Bishops, while a range of gospel sounds came from Betty Jean Robinson, Wait Mills, Jeff & Sherri Easter, Connie Smith, the Jerichos, and the Florida Boys. The music was complemented by the gospel message as presented by Monroe's old friend the Reverend Paul Baggett, known to his Millersville, Tennessee, congregation as "the Happy Pastor."

The 1994 June festival—the twenty-eighth annual—seemed to echo the previous year, with Alison Krauss as a headliner who also introduced the Cox Family, with whom she had just recorded a brilliant bluegrass project. Petticoat Junction returned, joining a mostly familiar group of artists: Jim & Jesse, Eddie Adcock, the Goins Brothers, the Sullivan Family, J. D. Crowe, and of course Ralph Stanley and Bill and James Monroe. Bill led the Blue Grass Boys (Robert Bowlin, Dana Cupp, Tater Tate, and Tom Ewing) and also did a guest appearance, without his mandolin, on Jim & Jesse's set. He was using a cane to help him get around at times, and in a remarkable photographic double exposure published later in *Bluegrass Unlimited,* he is seen at the 1994 June festival both leaning on the cane and playing mandolin.[29]

The fall festival, held on September 9–11, 1994, was presented under a new name, no doubt inspired by the new prominence at the park of Bill's transplanted

Bluegrass Hall of Fame and the rebuilt icon of Uncle Pen's Cabin. Billed as "the 20th Annual Hall of Fame and Uncle Pen Day" festival, the event's name resonated in the memories of longtime Bean Blossom regulars because of the Hall of Fame shows held there more than twenty years before. The weekend event brought in the Bluegrass Cardinals, Eddie Adcock, the Country Gentlemen, Del McCoury, Jim & Jesse, the Lewis Family, Larry Sparks, Gary Brewer, Petticoat Junction, Wendy Smith, the Carroll County Ramblers, and a new group: Glen Duncan, Larry Cordle, and Lonesome Standard Time.

Bill Monroe's last appearance at Bean Blossom came during the fall festival of 1995. Friends and fans often commented on the effects of his advancing age, noting that he had "slowed down" when he was offstage and would sometimes "nod off" while sitting in a chair talking to fans. Yet the act of musically performing invariably revived his energies, and he appeared alert and vigorous as soon as he stepped onstage. In the spring of 1996, Bill suffered a stroke from which he never recovered. During the June festival that year, rumors circulated that he would make a brief appearance, but his ill health prevented that hoped-for event.

When Bill Monroe died on September 9, 1996, James Monroe inherited the Bean Blossom music-park property and announced that he planned to continue operating the festivals. James had played a growing role in the financial management of his father's enterprises since about 1987.[30] James hosted the thirty-first annual June festival in 1997 and likewise promoted the "23rd Annual Hall of Fame and Uncle Pen Day Festival," but speculation almost immediately began that James might be interested in selling the property.

Two tales quickly gained currency among the scattered bluegrass faithful. The first held that the property was going to become a housing development, with a variety of dwellings on various-size lots. The second persistent rumor in 1997 and early 1998 was that Ricky Skaggs was interested in buying the park, possibly in association with Vince Gill, and that they were discussing the issue with James.

The development rumor had some factual basis. Nina Jo McDonald, the entrepreneurial wife of grocer Jack McDonald, did contemplate such a development. At her request, a survey-based plan of the property was created by a regional firm, Franklin Engineering. Although McDonald's plans did not proceed, the survey map illustrated their vision of the fifty-one-acre site laid out in house lots, with more than one hundred single-family dwellings, twenty-eight duplex dwellings accommodating fifty-six "elderly" families, and forty-nine cabins overlooking the small lake.

To local residents and fans of the old music park, the end seemed very near. But yet another chapter in the venerable music park's history was about to unfold.

# 11

# Renaissance, Continuity, and Change, 1998 and After

In early 1998, the swirl of Bean Blossom rumors ended with word that a former Blue Grass Boy—Dwight Dillman, of Peru, Indiana—had bought the music park from James Monroe. Using the corporate name "Brown County Jamboree," Dillman acquired the park on March 19, 1998.

After leaving the professional music business, in which he had been a banjo player for both Bill Monroe and Jimmy Martin, Dwight Dillman prospered as a furniture dealer. His success enabled him to purchase the park from James Monroe for about $750,000.[1] Of greater interest than the price was the welcome news that Dillman intended to renovate the music park and campground, dedicated to the memory of Bill Monroe.

Jim Peva immediately spread the word to the widespread bluegrass community via the BGRASS-L Listserv: "Dwight has purchased the Bean Blossom property from James Monroe and will be managing the festivals there starting June 18–21 this year. In my opinion, Dwight has the perfect combination of skills and background to bring this festival back to its glory days of the late 60s and early 70s. See his website at beanblossom.com and please spread the word."[2]

Within days Dillman began work on two fronts: publicity and physical improvements. He seemed to tackle both with energy and intensity, immediately demonstrating a different management style than *all* the park's prior managers, from the Runds to James.

First came advertising flyers. Single-page eight-and-a-half-by-eleven-inch flyers had long been used to promote festivals, but Dillman's first flyer for the June 1998 festival at Bean Blossom set a higher standard, employing a full four-color process printed on coated paper and offering a professionally designed page with many small photos of featured performers. The new flyer practically screamed "NEW MANAGEMENT!" yet seemed, still, to emphasize tradition and continuity. It was a new era at Bean Blossom.

Dillman's crews, preparing for the June 1998 festival, repaired and repainted all remaining Monroe-era buildings like food-concession and record-vending stands. The first round of renovations even included the outhouse Birch built in the early 1970s, originally a double-sided three-holer sited charmingly close to the woods' edge, near the lake, east of the museum.

Dillman's decisions to fix up that old outhouse and other remaining Monroe-era features seemed to succeed, both sentimentally and commercially. Dwight understood the sensibilities of bluegrass fans and of the Bean Blossom family in particular. He had worked and played this park as a Blue Grass Boy and as a Sunny Mountain Boy with his own musical heroes, Bill Monroe and Jimmy Martin.

Revitalizing the park required big investments. Dillman moved forward, taking the old country music park through several major rounds of transformation, developing it for a modern age. It was a physical and management renaissance at the old country music park.

First came upgrading the unsatisfactory toilets. With soil hydrology that was not well suited to permanent septic systems, Dillman simply set up self-contained semitrailer-size restrooms with holding tanks, with similar shower houses nearby. These respectably modern facilities were trucked in and set up at the northwest edge of the outdoor stage audience area (near the power-line clearing) and at the easternmost edge of the property, backing up to Brummett's field, up on Hippie Hill. The semipermanent portable facilities offered hot and cold running water in the sinks and showers and modern flush toilets kept clean and functional by a contracted maintenance staff during busy festival times. Though still modest, the new sanitary facilities were no longer the horrors that had inspired Bud Freedman's "Six-Day Bean Blossom Blues" a quarter century before.

Dillman forged on, employing heavy-equipment operators and other contractors as needed to reshape the land. Before his first June festival, workers applied 480 tons of crushed gravel to the park's alternately muddy or dusty roads. Huge amounts went into the deep ravine where "Campground Road" transitioned into the park's wooded north-central section containing the outdoor stage and amphitheater. All campground roads were built up and regraded. Dwight's construction people began installing a new network of permanent electric and water lines supplying graveled individually numbered campground parking slots, each with its own hookups, for the now dominant RV campers.

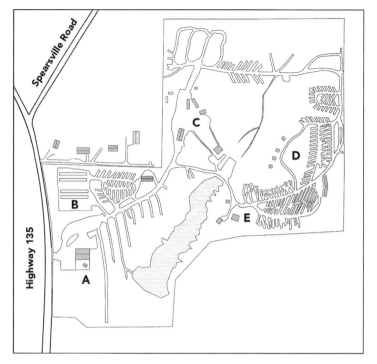

Dwight Dillman's Bill Monroe Memorial Music Park and Campground, ca. 2003. A: Bill Monroe Museum and Gift Shop, with Uncle Pen's Cabin. B: Flea-market pavilions. C: 1992 outdoor stage-amphitheater, with bluegrass vendor shelter. D: New cabins and RV hookups. E: Hippie Hill workshop stage and cabins.

When the festival faithful returned in June 1998, they found a transformed park. Dillman had created 109 permanent RV hookups, and more were planned. Less visible, but of even greater importance to the planned-for RV crowds of the future, were the two new underground dump stations.

Tent campers noticed improvements, too, particularly in the wooded campground sections north of the large east-west power line that paralleled the park's northern section. The clearing of brush and undergrowth that began with individual fans like Morris Barnett and hippies seeking privacy was extended by Dillman's workers, creating clearings suitable for modest groups of tent campers under the park's beautiful trees.

Some of the ubiquitous improvements seemed inconsequential at first sight. Dillman understood that memories of Bill Monroe and his peers and contemporaries were revered at Bean Blossom. So there were new signs designating each road and each part of the property. Entering the park grounds past the large sign still announcing "Bill and James Monroe's Festival Park and Campground," visitors found themselves directed by the ticket-booth staff to continue northeast on "Bill Monroe Avenue" or "Campground Road" to a series of parking lanes, on the right (east) side, each one named for performers: "Arnold Shultz Road" was succeeded on the right by "Kenny Baker Lane," "Curly Ray Lane," "Dave Akeman Road," "Earl Scruggs Lane," "Flatt Drive," "Goins Lane," and "Hank Williams Drive."[3] On the left (west) side of the road, where for years there had been fluidly arranged festival campground parking for RVs, now appeared a newly organized set of RV parking slots with hookups, all along "Charlie Monroe Circle." A year or two later, Dillman added four roofed sheds in the lowest elevations of this area, near Highway 135, to shelter a flea market.

Near the deep hollow just east of James Monroe's double-wide, Bill Monroe's oldest utility pickup truck, covered with picturesquely fading signatures and hand-painted notes and signs, was parked and labeled for all to see as "Bill Monroe's Truck." Where Campground Road divides, continuing north as Concession Lane on the west side of the amphitheater area or becoming Hippie Hill Road as it turns east past the head of Pastor Baggett Lake and rises to Hippie Hill, new signs bloomed amid a splendid June flower garden. West of Concession Lane, along the campground fence, was Peva Place, just south of the merchant camping area. The park's main east-west road, running beneath the high-voltage power line north of the amphitheater, was labeled James Monroe Drive on its west end and Brummett Road on the east. In the wooded RV camping area north of the power line—"the Woods"—roads were named for local heroes, and campers found Bernard Lee Drive, Jack Cox Drive, Lester Flatt Drive, and Jimmy Martin Drive. Up on Hippie Hill were Ralph Stanley Road and Wilma Lee Circle, designating an open-field area set up with thirty RV pads and hookups designed for long vehicles.

Dillman's signage not only labeled the functional new parking spaces and campground areas but also emphasized an internal geography of the park. Newcomers found a kind of introduction to the park's history and the culture of Bill Monroe and bluegrass music all around them. The actual Bill Monroe Bluegrass Hall of Fame and Museum, with Uncle Pen's re-created cabin, and the professionally run gift shop in the Hall of Fame's foyer reinforced a sense of historicity while offering souvenirs and CDs of bluegrass musicians.

The very cornerstone of modern promotion came next. By the fall of 1998, Dillman established a Web site, renamed http://www.beanblossom.us in 2010. Over the next decade, Jim Peva and others provided the Web master with historical photos, news, and stories of the park, and the Web site advertised the details of each upcoming year's music festivals. To the returning bluegrass festival family of fans, recovering from the shock of Bill's death and its consequent implications for the park, it would all be an inspiration and a delight.

Several weeks before the first Dillman-run festival (the thirty-second June bluegrass festival), Jim Peva made a special trip to the park to report the scope of the changes:

> By my estimate, Dwight has already spent several hundred thousands of dollars on facilities (water lines, new electric wiring & outlets, hot showers, toilets, etc.) for the comfort of fans who come in campers and tents to stay for the duration of the festival, as well as for the walk-in fans. The grounds are neatly manicured and little extra touches like flower beds bespeak the kind of effort that could only come from a deep commitment. But the old traditional charm of the place is still there—the tall hickory and beech trees reaching to the sky, the sloping, wooded amphitheater, the back woods and "hippie hill," now with many more camper conveniences. The respect for Bill Monroe and his music and the traditions of Bean Blossom is evident everywhere, especially in the museum and bluegrass hall of fame and the adjoining replica of Uncle Pen's cabin. After all, this was Big Mon's favorite place to perform and Dwight, a former Blue Grass Boy himself, has not forgotten that. The whole place stands as a memorial to the founder and father of bluegrass music and I know Bill would be pleased with what a former member of his band has done.[4]

Peva—who later that summer began to refer regularly to Bean Blossom as "the Mecca of bluegrass festivals"—was hardly alone in approving the new era. Former Country Music Hall of Fame curator Chris Skinker, an Indiana native and longtime Bean Blossom attendee, wrote a featured online story called "The Magic Returns" for the key country music Web site http://www.country.com, praising Dillman's improvements and illuminating the music park's value with the phrase, "It's not just a place, it's a state of mind."[5]

More innovations became evident that summer: Dillman instituted a festival shuttle bus, conveying daytime festival visitors from the named parking lanes near the museum to the main-stage amphitheater area. Next came a tractor-pulled "people-mover" with wooden passenger seats along both sides. Making many stops, and often manned by Dillman's immediate family members, this festival transportation ran continuously in a loop during the long days of the big festival's shows: from Concession Lane to Brummett Road past the Woods and Miller Hill, right on Ralph Stanley Drive to the top of Hippie Hill, then back down past the lake and the main stage to Concession Lane.

Dillman himself began a habit of circulating through the crowd in golf carts, ATVs, or small jeeps. During each festival, those newer vehicles were complemented by Dillman's fleet of buses, pick-up trucks, and other vehicles. Jimmy Martin approvingly noted, "He's always askin' 'Do you need anything?,' 'Just let us know, now.' You know, a festival, to have a crowd, it takes the promoter to work just as hard as his talent."[6] Dillman's movements through the festival hardly compare to Monroe's strolls through his beloved park being acknowledged by the fans. Dwight circulated at all hours, driving a golf cart or four-wheel ATV, stopping often to make eye-level contact with festivalgoers and checking their satisfaction, offering campers some firewood, speeding off to take care of a sudden critical RV-parking issue, talking all the while with key staff and family members on two-way radios or a cell phone. At the 1998 festival and those of the next few years, he brought free firewood to all campers who wanted it. The returning Bean Blossom family of fans and local merchants all loved it.

Dillman's redevelopment of the music park was rooted in a plan for its more intensive use. There had to be more than two festival weekends a year, so the calendar of expansion began right away. A month after Dillman's first June Bean Blossom Festival came the "First Annual Bean Blossom Jam Fest," a two-day weekend festival held July 30 and August 1, 1998. It featured the Lonesome River Band, the Fox Family, Jeff White, Unlimited Tradition, Talmadge Law & the Bluegrass Sounds, John Hartford, Continental Divide, Ernie Thacker & Highway 23, and Rambler's Choice. The lineup signaled Dillman's commitment to bluegrass and Bean Blossom tradition but also seemed planned to attract a new, younger audience with a more "progressive" and contemporary show. After Dillman's first fall festival, Jim Peva noted further new developments and reviewed Dwight's hands-on and personal touch in action:

> Every effort is expended to make the fans leave the festival in a happy mood. And dedication doesn't escape Dwight's notice either. When WM Bentley suggested that the weeds and brush be cleared from the edge of the lake so Bill Monroe's old walking trail could be restored for the fans to use, Dwight agreed, and had signs prepared for the "Monroe/Bentley" walking trail. An attractive archway entrance to the trail was constructed near the museum, and a formal ribbon-cutting ceremony was held on Saturday morning, attended by Jimmy Martin, Mr. Jackson, the show MC, and others. Little Dana Dillman, dressed to the hilt in a flowered dress, cut the ribbon, and Dwight and WM Bentley were the first through the arch. You could see the pride in Bentley's eyes—he has become a celebrity at Bean Blossom—and his recognition is well deserved. A jam session

involving Dwight, Derek, and Myron Dillman, Vernon Derrick, Talmadge Law and many others followed the ribbon cutting.[7]

Dillman moved rapidly to make the facility ever more profitable in both its music-festival and its campground functions. Mindful of Francis Rund's 1940 "tourist cabins," Dillman began to build rentable cabins in various parts of the park. These all suggest a Brown County "log cabin" look, not at all based on southern Indiana's actual traditions of British Isles and German log architecture. The new cabins with their rusticated appearance were built in a wide range of size and facilities. The first five cabins were plain, offering little more than a roofed room with a sheltered doorway, with electric lights and power and platforms on which three or four campers could place their own pads, cots, or sleeping bags. Over the next few years, more elaborate cabins came along. The biggest were fully furnished and equipped units, with heat and air-conditioning, porches with benches and swings, furnished kitchens, showers, and bedrooms or lofts (or both) with double beds.

The worldwide bluegrass music community noted the renaissance at Bean Blossom in several ways. In 1999, the Indiana General Assembly, by resolution, designated the part of State Highway 135 from Morgantown south to Nashville, which passes through Bean Blossom, the Bill Monroe Memorial Highway. In the fall of 2000, the bluegrass music industry (as embodied in the IBMA) declared the thirty-fourth June festival to be the "event of the year." Just a few months later, in May 2001, the Bill Monroe Memorial Bean Blossom Bluegrass Festival was added to the Library of Congress's "Local Legacies" program, intended to identify and highlight significant and historic places across the country.

Despite such acclaim, Dillman recognized that the music park could not be promoted the same way after Bill's death as it had before. So from the start, Dillman chose to emphasize a role for Jimmy Martin, his *other* former bluegrass bossman. Martin not only became a regular Bean Blossom performer again in the Dillman era but also served until his death in May 2005 as "ambassador" for the reborn music park. Dillman gave Martin the regular use of a newly leased and brightly painted bus that announced not only Jimmy Martin's "King of Bluegrass" presence everywhere it traveled but also the preeminence, longevity, and excitement of the annual bluegrass festivals at Bean Blossom.

Jimmy Martin, though controversial among some bluegrass fans for his long-standing problems with alcohol abuse, was also loved for his willingness to mingle with the fans at Bean Blossom.[8] As in the early festival years, he would stay for the whole duration of the festival and soon became renowned for his regular participation in nighttime jam sessions with the campground pickers. Jimmy loved meeting like-minded fans: "On Saturday night when my show is through, and I get my old clothes on, [Dwight] gets me in that cart with him, and we go around and meet people. We met some up there last September, wanted me to come up to Kentucky and hunted with 'em, which I did. And went up there huntin' for a week. And they're up there—if it's four days, they up there four days, if it's eight days, they up there."[9]

Martin's reputation as a hunter and appreciator of traditional southern country food also annihilated any remaining social distance between fans and performers through memorable shared events cemented by offerings of country food. MaryE Yeomans described the performers sharing "free" food with the fans after Dillman began to run the park: "Jimmy Martin was there in all his glory (and probably his red boiler suit and ball cap) serving up venison and rabbit and I don't know what all to HUNDREDS of folks who came along with plates and had them filled up—for free—with beans and corn bread and all that wild game meat, much of which I was told Jimmy shot himself. Now do you reckon you'd be invited to such a thing at a rock festival? Or even a country music festival? Not on your life!"

The Bean Blossom family quickly came to think of Martin's yearly offerings of food as "the traditional Jimmy Martin Sunday-morning squirrel breakfast." Martin was not alone in extending his country-style hospitality. James King equally impressed Yeomans with an impulsive gesture at the 2006 June festival: "James King went to the store and bought a bunch of white bread and cheese and big huge boxes of juicy tomatoes and told everyone on stage he was making everyone 'mater sandwiches and he sure did and the line formed and folks had a real good time with that. The food vendors were NOT happy, but the fans loved James to death for that."[10]

Although most of the modern recognition that Bean Blossom has drawn came from the place's long association with Bill Monroe and his own bluegrass festivals, Dillman quickly began to also use his park for nonbluegrass music festivals. He began staging them (or leasing the park for them) in ever-greater numbers. Since 1999, an enduring new event has been the "Bean Blossom Gospel Jubilee," which juxtaposes the bluegrass-gospel approach of familiar artists like Doyle Lawson and Paul Williams & the Victory Trio with southern gospel acts like the Stamps Quartet, Lulu Roman, and the Primitive Quartet. Another effort in 1999 was the two-day September "Country Music Hall of Fame Festival," offering a mix of contemporary country artists like Tracy Lawrence and Daryle Singletary and stars of yesteryear like Kitty Wells, Stonewall Jackson, and Del Reeves.

This underattended show, never repeated, was followed two weeks later by the long-established and successful "25th Annual Bluegrass Hall of Fame & Uncle Pen Days Festival." Dillman kept on known Bean Blossom stalwarts like Ralph Stanley and J. D. Crowe but also added newer, lesser-known groups: Mountain Heart, Goldwing Express, and the Shankman Twins, all welcomed eagerly by the fans. A late-season experimental venture was 1999's monthlong "Brown County Glittering Nights"—a December Christmastime drive-through display featuring fifty-three animated computer-controlled displays and more than a half-million lights. Some of the displays were based on Brown County and Bean Blossom themes: a log cabin next to a flowing waterfall and stream or a grouping of three cowboy-hatted musicians playing washtub bass, harmonica, and banjo. The 1999 Brown County Glittering Nights was apparently not an unqualified financial success, but it reflects Dillman's sensible desire to keep the park working at a season when few people camp in Brown County. Whereas the improved campground could be kept open throughout December, with RVs welcomed, Dillman's new hookups were still seasonal, since freezing conditions shut off the water.

Other kinds of park events proved successful, too, and the new music-park owner built on precedents as he could. The Indiana chapter of a national motorcycle group called ABATE—American Bikers Aimed towards Education—had conducted an annual party called the "Bean Blossom Boogie" right next door to the music park, on land owned by Carl Brummett, abutting his drag strip. The biker parties were held each summer from 1982 to 2002 and kept using the name Bean Blossom Boogie even after the event moved in 2003 to a new site at the Lawrence County Recreational Park. But plenty of the ABATE bikers had enjoyed being at Bean Blossom, and so a new fall-weekend motorcycle festival event was created in 2003 at Dillman's music park under the name "Bean Blossom Biketober Fest." The name changed after a couple years to "Bean Blossom Biker Bash." Bash attendees enjoy a big weekend music festival; set up a swap meet, bonfire, and bike show; and—except for the relative lack of parking-lot picking—function as a temporary festive community similar in some ways to that of the bluegrass fans who regather in June and September. Web sites devoted to Biketober Fest or the Bash reveal that the low spot where the road to Hippie Hill passes the north end of Pastor Baggett lake is now a particularly popular place for bikers to have photos taken of themselves on their beautifully painted and chromed custom machines.

Although Bash organizers make good use of the outdoor stage and amphitheater, staging concerts with hired bands, most other new events at the park are still music festivals but focused on forms other than traditional bluegrass music.

For instance, MagnoliaFest, an Americana, bluegrass, and acoustic roots festival established at Florida's Spirit of the Suwanee music park in 1998, staged "MagnoliaFest Midwest" at Bean Blossom in 2005. Similarly, the Bean Blossom Blues Fest was begun by harmonica player John Hall in 2004, bringing crowds of blues fans to "the Bean" each September for a weekend of acoustic jams, barbecue, and concerts on the amphitheater stage. The "Friends uv Nature & Knowledge" [*sic*] stage their annual "FUNK Fest" at the park each year, and a Dillman-sponsored weekend festival emphasizing parking-lot and campground picking continues today as the annual "W. M. Bentley Hillbilly Wagon Train Jam." W. M. Bentley continues to work for Dwight Dillman, as he formerly did for Bill Monroe, helping maintain and oversee the park.

Though Dwight Dillman has been the central figure at Bean Blossom ever since he bought the music park, independent forces also added to the escalating fame of the town and its music-park heritage. In 1999, SHS International, then a twelve-year-old Indianapolis-based sound-reinforcement company, complemented its American-made professional audio product lines (speakers, amplifiers, and microphones) with a new line of imported acoustic stringed instruments. These were initially introduced under the product-line names "Indiana" and "Morgan Monroe," but bluegrass-related instruments were soon given their own product-line name.[11] Since then, "Bean Blossom" banjos, guitars, resonator guitars, and mandolins have been marketed nationally. The upper end of the Bean Blossom line now carries the imprint "Bean Blossom, by Morgan Monroe."[12]

In 2007, after hosting bluegrass festivals for ten years, Dwight Dillman welcomed the June festival fans with the announcement that once again the historic site would be for sale. Dillman said he was seeking a potential buyer "to take the park and campground to the next level." The sale would transfer ownership of *all* of the park's current contents and assets, as inherited first from Bill Monroe and then from Dillman himself: the museum and its photos, documents, and instruments as well as the music stages, signs, tractors, vehicles, Web site ownership, and fan contact information. Dillman said he was looking for a buyer who would keep putting on the Bill Monroe bluegrass festivals, at least for some period of time, and he noted that even as the news of a sale was emerging, his staff were accepting reservations and proceeding with booking and promotion plans for the next year's events. With the festivals continuing but managed by some other owner, continued Dillman, he might once again enjoy future bluegrass festivals at Bean Blossom as a fan and picker.

Whatever course lies ahead, the old rural country music park in Brown County can be celebrated today for its persistence through more than sixty years. Through periods of success, neglect, controversy, and rapid change, the park's history has reflected in microcosm the nearly inconceivable social and technological changes that doomed or transformed other such parks and go on powerfully influencing vernacular music and musicians of many backgrounds. The site has been a source of pride or embarrassment to generations of Brown Countians and a wellspring of entertainment and fellowship for western, folk, country, and bluegrass music fans and performers at every level.

Though the Brown County Jamboree and the music park neither began nor ended with Bill Monroe, they are forever tied to his name and memory. For pickers in the style derived largely from his musical leadership, the park remains the "University of Bluegrass." For millions of Monroe's fans or followers, the place is synonymous with "traditional bluegrass music," whose story is today correctly recognized as a permanent, venerable, and valuable part of the interconnected story of all American vernacular music.

But tiny Bean Blossom is bigger than bluegrass. Bean Blossom is more than a little Indiana town, or a musical site, or even a local legacy; it is an idea. It will remain, for a while longer at least, as a vital, world-famous American cultural scene, a place where music-as-work and music-as-play routinely intersect. In the living, changing scene that is Bean Blossom, social music making goes on, enriching the lives of all who are lucky enough to live any piece of it there.

# Notes

## Introduction

1. Historian Lyman H. Butterfield was said by Cooperstown Graduate Program professor Bruce Buckley to have originated this pithy phrase, though no more specific citation has been found. Butterfield directed the Institute of Early American History and Culture at Williamsburg, Virginia, in the early 1950s, helped to edit *The Papers of Thomas Jefferson* at Princeton, and edited John Adams's presidential papers.

2. Rosenberg, *Bluegrass: A History,* 96; R. D. Smith, *Can't You Hear Me Callin',* 135; Rinzler, "Bill Monroe."

3. A very recent midwestern example of such parks' core elements is Lonesome Acres Park, developed by Glen and Nancy Brogan at their farm near Miamisburg, Ohio, in 2007, and documented with photos at http://lonesomeacrespark.com.

4. Koretzky, "Night Falls on Sunset Park."

5. Rosenzweig and Blackmar, *Park and People,* 4.

6. Lorzing's 2001 work, *Nature of Landscape,* presents some historical background on parks, including such "rationalized, romantic parks" as the Parc de Versailles, but his historical citations mostly illustrate an unconventional analysis of the concepts of parks and landscapes. A general history more directly pertinent to this introduction is Roberts, *Royal Landscape.*

7. Futrell, *Amusement Parks of Pennsylvania,* 3.

8. Ibid., 25–27.

9. Cox, "Rise and Decline of Willow Grove Park."

10. Library of Congress, "Religion and the Founding of the American Republic." This interactive illustrated essay was created in 1998 by the Library of Congress to complement an exhibit developed and presented at the Library of Congress that year. See also

Malone, *Southern Music—American Music,* 166, which notes the particular relevance of Boles's *Great Revival* and Bruce's *And They All Sang Hallelujah* to questions of the musical heritage of rural southern whites.

11. Canning's recent history of Chautauqua, *Most American Thing in America,* discusses the movement's relationship to mainstream theater and to many other types of American cultural performance and how the Chautauquas both reflected and affected changing values in American social life.

12. Several American folk-fiddling histories cite a Hanover County, Virginia, contest of November 30, 1736, that awarded prizes for "foot-ball play" as well as for fiddling and other arts. Orr's "Fiddlers and Fiddlers' Conventions" and Charles Wolfe's *Devil's Box* provide additional examples.

13. Rosenberg, *Bluegrass: A History,* 145.

14. This formulation follows the seminal "core-domain-sphere" model proposed by Meinig for his 1965 study of the Mormon culture region and subsequently adopted by a majority of cultural geographers. Meinig's model is concisely explained in Zelinsky's *Cultural Geography of the United States,* 114–16.

15. "Little Oprys" are studied in detail in folklorist Amy Noël Davis's thesis, "'When You Coming Back?'"

## Chapter 1. Brown County History and Roots

1. Rosenberg called the 1965 weekend event at Roanoke, Virginia, "the first bluegrass festival" in his seminal *Bluegrass: A History,* 85.

2. Essential county history is reviewed in the Brown County Historical Society's overview, *History and Families.*

3. Jack McDonald remarked several times in conversations that he recalled receiving instruction about the glaciers' effects on Brown County when he was in elementary school in the 1930s.

4. The classic reference for the history of Indiana drift and bedrock geology with respect to glaciation is William Wayne's *Thickness of Drift.* Wayne's maps clearly show the phases of glacial advance, which at their greatest extent covered more than two-thirds of the state.

5. Bustin, *If You Don't Outdie Me,* 4.

6. Esarey's two-volume work, *A History of Indiana,* vol. 1, *1915,* and vol. 2, *1918,* 1:28–125, offers a lengthy and helpful overview of several centuries of deteriorating relationships between Native Americans and Euro-Americans and their consequences for the state's settlement.

7. In his first book, *Pattern in the Material Folk Culture,* 37–39, folklorist Henry Glassie (who has often attended bluegrass festivals at Bean Blossom since the 1970s) mapped the historical "movement of ideas" in traditional cultures from three major cultural hearths in the eastern United States. His maps show folk cultures of south-central Indiana being imported from mid-Atlantic and southern source regions by diffusion and migration.

8. Esarey, *History of Indiana,* 2:629.

9. Baker and Carmony, *Indiana Place Names*, 9–10.

10. Knowlton, "First Impressions of Bean Blossom," 5.

11. "Ernie Pyle's Brown County," reprint of 1940 Scripps-Howard column in the *Brown County Democrat*, April 18, 1973.

12. Nicholson, "Swine, Timber, and Tourism."

13. Buston, *If You Don't Outdie Me*, 8.

14. The phrase "Hills o' Brown" lives on in business advertising and common speech today in Brown County. It likely reflects the memory of photographer Frank Hohenberger's popular Sunday column that ran from 1936 to 1954 in the *Indianapolis Star*, called "Down in the Hills o' Brown County."

15. Ibid., 9.

16. In *Citizen Klansmen*, Moore notes that the surging Klan prominence in the 1920s was very different from the national Klan's white-supremacy antecedents in the post–Civil War years and white-supremacy followers in the civil rights era of the 1960s. In the 1920s, the Ku Klux Klan's interests in Indiana and elsewhere lay strongly in political power and espoused "a more complex creed of racism, nativism, Americanism; the defense of traditional moral and family values; and support for Prohibition" (3).

17. Brown County Historical Society, *Brown County Remembers*, includes Chattie Wade Miller's reminiscence of the Whitecappers of Brown County.

18. The complex symbology of the term *hillbilly* is explicated in Archie Green's groundbreaking essay, "Hillbilly Music."

19. The horde at one point included my parents, refugee Austrian physicians who repeatedly came from their Chicago home to vacation at the state park's Abe Martin Lodge several times in the 1950s and early 1960s.

20. *Brown County Democrat* column, "Old Time' Pictures of Brown County," featured Schrock in his Abe Martin outfit, November 21, 1957.

21. Brewster's book *Ballads and Songs of Indiana* includes more than a hundred traditional song texts from eighteen Indiana counties, mostly south of Indianapolis, but none from Brown County.

22. The story of one fiddler and violin builder, Williamson Hamblen, was preserved in "A History of the Hamblen and Allied Families," by Armeanous Porter Hamblen, ca. 1940, and recounted in a newspaper article by Joanne Nesbit, "Fiddlin'," *Brown County Democrat*, June 30, 1993, 1.

23. The "vaudeville tour" photograph appears in Peva, *Bean Blossom*, 2.

24. On April 22, 1939, the Van Buren String Busters played a live radio show on the *High School Hour* on WFBM in Indianapolis, as duly noted in the local paper: "Brown County People Broadcast over WFBM," *Brown County Democrat*, April 27, 1939.

25. Boldly illustrated advertisements for such WLW Boone County Jamboree shows appeared in both big-city and small-town newspapers in Indiana, Ohio, and Kentucky. The *Lulu Belle & Scotty* WLW show cited here appeared in the *Indianapolis Times*, April 17, 1941.

## Chapter 2. Origins of the Brown County Jamboree, 1939–41

1. Principal sources for this material were Jack McDonald, Jack Cox, Marvin Hedrick (transcribed interview by Neil V. Rosenberg), Denzel Ragsdale, Maurice Duckett, and Owen Duckett.

2. Painstaking scrutiny of six decades worth of the local weekly newspaper, the *Brown County Democrat,* beginning in early January 1936, yielded no direct references to the Brown County Jamboree before 1941; there is therefore no print-based corroboration of a 1939 date. The earliest print reference to the Brown County Jamboree appeared on August 28, 1941.

3. For instance, the *Edinburg (Ind.) Daily Courier*, October 10, 1941, said that Dan Williams "inadvertently set off the Sunday night gatherings *last spring*" (emphasis added). A series of notes and short articles mentioning the Sunday-evening free shows appeared in the *Brown County Democrat* beginning in early August 1941.

4. Jack McDonald wrote his account of the Brown County Jamboree's origins in late 1993, at the request of the late Frank Overstreet (1925–2002), a devoted bluegrass musician and supporter from Indianapolis. Overstreet was also editor of *Bluegrass Music News,* issued by the Society for the Preservation of Blue Grass Music in America.

5. I date Smith's departure from the last appearance of his name in prominent advertising materials and from the discontinuance on handbills and posters of the term *Beanblossom Jamboree.*

6. Transcribed tape provided by Neil Rosenberg of Denzel Ragsdale emceeing the Brown County Jamboree Old Timers' Reunion Day on October 31, 1965.

7. Bunge, interview, June 17, 2000.

8. McDonald, interview, September 25, 1999.

9. Numerous musicians used the nickname "Kentucky Slim" at one time or another. The one recalled by Maurice Duckett and others from the early Brown County Jamboree is unknown. Bean Blossom's Kentucky Slim was not the 275-pound dancer Charles Elza, known as both "Kentucky Slim" and "Little Darlin'," who worked for some years with the Lester Flatt and Earl Scruggs show.

10. Wallace wrote a short series of lighthearted columns describing his shows and those of other self-styled hillbilly or cowboy musicians in central Indiana. These appeared in the regional periodical the *Jamboree,* in which Wallace also bought display ads touting his availability for shows.

11. The short-lived Indiana-based magazine the *Jamboree* reported on many local music venues in a number of states. With that wider perspective, the magazine's name attempted to represent them all. More background on the *Jamboree* appears in the next chapter.

12. Gladys McDonald as quoted in Dick Reed, "Brown County Folks," *Brown County Democrat,* December 6, 1973.

13. *Morgantown News,* June 26, 1941.

14. Mike Lewis, "Before Bill," *Brown County Democrat,* n.d., from scrapbook of William Bernard Lee; Helen Ayers, "Hendersons Recall Musical History in Their Lifetimes," *Brown County Democrat,* May 30, 1984. *Open-air platform* was the term repeatedly used

by emcee "Spurts" or "Silver Spur" Ragsdale to describe the Jamboree's first performance site.

15. Helen Ayers, "'Doc' and 'Hep' Gave Country Music Its First Home," *Brown County Democrat,* October 28, 1981.

16. *Brown County Democrat,* August 14, 1941.

17. *Brown County Democrat,* August 28, 1941.

## Chapter 3. The Rund Family's Brown County Jamboree, 1941–51

1. Rund genealogy is from Brown County Historical Society, *History and Families,* 265–68.

2. *Brown County Democrat,* December 1, 1938.

3. *Brown County Democrat,* August 1, 1940. The cabins are often recalled by former Blue Grass Boys such as Eddie Adcock, Roland White, Vic Jordan, and Doug Hutchens. Monroe's sidemen stayed in these poorly built structures while they worked at, and on, the park.

4. When bought by Bill and Birch Monroe in late 1951, the Brown County Jamboree park comprised 50.19 acres. Rund kept the other 10 or so acres—his own cabin site and adjoining land—which were later sold in lots to (among others) Jack McDonald.

5. Guylia Bunge scrapbook, untitled newspaper clipping.

6. The tent-rental contract is in a scrapbook collected by Mrs. Guy Smith, now owned by her daughter, Guylia Lucille Smith Bunge, of Helmsburg, Ind.

7. Wallace, "News from the Hills of Brown County."

8. Frank M. Hohenberger (1876–1962) moved from Ohio to Nashville, Indiana, in 1917. His thirteen thousand photographs documenting Brown County from the second decade of the 1900s through the prewar years now constitute a special collection at the Lilly Library, Indiana University. Hohenberger's photos were also the basis for Dillon Bustin's book *If You Don't Outdie Me.*

9. Denzel "Silver Spurs" Ragsdale recorded at the Brown County Jamboree barn, October 31, 1965, during an "Old Timers' Reunion" show. Audiotape courtesy of Neil V. Rosenberg.

10. M. Hedrick, interview, August 18, 1972.

11. G. Hedrick, interview.

12. J. Cox, interview, August 15, 1999.

13. Cox misremembered his first tent-show appearance, claiming it was on Sunday, October 15, 1939—two years before the grand-opening tent show.

14. Ibid.

15. Handbill in Guylia Smith Bunge scrapbook.

16. From the *Jamboree,* n.d., preserved in Guylia Smith Bunge scrapbook.

17. Original sheet music for "The Brown County Jamboree" theme song, copyrighted January 7, 1942. Lyrics by Roy Wallace and melody by Pearl Clark. From Guylia Smith Bunge scrapbook.

18. Wallace, "Prof. Scrub-Board Wallace."

19. Ayers, "'Doc' and 'Hep'" (see chap. 2, n. 15). Beauchamp here erroneously cites Bill Monroe as the 1941 owner who underpaid him and demanded union membership.

20. Malone, *Don't Get above Your Raisin'*, 130–32.

21. Statistics and general history of Camp Atterbury are from http://www.indianamilitary .org.

22. According to Oscar and Juanita's son Sam, *Shehan* was the correct spelling. Shorty used *Sheehan* for stage appearances.

23. Per Neil V. Rosenberg.

24. Sizemore, "Early Country Music," 17–18.

25. L. Martin, interview.

26. Bunge, interview, June 17, 2000.

27. *Brown County Democrat,* September 3, 1942.

28. *Brown County Democrat,* October 23, 1941.

29. At the urging of Neil Rosenberg, the barn was measured and drawn to scale in 1977 by the author and Elizabeth Mosby Adler.

30. Though no known photos show a curtain concealing the stage, several informants mentioned it. Blue Grass Boy Jim Smoak confirmed that the stage's curtain was still in use in September 1952, when he first came to Bean Blossom.

31. J. Cox, interview, August 15, 1999; Rund, interview.

32. J. Cox, interview, August 15, 1999.

33. J. McDonald, interview, September 21, 2001.

34. *Brown County Democrat,* November 4, 1943.

35. "Festive Occasion at Jamboree Barn," *Brown County Democrat,* July 6, 1944.

36. A "bench show" is an exhibition of dogs or other small animals, thus named because the animals are usually placed on benches or raised platforms for viewing by judges and the public. The animals are judged for awards on the basis of their conformity to ideal standards for the breed.

37. "Folk Talent and Tunes."

38. Ayres, interview.

39. B. Thompson, interview.

40. Duncan, interview.

41. Parker, interview.

## Chapter 4. Bill Monroe's Brown County Jamboree Park, 1952–57

1. *Brown County Democrat,* April 10, 1952, 1. The quote is not an excerpt; it is the entire article.

2. Osborne, interview.

3. This is the earliest *corroborated* date of a Monroe Jamboree appearance known to the author.

4. Bill Monroe historian (and former Blue Grass Boy) Tom Ewing notes on this point in *The Bill Monroe Reader* that Monroe was playing many small and relatively low-paying percentage-based shows, as well as the rarer large and lucrative ones with a guaranteed fee, in the early fifties.

5. B. Monroe, interview.

6. "Land contracts" in Indiana are negotiated by the involved parties, with the buyer under contract to pay the seller directly. No transfer of the deed is recorded at that time; the actual deed transfer takes place when the contract is paid off.

7. In an interview, Raymond E. Huffmaster recalled Monroe's direct statement to him noting that the purchase came after Christmas and that the ground was frozen and in many places thick with ice. This description is consistent with published weather reports in Brown County for the week after Christmas 1951.

8. Duncan, interview.

9. Gentry, *Country, Western, and Gospel Music,* 110; H. Smith, interview, March 22, 2003.

10. Duncan, interview.

11. Cline, interview; Shehan, interview, July 14, 2009.

12. Email from Tom Ewing, based on a questionnaire sent to former Blue Grass Boys by Doug Hutchens.

13. Tex Logan's memories corroborate Monroe's Indiana trip the week before the recording session. Logan had been invited to fiddle on Monroe's recording of his 1948 composition but stayed in Texas instead. A week after the recording was made with Gordon Terry playing fiddle, Monroe played it to Logan over the phone, and Logan approved what he heard. See Tex Logan (as told to John Holder), "Christmas Time's a-Comin'," 60.

14. Huffmaster, interview.

15. R. D. Smith, *Can't You Hear Me Callin',* 194.

16. See chapter 3, n. 36.

17. *Brown County Democrat,* October 25, 1951, cites the Fall Fox Meet of the Brown County Fox Hunters Association that took place on October 20 and 21. On March 31, 1952, Decca Records released Decca 28045, "First Whippoorwill," backed with "I'm on My Way to the Old Home," an autobiographical ("true story") Monroe composition in which the first verse proclaims Monroe's specific nostalgia for fox hunting:

> Back in the days of my childhood,
> In the evening, when everything was still
> I used to sit and listen to the foxhounds
> With my dad in them old Kentucky hills.

Several Blue Grass Boys emphatically affirmed Monroe's love of fox hunting; Lucky Saylor, a Blue Grass Boy in 1956, noted that he, Bill, and Earl Taylor all loved fox hunting. Saylor was quoted on the subject in Gitlin, "Forgotten Blue Grass Boy": "At the time, he [Monroe] had about thirty dogs out there on the farm and we'd go up on the ridge and he'd turn 'em loose and they'd hit a fox, they'd run" (41).

18. In an interview, banjoist and former Blue Grass Boy Jim Smoak recalled several trips he made with Monroe from Nashville to Bean Blossom with "a trailer full of foxhounds."

19. *Brown County Democrat,* May 1, 1952.

20. Cline, interview.

21. The lowest value is from Jimmy Martin, the highest from Jack McDonald; James Monroe provided an intermediate figure.

22. Jim Bessire recalled in a telephone interview that Tex Watson, who lived for a time at the southern end of Nashville, Indiana, managed the Jamboree for a short time before Birch assumed that duty.

23. Warranty Deed #1129 between Francis Rund and Mae Rund of Johnson County and Birch Monroe of Morgan County, recorded in Brown County property records, August 21, 1959. A Brown County surveyor's map of the transferred property made on March 12, 1952, indicates the park's rough assets from the beginning of the Monroe era. Ownership of the park was finally transferred from Birch to Bill on May 28, 1976, as recorded in Brown County Warranty Deed #8993.

24. Lowry, interview, March 15, 2003.

25. Rosenberg, "Into Bluegrass," 32.

26. The earliest posters of this type were regularly used to promote boxing matches in the 1930s and were typically used by advertisers of blues shows in the mid-1950s.

27. The 1942 posters were printed by the Tribune Press of Earl Park, Indiana, printers of similar posters for Chicago blues artists and boxing promoters. Similar posters for the Brown County Jamboree were ordered beginning in May 1952 from the famous company Hatch Show Print of Nashville, Tennessee. After Hatch Show Print reputedly refused to extend credit to the Monroes in the 1970s, they turned again to the Tribune Press.

28. J. Martin, interview.

29. Many of Birch's tunes can be heard on the 1975 LP album *Brother Birch Monroe Plays Old Time Fiddle Favorites* (Atteiram APIL-1516). A subtitle on the jacket says *Twenty-four Years Brown County Jamboree,* corroborating the Monroes' first involvement with the Jamboree in 1951.

30. Lambert with Sechler, *Good Things Out Weigh the Bad,* vi.

31. This pattern of parking-lot talent recruitment was still much in evidence in the mid-1970s, when Birch first hired the Pigeon Hill String Ticklers, a bluegrass band composed of four Indiana University graduate students in folklore: Jens Lund, Gary Stanton, Roby Cogswell, and the author. We played several times as a last-minute opening act with no publicity or billing at all, but were eventually featured on posters for shows with the McCormick Brothers, Bryant Wilson, and others.

32. *Brown County Democrat,* November 1, 1951.

33. Wilkinson, "The Lattie Moore Story," presents both a musical biography and a discography.

34. J. Martin, interview.

35. Wells, interview.

36. *Billboard,* August 2, 1952, 148.

37. In addition to Grandpa Jones, the Brown's Ferry Four consisted of the Delmore Brothers and Merle Travis.

38. Clark's sporadic Opry performances with Monroe are cited on the Renfro Valley Entertainers Web site, http://www.renfrovalley.com/entertainment/bios/old_joe_clark.html.

39. Lunn was forty years old in 1952 but had begun performing on the Grand Ole Opry in 1935, when he was twenty-three; there Judge George D. Hay soon billed him as "the Talking Blues Man."

40. As recounted on Sonny Osborne's Web site, http://www.osbornebros.com/sonny
.html.

41. Peva's observations about one such firing are cited below, in chapter 8. According
to Charles Wolfe's extensive notes to *Bill Monroe: 1970–1979,* Jack Hicks was offered
the banjo-playing job by Monroe "when Rual Yarbrough quit," while Hicks was at Bean
Blossom. Similarly, Doug Hutchens has carefully described in an online testimonial for
Peva's book *Bean Blossom* how in 1970 Monroe asked him to start regularly working for
him the following summer; that year Hutchens replaced Joe Stuart on bass. See http://
www.buybooksontheweb.com/product.aspx?ISBN=0-7414-3210-2.

42. Gordon Terry and Garry Thurmond, "Since He's Not Here, Let's Talk about
Him," in *Howdy, Folks, Howdy,* ed. Hutchens, 12.

43. R. D. Smith, *Can't You Hear Me Callin',* 123–25.

44. Haney, interview.

45. Parker, interview.

46. Carlton Haney, quoted from audiocassette of "mid-1950s" Brown County Jamboree performance provided by Loren Parker.

47. M. Hedrick, interview, August 18, 1972.

48. Rosenberg, *Bill Monroe and His Blue Grass Boys,* 66, 71.

49. Melvin Goins, recorded at a public workshop at Bean Blossom during "Uncle Pen
Days," at the Hippie Hill workshop stage, September 24, 2004.

50. *Brown County Democrat,* July 29, 1956.

51. Ron Teofan, from email correspondence prompted by his posts to BGRASS-L,
1997.

## Chapter 5. Survivals, Revivals, and Arrivals, 1958–66

1. Kenny Baker quoted in Rooney, *Bossmen,* 71.

2. "Brown County Jamboree Barn Partially Burns," *Brown County Democrat,* April
24, 1958 (front-page article with photos).

3. Rosenberg, "From Sound to Style."

4. Cravens, interview; Bray, interviews, August 11, September 17, 20, 2003.

5. Hartford's surname was then still "Harford"; he changed it in the mid-1960s at
Chet Atkins's request.

6. Cravens, interview.

7. Adcock, interview; Cravens, interview. Cravens noted that the platform was gone
by about 1960.

8. Brower, "Harley Bray—Bluegrass Gentleman," 64.

9. B. Monroe, interview.

10. On their 1962 Liberty album (Liberty LST 7214), they were the "Bluegrass Gentlemen," but they were better known as the Bray Brothers.

11. Lomax, "Bluegrass Background—Folk Music with Overdrive."

12. Rosenberg, "From Sound to Style."

13. Rosenberg, *Bluegrass: A History,* 181.

14. R. L. Smith, in "If I Had a Song . . . ," states that from 1945 to 1967, Swarthmore

College hosted the first of the annual college-based folk festivals. In the 1940s, featured artists included Richard Dyer-Bennet, John Jacob Niles, Lead Belly, and Woody Guthrie. Some later performers were Pete Seeger, Odetta, the New Lost City Ramblers, and, in 1959, Swarthmore alumnus Ralph Rinzler.

15. Rooney, *Bossmen*, 77.

16. Von Schmidt and Rooney, *Baby, Let Me Follow You Down*, 157–59.

17. Rinzler, "Bill Monroe," 204.

18. Rinzler, "Bill Monroe—Daddy."

19. Rinzler, liner notes to *Monroe and Watson, Live Duet Recordings*.

20. Rinzler's approach to Monroe, with some help from Tex Logan, took place at a party at the New York home of folksinger Oscar Brand and is recounted in detail in R. D. Smith, *Can't You Hear Me Callin*,' 172.

21. Ibid.

22. Rothman, "Rambling in Redwood Canyon," 58–66.

23. Rosenberg, "Picking Myself Apart," 279.

24. Ibid.

25. Dorson reviewed the history of his 1950 coinage *fakelore* in "Folklore, Academe, and the Marketplace," the introduction to his collection of essays *Folklore and Fakelore*.

26. Jim Peva, "How Did You Get into BG?" email to BGRASS-L, July 2, 1998.

27. Peva, "Thirty Years of Bean Blossom Recollections."

28. Such different country musicians as old-time fiddler Clayton McMichen (who began his recording career with the Skillet Lickers in 1926) and singer Johnny Cash appeared at the Brown County Jamboree during this time period with little or no newspaper advertising.

29. Rosenberg, *Bill Monroe and His Blue Grass Boys*, 22.

30. Neil V. Rosenberg, unpublished letter to Ralph Rinzler, November 25, 1963, in the Smithsonian Institution's Center for Folklife, Rinzler files, Box RR343, Box 9.

31. Details of Rinzler's appeal to Bill Monroe to let Neil Rosenberg manage the Jamboree are recalled by Jim Rooney in von Schmidt and Rooney, *Baby, Let Me Follow You Down*, 157–62.

32. The rule banning two Bills was ignored by Monroe during the tenures of other Blue Grass Boys, like guitarist Bill Box and banjoist Bill Holden.

33. John Wright, email to BGRASS-L, July 7, 1996.

34. Neil V. Rosenberg, interview by Brance Gillihan, TheBluegrassBlog.com, posted March 30, 2006.

35. Ibid.

36. Marvin Hedrick to Ralph Rinzler, August 22, 1963.

37. Sandy Rothman's fine account of this trip can be found at http://eyecandypromo.com/SR/jgbanjo.html.

38. G. Hedrick, interview.

39. Rothman, http://eyecandypromo.com/SR/jgbanjo.html.

40. Interesting reports of Garcia and Rothman's trip to Bean Blossom are found in McNally's *Long Strange Trip* and in Jackson's *Garcia: An American Life*. Both accounts emphasize the intimidation that Garcia and Rothman felt in the presence of Bill Monroe.

41. Eddie Adcock, quoted in "Adcock's News Update," email newsletter, November 29, 2005.

42. Rosenberg describes the synthesis of familiar and novel elements at Haney's first festival in *Bluegrass: A History,* 205–7, and notes Rinzler's key "behind the scenes" role in its production.

43. Duncan, interview.

44. Ibid.

45. Carlson's 1968 publication, the *Bluegrass Handbook,* was mimeographed onto the unused backs of academic entomology and agricultural handouts, obtained while he studied at Purdue University. The handbook proffered Carlson's artistically conservative bluegrass advice and insights on matters ranging from "show tips" to getting more bluegrass on the radio. He told readers how to produce their own bluegrass shows locally and provided voluminous contact information for related publishers and organizations from tape-exchange and fan clubs to record vendors, discographers, and academic departments. His stated goal, at a time when few others even conceived of a bluegrass community, was "making the bluegrass community more tightly knit and powerful."

46. Carlson, "Stanley Brothers Fan Club," 31.

47. Carlson, "Indiana Shows Reviewed," 6.

48. Carlson, "Brown County Jamboree," 4.

49. Ibid. Jerry Wilson wrote a biography of his father titled *The Kentucky Rambler* and printed a small number of copies. The full text, with discography and some musical samples, is available at http://wilstar.com/ky-ramb.htm.

50. Carr and Munde, *Prairie Nights to Neon Lights,* 104–5.

51. Logan, interview.

52. Lamar Grier, interviewed by Jim Moss via email; the full interview is at http://www.candlewater.com/interviews/LamarGrier_Part1. Monroe's "stake-bodied truck" had removable sides so it could carry oversize loads and be loaded from any side.

53. Carter Stanley, recorded at Bean Blossom, October 16, 1966.

## Chapter 6. Building the Festivals, 1967–68

1. Documented in 1972 in a group of Brown County Jamboree posters compiled by Neil V. Rosenberg and photographed by Carl Fleischhauer.

2. Rinzler reported the estimated audience size and noted that they came from twenty-two states in "Blue Grass Fest a 'Picknic.'"

3. Bickel, interview, July 30, 2006.

4. Rosenberg's *Bluegrass: A History* shows a photo of Monroe's first Bean Blossom bluegrass festival poster by Carl Fleischhauer (opposite p. 304). Frank Brown's nickname is usually spelled "Hylo."

5. Martin reminded the crowd of Rudy Lyle's reputation as a banjoist but noted that he had been playing electric guitar lately in their act; both Martin's statement and the sounds of Lyle's electric guitar are on a tape of the show for Saturday, June 24, 1967, provided by collector Don Hoos of Evanston, Illinois.

6. Roland White said of his early tenure as a Blue Grass Boy, "You have to remember,

I wasn't a guitar player 'til that band. Well, I knew the chords. . . . I knew the chords to all the songs. I knew the lyrics to most of everything he recorded to date" (from an interview published by Jim Moss at http://www.rentalfilm.com/MonroeChristmas/).

7. Robins, *What I Know 'bout What I Know*, 50–52.

8. White, interview.

9. Wright, *Traveling the High Way Home*, 12–13.

10. This fact has been duly reported in recent years—for example, in Peva's 2006 souvenir book, *Bean Blossom*, 59.

11. The modest attendance was noted by stringed-instrument dealer George Gruhn, who attended Bean Blossom and other early bluegrass festivals regularly for years. James Monroe, in an interview in 2000, recalled the low profit produced for Monroe by the "Celebration."

12. Letter to the *Bill Monroe Fan Club Newsletter*, ca. early 1967.

13. Sullivan and Sullivan, *Sullivan Family*, 90–91.

14. Cantwell, "Believing in Bluegrass."

15. White, interview.

16. Glen Duncan, contemplating Carlton Haney's encouragement of Roger Smith and other good musicians to move to the area, termed the practice "running a farm team for Blue Grass Boys."

17. Duncan, interview. Duncan's reminiscence of these events was also cited in Devan, "Duncan, Cordle, and Lonesome Standard Time."

18. Jordan, interview, April 5, 1997.

19. T. Williams, "Talking Feet: Mike Seeger," cites Seeger's recollection of New River Ranch music-park seating. The original benches at Bean Blossom lasted only a few years and were never replaced. Most festival ads from the late 1960s onward routinely instructed fans to "bring lawn chairs" (43).

20. White, interview.

21. The quoted phrase, indicating the special, ritualized nature of festival events, is borrowed from Falassi's compilation, *Time Out of Time*.

22. Cornell, interview.

23. The groundbreaking Oscar-winning movie *Bonnie and Clyde* premiered at the Montreal Film Festival on August 4, 1967, and utilized Flatt and Scruggs's 1949 recording "Foggy Mountain Breakdown" to great effect in its chase scenes.

24. Turner, "Luke and Cecil Thompson," 52.

25. Bill Monroe, addressing the Brown County Jamboree audience at a show featuring Loretta Lynn, August 18, 1968.

26. *Bluegrass Unlimited* 15, no. 4 (1980): 14.

27. Available for institutional (only) rental from the Film-Makers Cooperative, c/o Clocktower Gallery, 108 Leonard Street, 13th Floor, New York, NY 10013.

28. Bill Grant, quoted in *Bluegrass Unlimited* 17, no. 1 (1982): 34.

29. Hoffman, "Reflections on Taping."

30. Bill Monroe at Brown County Jamboree, August 18, 1968.

31. "Robert Hall" was a large national chain of discount clothing stores that operated

from just after World War II until its liquidation in 1977. Rosenberg cites the "Derriere!" bit in "Picking Myself Apart," 280.

## Chapter 7. The Festival Becomes a Landmark, 1969–71

1. The numbers are based on a count of names included in prefestival advertising and included important sidemen such as Neil Rosenberg and Byron Berline as well as famous radio deejays such as Paul Mullins and Grant Turner, who worked the Bean Blossom festivals mostly as emcees.

2. Carney, "Bluegrass Grows All Around," includes maps with the distribution of early bluegrass festivals; data provided by Peggy Logan, then on the editorial staff of *Muleskinner News.*

3. Robins, *What I Know 'bout What I Know,* 59.

4. All "food events," in the synaptic model of food and culture propounded by folklorist Charles Camp, link cooks and eaters in complex ways, even in cases that seem to be most ordinary or mundane. By providing annual festivalgoers with "free" food—especially foods that are inexpensive and regional—the Monroe festivals strengthened the traditional social bond between hosts and music fans. See Camp, *American Foodways,* chap. 3, "The Food Event."

5. Rooney, *Bossmen,* 101; DeJean, "Bluegrass: The People's Choice," 29.

6. Royce Campbell, *Bill Monroe Fan Club Newsletter,* Summer 1970; Saal, "Pickin' and Singin.'"

7. Cantwell, *Bluegrass Breakdown,* 252.

8. Many 1970 Bean Blossom festival photos accompany helpful discussions of public and private performance at Bean Blossom in Fleischhauer and Rosenberg, *Bluegrass Odyssey.*

9. "Scruggs to Play at Blue Grass Festival," *Bloomington (Ind.) Herald-Telephone,* June 18, 1970.

10. Spencer Sorenson, email to BGRASS-L, March 25, 1998.

11. Plous, "Farm Where Bluegrass Music Grows."

12. From notes taken by Judith McCulloh, June 20, 1970.

13. Bettie Leonard, *Bill Monroe Fan Club Newsletter,* Summer 1970.

14. Greg Temple, "2 Music Conventions Planned at Beanblossom," *Brown County Democrat,* September 3, 1970, 3. Popejoy's anecdote, if based even slightly on a real event, could not have taken place at the Brown County Jamboree, which had no stage curtain at that time and no janitor.

15. Bill's commanding attitude and sometimes off-putting actions toward his older brothers, Charlie and Birch, were interpreted by some Blue Grass Boys as "payback" for their superior and condescending treatment of him in their childhood.

16. Melvin Goins, at a "storytelling" workshop at the Bill Monroe Memorial Music Park's Hippie Hill workshop stage, September 24, 2004.

17. *Brown County Democrat,* June 17, 1971.

18. Overstreet, "Bill Monroe's Fifth Annual Bluegrass Festival."

19. Black, *Come Hither to Go Yonder*, 23.

20. Artis, *Bluegrass*, 127. The quote is from a brilliant pastiche of Artis's own festival experiences, which constitutes a chapter aptly titled "The Endless Festival" in his classic book.

21. Along with bassist Randy Scruggs, these musicians had helped Hartford record his groundbreaking album *Aereo-Plain* (Warner Brothers Records WS1916), released January 1, 1971.

22. Doug Hutchens, email to BGRASS-L, August 28, 2003.

23. White, "Sam Bush," 20.

24. Doug Hutchens, email to BGRASS-L, January 4, 2000.

## Chapter 8. The Festival's Golden Age, 1972–82

1. Blue Grass Boy Wayne Lewis evoked Bill Monroe's deliberately old-fashioned ways with this phrase at a storytelling workshop at the park on September 24, 2005. Imitating Monroe's distinctive voice and diction, Lewis told how his efforts to use modern tools and methods to build a corncrib were repeatedly stymied by his employer's focus on the past.

2. Carney, "Bluegrass Grows All Around," 41.

3. The exceptions were in 1975, 1976, and 1984, when the festival dropped back to five days, beginning on Wednesday and ending Sunday.

4. Despite the ongoing distraction of Nashville, Indiana's centennial in 1972, the *Brown County Democrat* continued to note the growing size and drawing power of Monroe's bluegrass music festival.

5. See the photo included on an unnumbered page at the end of chapter 10 of Rosenberg, *Bluegrass: A History*, depicting the Bluegrass Alliance on stage at this festival.

6. For most of the Bean Blossom festival years, the McDonald's Bean Blossom grocery store was part of the Independent Grocers Association, the world's largest voluntary supermarket chain. Still often called "the IGA" in conversation, it has been part of the ShopWorth grocery alliance for the past few years.

7. Marshall, "Conversation with Jim McReynolds"; *Brown County Democrat*, December 27, 1972.

8. Information about this mandolin and the circumstances of its sale is from an email post to BGRASS-L on May 10, 2004, by Joe Cline, citing "noted Loar and Monroe expert" Tom Isenhour. Jack Lawrence verified the 1972 purchase date and general memories of the jam session.

9. Joe Ross, "Another Success in Norco," 28.

10. Goldsmith, introduction to *The Bluegrass Reader*, 26.

11. Filiatreau, "Bluegrass May Be a Changin,'" with photos by folklorist Howard W. Marshall, then a mandolin player and graduate student at Indiana University.

12. Rooney, "Sketches of Bill Monroe."

13. I witnessed the stage director's insistent cues, which angered some fans sitting near me. Tom Ewing recalled that audience participation was first prompted by the flashing red light.

14. R. D. Smith, *Can't You Hear Me Callin',* 223.

15. Lester Flatt performed annually from 1971 through 1978. Booked to perform in 1979 as well, Lester passed away that May.

16. After Stoney's March 1977 death, Wilma Lee persevered as the leader of the Clinch Mountain Clan, making many more appearances at Bean Blossom.

17. Jim Moss, email to BGRASS-L, August 27, 2003. Many of Moss's interviews and photographs from Bean Blossom can be found on his two extensive Web sites, http://www.mossware.com and http://www.candlewater.com.

18. Raymond W. McLain, email to the author, October 30, 2003.

19. Raymond E. Huffmaster, email to BGRASS-L, August 28, 2003.

20. Cantwell, "Is the 'Scene' Grass?" 38.

21. H. Smith and B. Smith, interview, February 6, 2004.

22. *Bluegrass Unlimited* 11, no. 7 (1977).

23. Henry's Web site, http://www.murphymethod.com, provides links to both her instrumental instructional materials and a subject listing for her occasional magazine, *Women in Bluegrass.*

24. This poster is in the permanent collection of the International Bluegrass Music Museum, Owensboro, Kentucky. The band in question was actually the "Pigeon Hill String Ticklers," composed of four graduate students from Indiana University's Folklore Institute: Jens Lund, Gary Stanton, Roby Cogswell, and the author.

25. H. Smith, interview, February 6, 2004.

26. Peva's mid-1980s photograph showing Bill happily giving such a wagon ride is in Peva, *Bean Blossom,* 29.

27. R. D. Smith, *Can't You Hear Me Callin',* uses this phrase as the title of the seventh chapter in his biography of Monroe, covering the period 1965 to 1983.

28. Black, *Come Hither to Go Yonder,* 69–71.

29. *Bluegrass Unlimited* 10, no. 9 (1976): 26.

30. Wayne Lewis, Uncle Pen Days Storytelling Workshop, September 24, 2005.

31. *Pickin'* 3, no. 8 (1976): 45. The "other" Tom Adler is a bluegrass and old-time banjoist and songwriter living in New Mexico.

32. Bettie Leonard, letter to *Bill Monroe Fan Club Newsletter,* September 1978.

33. *Bluegrass Unlimited* 14, no. 2 (1979): 11.

34. Mike Donathan, letter to *Bill Monroe Fan Club Newsletter,* November 1979.

35. R. D. Smith, *Can't You Hear Me Callin',* 234.

36. Dave Underwood, letter to the editor, *Brown County Democrat,* May 14, 1980.

37. The name of the bass player is unfortunately forgotten; the banjo player was the author.

38. *Brown County Democrat,* June 18, 1980.

39. Betty Scott, letter to the editor, *Brown County Democrat,* July 23, 1980.

40. *Bluegrass Unlimited* 15, no. 10 (1981): 9.

41. Raymond Huffmaster, email to BGRASS-L, January 18, 2007.

## Chapter 9. Festival People and Lore

1. Jack Lawrence, email to BGRASS-L, May 11, 2004.
2. A hamburger cookout for and by Japanese fans at Jim Peva's campsite grill is pictured in Peva, *Bean Blossom*, 25.
3. Bud Freedman, "Six-Day Bean Blossom Blues," recorded ca. 1971–72 by Jim Peva.
4. Peva posted this tale on the Bean Blossom internet site as "The Outhouse Scare," at http://www.beanblossom.com/History/Memories/OuthouseScare.html; another version is in Peva's book *Bean Blossom*, 72.
5. M. Barnett, interview, June 18, 2001.
6. Ibid.
7. Hannemann, interview.
8. Black, *Come Hither to Go Yonder*, 78.
9. Andrea Roberts, informal interview, April 20, 1996, Scottsville, Ky.
10. H. Smith, interview, February 6, 2004.
11. MaryE Yeomans, email to BGRASS-L, March 16, 2003.
12. Paul Birch, email to BGRASS-L, December 13, 2005.
13. H. Smith, interview, February 6, 2004.
14. Doug Hutchens, email to BGRASS-L, August 28, 2003.
15. Jack Derry, email to BGRASS-L, July 21, 1998.
16. Bickel, interview, August 5, 2006.

## Chapter 10. Bill and James Monroe's Festival Park, 1983–97

1. R. D. Smith, *Can't You Hear Me Callin,'* 245.
2. "Jamboree Remodeling Done without Approval," *Brown County Democrat,* July 13, 1983.
3. Thomas, "Dixie Flyers," 59.
4. *Bluegrass Unlimited* 19, no. 2 (1984): 14.
5. Hutchens, "Bill Monroe Museum."
6. Drudge, "Commercialism," 63.
7. R. D. Smith, *Can't You Hear Me Callin,'* 254–55.
8. Duncan, interview.
9. Email to BGRASS-L, August 31, 2004.
10. Rattlesnake Annie, email to author, February 10, 2006.
11. *Brown County Democrat,* June 18, 1986.
12. The second mandolin damaged in the November 13, 1985, attack was serial no. 72214, dated February 26, 1923, bought by Monroe from the original owner's widow in 1972.
13. Monroe, interview.
14. Barnett, interview, June 18, 2001.
15. *Brown County Democrat,* October 22, 1986.
16. Overstreet's title evokes the then-popular song "Ashes of Love," written by Johnnie

Wright and Jack Anglin, and recorded as a bluegrass number by Jim and Jesse McReynolds & the Virginia Boys and many others.

17. Email to BGRASS-L, August 31, 2004.

18. Cotton Ginnee, email to BGRASS-L, September 1, 2004.

19. *Bluegrass Unlimited* 22, no. 10 (1988): 86.

20. Putnam, "Bill Monroe."

21. Tolbert, "Letters," 10.

22. Black, *Come Hither to Go Yonder,* 140–43.

23. Rosenberg and Wolfe, *Music of Bill Monroe,* 239.

24. After Dwight Dillman's acquisition of the park in 1998, this "Mecca" metaphor began to be repeatedly uttered and written by Jim Peva, who nonetheless denies authorship of the phrase.

25. Barnett, interview, June 18, 2001.

26. Tottle, "Moveable Feast," 45.

27. Stephen Gebhart quoted in Humble, "Monroe: Captured on Film."

28. A clear view of the just-constructed 1992 stage is provided in Peva, *Bean Blossom,* 39. On the next page, Peva also illustrates and discusses the stage's signature "Back Home Again in Indiana" signs, old and new.

29. Putnam, "What's Wrong with This Picture?" 27.

30. Adcock, interview, September 29, 2002.

## Chapter 11. Renaissance, Continuity, and Change, 1998 and After

1. The amount was reported to the author by Jimmy Martin (interview).

2. Jim Peva, email to BGRASS-L, March 30, 1998.

3. The new road and lane names first appeared on a crude freehand hand-lettered map of the park given out to visitors in 1998. Several years later, with many changes, a professionally drawn park map was created to show the newly built cabins and changing park layout.

4. Jim Peva, email to BGRASS-L, May 24, 1998.

5. Skinker, "The Magic Returns."

6. J. Martin, interview.

7. Jim Peva, email to BGRASS-L, October 24, 1998.

8. The late Jimmy Martin's loud personality and alcohol-abuse problems were highlighted in the opening pages of Piazza's *True Adventures.*

9. J. Martin, interview.

10. MaryE Yeomans, email to BGRASS-L, January 18, 2007.

11. SHS International's product lines all bear Indiana place-names. Despite fanciful early company advertisements about the heritage of fine craftsmanship practiced by a fictitious man named "Morgan Monroe," Indiana residents recognize the name as being derived from two counties adjacent to Brown County and from the Morgan-Monroe State Forest, a twenty-four thousand–acre recreational tract established five miles south of Martinsville by the state in 1929.

12. Mike Schwab of SHS International, email to the author, July 29, 2003.

# Interviews

All interviews except those marked as "unrecorded," "telephone," or "email" were tape-recorded and transcribed by the author.

Adcock, Edward W. September 29, 2002; September 2, 2003 (email).
Ayres, Roy. August 12, 2004 (email).
Bakalar, Bob. September 24, 2005.
Baker, Kenny. October 24, 2000; September 28, 2002 (unrecorded).
Banister, Roger L. November 2, 2002.
Barnett, Morris C. June 18, 2001; September 28, 2002 (unrecorded).
Bessire, Jim. April 14, 1999 (telephone).
Bickel, Harry. July 30, 2006; August 5, 2006 (telephone).
Bray, Harley O. August 11, 2003 (telephone); September 17, 2003 (telephone);
    September 20, 2003.
Brock, Roger. September 23, 2006.
Bunge, Guylia S. June 17, 2000; September 23, 2000.
Clayton, James D. June 16, 2001 (unrecorded).
Clements, Vassar. July 17, 1999 (unrecorded).
Cline, Charlie. March 26, 2003 (telephone).
Cornell, Jim. January 14, 2006 (unrecorded).
Cox, Harold. June 15, 2002.
Cox, Jack. October 9, 1998; August 15, 1999 (unrecorded); September 25, 1999
    (unrecorded); September 21, 2001 (unrecorded); September 22, 2002.
Cox, Ruth. June 15, 2002.
Cravens, Robert "Red." August 25, 2003 (telephone).
Dillman, Dwight. October 20, 1999.
Duckett, Maurice. November 2, 2002; October 29, 2006 (telephone).

Duckett, Owen "Tex." January 11, 2003.

Duncan, Glen. February 7, 2004.

Edwards, Joe. January 14, 2003 (telephone); February 7, 2003.

Fuller, Mary C. September 29, 2002.

Haney, Carlton. September 18, 2003 (telephone).

Hannemann, Robert M. September 27, 2002.

Hedrick, David. April 23, 1999 (telephone).

Hedrick, Gary. November 9, 2002.

Hedrick, Marvin. Interview by Neil V. Rosenberg and Carl Fleischhauer, 1968; 1972 transcriptions provided by Neil V. Rosenberg.

Hoos, Don. November 20, 2003 (telephone).

Huffmaster, Raymond E. June 18, 2001 (unrecorded).

Hutchens, Doug. November 12, 2005.

Jordan, Vic. April 5, 1997; June 18, 2001 (unrecorded).

Keeney, Dan. September 22, 2001.

Kegley, Jack. September 25, 1999 (unrecorded).

Lappin, Brian. December 13, 2003.

Law, Aaron. June 21, 2003.

Law, Talmadge. September 22, 2000.

Lee, Genevieve. August 15, 1999; September 21, 2001 (unrecorded).

Lee, William Bernard. August 15, 1999; September 21, 2001 (unrecorded).

Lewis, Jimmy. January 13, 2007 (telephone).

Lewis, Wayne. September 24, 2005.

Logan, Benjamin "Tex." December 20, 2005 (telephone).

Lowry, Harold. December 1, 2002 (telephone); March 15, 2003.

Martin, Jimmy. April 19, 2003.

Martin, Linda Lou. October 26, 2003 (telephone).

Martin, Mac. August 18, 2005 (telephone).

McDonald, Jack. September 25, 1999 (unrecorded); September 21, 2001; September 27, 2002 (unrecorded); January 28, 2007 (telephone).

Monroe, Birch. September 26, 1977.

Monroe, James. February 26, 2000.

Moore, Lattie. February 1, 2003.

Neat, Frank. July 16, 1999 (unrecorded).

Osborne, Sonny. June 19, 2003 (unrecorded).

Parker, Loren. June 16, 2000.

Peva, James R. June 15, 1996; September 23, 2000 (unrecorded); June 17, 2001 (unrecorded); September 27, 2002 (unrecorded); September 28, 2002 (unrecorded); March 2, 2004 (email); December 28, 2004 (email).

Robins, Joseph "Butch" C. June 21, 2003.

Rund, Lettie Mae "Sandy." June 27, 1999.

Schmaltz, Jim. September 23, 2005.

Seeger, Mike. February 27, 2005.

Shehan, Sam. July 12, 2009; July 14, 2009 (telephone).

Sizemore, James. March 13, 2003 (telephone).

Smith, Hazel. March 22, 2003 (telephone); February 6, 2004.

Smith, Roger. September 21, 2001 (unrecorded).

Smoak, Jim. August 5, 2006 (unrecorded).

Stamper, Pete. October 26, 2003 (telephone).

Stanley, Ralph. September 11, 1999 (unrecorded).

Stedman, William J. September 27, 2003.

Taggart, David Bruce. November 3, 2002.

Terry, Arnold. November 26, 2002 (telephone).

Thompson, Bob. June 19, 1998.

Thompson, Luke. December 1, 2002 (telephone).

Wells, Kyle. November 3, 2002.

White, Roland. October 21, 1999.

Yates, Bill. June 18, 2005.

# Bibliography

Artis, Bob. *Bluegrass*. New York: Hawthorn Books, 1975.

Baker, Ronald L., and Marvin Carmony. *Indiana Place Names*. Bloomington: Indiana University Press, 1975.

Black, Bob. *Come Hither to Go Yonder: Playing Bluegrass with Bill Monroe*. Urbana: University of Illinois Press, 2005.

Boles, John. *The Great Revival, 1787–1805: The Origins of the Southern Evangelical Mind*. Lexington: University Press of Kentucky, 1972.

Boomhower, Ray. "A 'Dapper Dan with the Soul of an Imp': Kin Hubbard, Creator of Abe Martin." *Traces of Indiana and Midwestern History* 5, no. 4 (1993).

Brewster, Paul G. *Ballads and Songs of Indiana*. Folklore series, no. 1. Bloomington: Indiana University Publications, 1940.

Brower, Barry. "Harley Bray—Bluegrass Gentleman." *Bluegrass Unlimited* 19, no. 1 (1984): 60–68.

Brown County Historical Society. *Brown County Remembers*. Comp. Dorothy B. Bailey. Nashville, Ind.: Rever Press, 1986.

———. *History and Families, Brown County, Indiana, 1836–1991*. Comp. *Brown County Democrat*. Paducah, Ky.: Turner Publishing, 1991.

Bruce, Dickson, Jr. *And They All Sang Hallelujah: Plain-Folk Camp Meeting Religion, 1800–1845*. Knoxville: University of Tennessee Press, 1974.

Bustin, Dillon. *If You Don't Outdie Me: The Legacy of Brown County*. Bloomington: Indiana University Press, 1982.

Camp, Charles. *American Foodways: What, When, Why, and How We Eat in America*. Little Rock: August House, 1989.

Canning, Charlotte. *The Most American Thing in America: Circuit Chautauqua as Performance*. Iowa City: University of Iowa Press, 2005.

Cantwell, Robert. "Believing in Bluegrass." *Atlantic Monthly,* March 1972, 52–54.

——. *Bluegrass Breakdown: The Making of the Old Southern Sound.* Urbana: University of Illinois Press, 1984.

——. "Is the 'Scene' Grass?" *Bluegrass Unlimited* 8, no. 10 (1974).

Carlson, Norman. "Brown County Jamboree." *Bluegrass Unlimited* 1, no. 6 (1966): 4.

——. "Indiana Shows Reviewed." *Bluegrass Unlimited* 1, no. 4 (1966): 5–6.

——. "Inside Folklore." *Ralph Stanley International Fan Club Newsletter,* June 1969, 12–18.

——. "The Stanley Brothers Fan Club and a Twenty-Year Bluegrass Odyssey." *Bluegrass Unlimited* 21, no. 7 (1987): 29–34.

Carney, George O. "Bluegrass Grows All Around: The Spatial Dimensions of a Country Music Style." *Journal of Cultural Geography* 73, no. 4 (1974): 34–55.

Carr, Joe, and Alan Munde. *Prairie Nights to Neon Lights: The Story of Country Music in West Texas.* Lubbock: Texas Tech University Press, 1995.

Carrier, Jim. "Images of Bean Blossom." *Bluegrass Unlimited* 19, no. 9 (1985): 82–83.

Cox, Harold E. "Rise and Decline of Willow Grove Park." Paper presented at the Old York Road Historical Society, Jenkintown, Pa., March 19, 1963.

Davis, Amy Noël. "Local Oprys in Kentucky: The Grassroots Support of Country Music." In *Kentucky Folklife Festival Program Book.* Frankfort: Kentucky Historical Society, 1998.

——. "'When You Coming Back?': The Local Country-Music Opry Community." Master's thesis, University of North Carolina, 1998.

DeJean, David. "Bluegrass: The People's Choice." *Louisville Courier-Journal and Times Magazine,* August 3, 1969, 28–36.

Devan, Brett F. "Glen Duncan, Larry Cordle, and Lonesome Standard Time." *Bluegrass Unlimited* 28, no. 1 (1993): 20–28.

Dorson, Richard M. *Folklore and Fakelore: Essays toward a Discipline of Folk Studies.* Cambridge: Harvard University Press, 1976.

Drudge, Mike. "Commercialism: Does Bluegrass Need It?" *Bluegrass Unlimited* 21, no. 9 (1987): 63–66.

Esarey, Logan. *A History of Indiana: From Its Exploration to 1850.* Vols. 1–2. Indianapolis: Hoosier Heritage Press, 1970.

Ewing, Tom, ed. *The Bill Monroe Reader.* Urbana: University of Illinois Press, 2000.

Falassi, Alessandro. *Time Out of Time: Essays on the Festival.* Albuquerque: University of New Mexico Press, 1987.

Fields, Cary Allen. "Bill Monroe's Legacy: Alive and Well and Living in Central Indiana." *Bluegrass Journal* (Winter 2006): 1, 6–7.

Filiatreau, John. "Bluegrass May Be a Changin' in Them Indiana Woods." *Country Music* 1, no. 2 (1972): 40–46.

Fleischhauer, Carl, and Neil V. Rosenberg. *Bluegrass Odyssey: A Documentary in Pictures and Words, 1966–86.* Urbana: University of Illinois Press, 2001.

"Folk Talent and Tunes." *Billboard,* May 15, 1948.

Futrell, Jim. *Amusement Parks of Pennsylvania.* Mechanicsburg, Pa.: Stackpole Books, 2002.

Gentry, Linnell. *Country, Western, and Gospel Music: A History and Encyclopedia of Composers, Artists, and Songs.* Nashville: McQuiddy Press, 1961.

Gitlin, Ira. "A Forgotten Blue Grass Boy: Lucky Saylor." *Bluegrass Unlimited* 27, no. 11 (1993): 38–43.

Glassie, Henry. *Pattern in the Material Folk Culture of the Eastern United States.* Philadelphia: University of Pennsylvania Press, 1968.

Goldsmith, Thomas, ed. *The Bluegrass Reader.* Urbana: University of Illinois Press, 2004.

Green, Archie. "Hillbilly Music: Source and Symbol." *Journal of American Folklore* 78 (1965): 204–22.

Green, Douglas B. "Pete Pyle: Bluegrass Pioneer." *Bluegrass Unlimited* 12, no. 9 (1978): 22–25.

Grelle, Clarence. "Hops, Hoedowns, and Frolics: Country Music in Indiana, 1930 to 1960." *Old Time Country* 10, no. 2 (1994): 4–7.

Hawes, David S. *The Best of Kin Hubbard: Abe Martin's Sayings and Wisecracks, Abe's Neighbors, His Almanack, Comic Drawings.* Bloomington: Indiana University Press, 1995.

Hoffman, Robert L. "Reflections on Taping and the Alleged Future of Bluegrass Music." *Bluegrass Unlimited* 3, no. 3 (1968).

Humble, Kelly. "Monroe: Captured on Film." *Bluegrass Unlimited* 27, no. 10 (1993): 54–57.

Hutchens, Doug. "The Bill Monroe Museum and Bluegrass Hall of Fame: The Dream Comes True." *Bluegrass Unlimited* 19, no. 4 (1984): 10–11, 31–34.

———, ed. *Howdy, Folks, Howdy.* Vol. 1, *Stories of Bill Monroe and the Blue Grass Boys, by the "Men Who Wore the Hats."* Pippa Passes, Ky.: Pippa Valley Printing, 2003.

Jackson, Blair. *Garcia: An American Life.* New York: Penguin Books, 2000.

Kelly, Fred C. *The Life and Times of Kin Hubbard, Creator of Abe Martin.* New York: Farrar, Strauss, and Young, 1952.

Kingsbury, Paul, ed. *The Encyclopedia of Country Music: The Ultimate Guide to the Music.* New York: Oxford University Press, 1998.

Knowlton, Bill. "First Impressions of Bean Blossom." *Bluegrass Unlimited* 6, no. 2 (1971): 5–6.

Koretzky, Henry. "Night Falls on Sunset Park." *Bluegrass Unlimited* 37, no. 7 (2003): 28–30.

Lambert, Jake, with Curly Sechler. *The Good Things Outweigh the Bad: A Biography of Lester Flatt.* Hendersonville, Tenn.: Jay-Lyn, 1982.

Lehmann-Haupt, Christopher. "Out of My Mind on Bluegrass." *New York Times Magazine,* September 13, 1970, 36–37.

Letsinger-Miller, Lyn. *The Artists of Brown County.* Bloomington: Indiana University Press, 1994.

Library of Congress. "Religion and the Founding of the American Republic." Chapter 7, "Religion and the New Republic." http://www.loc.gov/exhibits/religion/religion.html.

Logan, Tex, as told to John Holder. "Christmas Time's a-Comin.'" *Bluegrass Unlimited* 17, no. 6 (1982).

Lomax, Alan. "Bluegrass Background: Folk Music with Overdrive." *Esquire,* October 1959, 108.

Long, Kevin. "Berea Bluegrass: Phuzz Street Knucklebusters." *Bluegrass Unlimited* 12, no. 10 (1978): 79–84.

Lorzing, Han. *The Nature of Landscape: A Quest into the Nature of Landscape.* Netherlands: Uitgeverij 010 Publishers, 2001.

Malone, Bill C. *Don't Get above Your Raisin': Country Music and the Southern Working Class.* Urbana: University of Illinois Press, 2002.

———. *Southern Music—American Music.* Lexington: University Press of Kentucky, 1979.

Malone, Bill C., and Judith McCulloh, eds. *Stars of Country Music: Uncle Dave Macon to Johnny Rodriguez.* Urbana: University of Illinois Press, 1975.

Marshall, Howard Wight. "A Conversation with Jim McReynolds." *Country Music* 1, no. 2 (1972): 53–54.

Martin, Linda Lou. *One Armed Banjo Player: Early Years of Country Music with Emory Martin.* Berea, Ky.: Kentucke Imprints, 1991.

Meinig, Donald W. "The Mormon Culture Region: Strategies and Patterns in the Geography of the American West, 1847–1964." *Annals of the Association of American Geographers* 55 (1965): 191–220.

Menius, Art. "A Bluegrass Hall of Fame." *Bluegrass Unlimited* 18, no. 8 (1984): 10.

McCloud, Barry. *Definitive Country: The Ultimate Encyclopedia of Country Music and Its Performers.* New York: Perigee Books, 1995.

McNally, Dennis. *A Long Strange Trip: The Inside History of the Grateful Dead.* New York: Broadway Books, 2003.

Moe, John F. "Folk Festivals and Community Consciousness." *Folklore Forum* 10, no. 2 (1977): 31–40.

Moore, Leonard J. *Citizen Klansmen: The Ku Klux Klan in Indiana, 1921–1928.* Chapel Hill: University of North Carolina Press, 1991.

Nicholson, Howard Lee. "Swine, Timber, and Tourism: The Evolution of an Appalachian Community in the Middle West, 1830–1930." Ph.D. diss., Miami University, 1992.

*Official WSM Grand Ole Opry History-Picture Book* 2, no. 2 (1961).

Orr, Jay. "Fiddle and Fiddler's Conventions." In *Encyclopedia of Southern Culture,* ed. Charles Reagan Wilson and William Ferris, 1056–57. Chapel Hill: University of North Carolina Press, 1989.

Overstreet, Frank. "Ashes of Bean Blossom." *Bluegrass Unlimited* 21, no. 10 (1987): 47.

———. "Bill Monroe's Fifth Annual Bluegrass Festival." *Bluegrass Unlimited* 6, no. 2 (1971): 6–7.

———. "40 Years+—Roger Smith: Musician, Teacher, Promoter." *Bluegrass Unlimited* 28, no. 11 (1994): 36–38.

Peva, Jim. *Bean Blossom: Its People and Its Music.* West Conshohocken, Pa.: Infinity, 2006.

———. "Thirty Years of Bean Blossom Recollections." *Bluegrass Unlimited* 32, no. 7 (1998): 34–38. Reprinted in *The Bill Monroe Reader,* ed. Tom Ewing, 264–69. Urbana: University of Illinois Press, 2000.

Piazza, Tom. *True Adventures with the King of Bluegrass: Jimmy Martin.* Nashville: Vanderbilt University Press, 1999.

Plous, F. K., Jr. "A Farm Where Bluegrass Music Grows." *Midwest (Chicago Sun-Times)*, August 9, 1970, 10–14.

Putnam, Michelle. "Bill Monroe: A Tradition Ends, a New Venture Begins." *Bluegrass Unlimited* 23, no. 2 (1988): 54–55.

———. "What's Wrong with This Picture?" *Bluegrass Unlimited* 32, no. 3 (1997): 26–28.

Rhodes, Don. "Monroe the Father, Monroe the Son." *Bluegrass Unlimited* 12, no. 8 (1978): 12–17.

Rinzler, Ralph. "Bill Monroe." In *Stars of Country Music: Uncle Dave Macon to Johnny Rodriguez,* ed. Bill C. Malone and Judith McCulloh, 202–21. Urbana: University of Illinois Press, 1975.

———. "Bill Monroe: The Daddy of Blue Grass Music." *Sing Out!* 13, no. 1 (1963): 5–8.

———. "Blue Grass Fest a 'Picknic': Top Names Mark 1st Event." *Billboard,* September 18, 1965.

———. Liner notes to *Bill Monroe and Doc Watson, Live Duet Recordings, 1963–1980: Off the Record.* Vol. 2. Smithsonian-Folkways SFW 40064, 1990.

Roberts, Jane. *Royal Landscape: The Gardens and Parks of Windsor.* New Haven: Yale University Press, 1997.

Robins, Butch. *What I Know 'bout What I Know: The Musical Life of an Itinerant Banjo Player.* Bloomington, Ind.: 1st Books, 2003.

Rooney, James. *Bossmen: Bill Monroe and Muddy Waters.* New York: Hayden Book, 1971.

———. "Sketches of Bill Monroe." *Country Music* 1, no. 2 (1972): 47–49.

Rosenberg, Neil V. *Bill Monroe and His Blue Grass Boys: An Illustrated Discography.* Nashville: Country Music Foundation Press, 1974.

———. *Bluegrass: A History.* Urbana: University of Illinois Press, 1985.

———. "From Sound to Style: The Emergence of Bluegrass." *Journal of American Folklore* 80 (1967): 143–50.

———. "A Front Porch Visit with Birch Monroe." *Bluegrass Unlimited* 17, no. 3 (1982): 58–63.

———. "Into Bluegrass: The History of a Word." *Muleskinner News* 5 (August 1974): 7–9, 31–33.

———. "Picking Myself Apart: A Hoosier Memoir." *Journal of American Folklore* 108, no. 429 (1995): 277–86.

———. "Strategy and Tactics in Fieldwork: The Whole Don Messer Show." In *The World Observed: Reflections on the Fieldwork Process,* ed. Bruce Jackson and Edward D. Ives, 144–58. Urbana: University of Illinois Press, 1996.

———, ed. *Transforming Tradition: Folk Music Revivals Examined.* Urbana: University of Illinois Press, 1993.

Rosenberg, Neil V., and Charles K. Wolfe. *The Music of Bill Monroe.* Urbana: University of Illinois Press, 2007.

Rosenzweig, Roy, and Elizabeth Blackmar. *The Park and the People: A History of Central Park.* Ithaca: Cornell University Press, 1992.

Ross, Joe. "Another Success in Norco." *Bluegrass Unlimited* 20, no. 9 (1986).

Rothman, Sandy. "Rambling in Redwood Canyon: The Routes of Bay Area Bluegrass." Pt. 2 of 4. *Bluegrass Unlimited* 25, no. 12 (1991): 58–66.

Saal, Herbert. "Pickin' and Singin.'" *Newsweek,* June 29, 1970, 85.

Satterlee, Dennis. "Luke Thompson: A Decade at Bean Blossom." *Bluegrass Unlimited* 37, no. 6 (2002): 52–55.

Sizemore, Jim. "Early Country Music and Bluegrass in East Tennessee." Pt. 2. *Pickin'* 1, no. 3 (1974): 16–19.

Skinker, Chris. "Bean Blossom." In *The Encyclopedia of Country Music: The Ultimate Guide to the Music,* ed. Paul Kingsbury, 31. New York: Oxford University Press, 1998.

———. "The Magic Returns." 1998. http://www.country.com/music/news/feature/bluegrass.html.

Smith, L. Mayne. "First Bluegrass Festival Honors Bill Monroe." *Sing Out!* 15, no. 6 (1966): 65–69.

Smith, Ralph Lee. "If I Had a Song . . ." *Swarthmore College Alumni Bulletin* (March 1997).

Smith, Richard D. *Can't You Hear Me Callin': The Life of Bill Monroe, Father of Bluegrass.* Boston: Little, Brown, 2000.

Stamper, Pete. *It All Happened in Renfro Valley.* Lexington: University Press of Kentucky, 1999.

Sullivan, Enoch, Margie Sullivan, with Robert Gentry. *The Sullivan Family: Fifty Years in Bluegrass Gospel Music.* Many, La.: Sweet Dreams, 1999.

Thomas, Alyssa. "The Dixie Flyers: A Canadian Bluegrass Tradition." *Bluegrass Unlimited* 20, no. 11 (1986).

Tolbert, Mike. "Letters." *Bluegrass Unlimited* 23, no. 4 (1988).

Tottle, Jack. "A Moveable Feast: The Ricky Skaggs Pickin' Party." *Bluegrass Unlimited* 26, no. 6 (1991): 43–47.

———. "Neil Rosenberg at East Tennessee [State] University." *Bluegrass Unlimited* 22, no. 4 (1987): 64.

Turner, Bill. "Luke and Cecil Thompson: Bayou State Bluegrass Trailblazers." *Bluegrass Unlimited* 27, no. 9 (1993): 49–55.

von Schmidt, Eric, and Jim Rooney. *Baby, Let Me Follow You Down: The Illustrated Story of the Cambridge Folk Years.* 2nd ed. Amherst: University of Massachusetts Press, 1994.

Wallace, Roy. "News from the Hills of Brown County." *Jamboree* (February 28, 1942): 9–10.

———. "Prof. Scrub-Board Wallace Says: 'Show Your Hand.'" *Jamboree* 3, no. 31 (1942): 3–5.

Wayne, William J. *Thickness of Drift and Bedrock Physiography of Indiana North of the Wisconsin Glacial Boundary.* Bloomington: Indiana Geological Survey, 1956.

White, Alana J. "Sam Bush." *Bluegrass Unlimited* 24, no. 3 (1989): 18–24.

"Who's Who, 1948–1959: News Taken from *Billboard*'s Weekly Country Music Columns." In *The Original County Music Who's Who,* ed. Thurston Moore, 86–99. First annual edition for 1960. Cincinnati: Cardinal Enterprises.

Wilkinson, Tony. "The Lattie Moore Story." *American Music Magazine* (Swedish Rock'n'Roll Club), no. 89 (September 2001): 4–15.

Williams, Michael Ann. *Staging Tradition: John Lair and Sarah Gertrude Knott.* Urbana: University of Illinois Press, 2006.

Williams, Toni. "Talking Feet: Mike Seeger." *Bluegrass Unlimited* 26, no. 8 (1992): 41–45.

Willis, Barry R. *America's Music: Bluegrass.* Franktown, Colo.: Pine Valley Music, 1997.

Wilson, Charles Reagan, and William Ferris, eds. *Encyclopedia of Southern Culture.* Chapel Hill: University of North Carolina Press, 1989.

Wolfe, Charles. *The Devil's Box: Masters of Southern Fiddling.* Nashville: Country Music Foundation Press / Vanderbilt University Press, 1999.

———. Liner notes to *Bill Monroe: 1970–1979.* Bear Family BCD 15606, 1994.

Wolmuth, Roger. "Bluegrass in Blossom." In "Here Comes Summer." Special section, *Time,* July 4, 1977.

Wright, John. *Traveling the High Way Home: Ralph Stanley and the World of Traditional Bluegrass Music.* Urbana: University of Illinois Press, 1993.

Zelinsky, Wilbur. *The Cultural Geography of the United States.* Foundations of Cultural Geography Series. Englewood Cliffs, N.J.: Prentice-Hall, 1973.

# Index

Only a Miner: Studies in Recorded Coal-Mining Songs    *Archie Green*
Great Day Coming: Folk Music and the American Left    *R. Serge Denisoff*
John Philip Sousa: A Descriptive Catalog of His Works    *Paul E. Bierley*
The Hell-Bound Train: A Cowboy Songbook    *Glenn Ohrlin*
Oh, Didn't He Ramble: The Life Story of Lee Collins, as Told to Mary Collins
    *Edited by Frank J. Gillis and John W. Miner*
American Labor Songs of the Nineteenth Century    *Philip S. Foner*
Stars of Country Music: Uncle Dave Macon to Johnny Rodriguez    *Edited by*
    *Bill C. Malone and Judith McCulloh*
Git Along, Little Dogies: Songs and Songmakers of the American West
    *John I. White*
A Texas-Mexican *Cancionero*: Folksongs of the Lower Border    *Américo Paredes*
San Antonio Rose: The Life and Music of Bob Wills    *Charles R. Townsend*
Early Downhome Blues: A Musical and Cultural Analysis    *Jeff Todd Titon*
An Ives Celebration: Papers and Panels of the Charles Ives Centennial
    Festival-Conference    *Edited by H. Wiley Hitchcock and Vivian Perlis*
Sinful Tunes and Spirituals: Black Folk Music to the Civil War    *Dena J. Epstein*
Joe Scott, the Woodsman-Songmaker    *Edward D. Ives*
Jimmie Rodgers: The Life and Times of America's Blue Yodeler    *Nolan Porterfield*
Early American Music Engraving and Printing: A History of Music
    Publishing in America from 1787 to 1825, with Commentary on Earlier
    and Later Practices    *Richard J. Wolfe*
Sing a Sad Song: The Life of Hank Williams    *Roger M. Williams*
Long Steel Rail: The Railroad in American Folksong    *Norm Cohen*
Resources of American Music History: A Directory of Source Materials from
    Colonial Times to World War II    *D. W. Krummel, Jean Geil, Doris J. Dyen,*
    *and Deane L. Root*
Tenement Songs: The Popular Music of the Jewish Immigrants    *Mark Slobin*
Ozark Folksongs    *Vance Randolph; edited and abridged by Norm Cohen*
Oscar Sonneck and American Music    *Edited by William Lichtenwanger*
Bluegrass Breakdown: The Making of the Old Southern Sound    *Robert Cantwell*
Bluegrass: A History    *Neil V. Rosenberg*
Music at the White House: A History of the American Spirit    *Elise K. Kirk*
Red River Blues: The Blues Tradition in the Southeast    *Bruce Bastin*
Good Friends and Bad Enemies: Robert Winslow Gordon and the Study of
    American Folksong    *Debora Kodish*
Fiddlin' Georgia Crazy: Fiddlin' John Carson, His Real World, and the World of
    His Songs    *Gene Wiggins*
America's Music: From the Pilgrims to the Present (rev. 3d ed.)    *Gilbert Chase*
Secular Music in Colonial Annapolis: The Tuesday Club, 1745–56    *John Barry Talley*
Bibliographical Handbook of American Music    *D. W. Krummel*
Goin' to Kansas City    *Nathan W. Pearson, Jr.*

Gone to the Country: The New Lost City Ramblers and the Folk Music Revival
    *Ray Allen*
The Makers of the Sacred Harp    *David Warren Steel with Richard H. Hulan*
Woody Guthrie, American Radical    *Will Kaufman*
George Szell: A Life of Music    *Michael Charry*
Bean Blossom: The Brown County Jamboree and Bill Monroe's
    Bluegrass Festivals    *Thomas A. Adler*

THOMAS A. ADLER is a folklorist, banjoist, radio show host, and the former executive director of the International Bluegrass Music Museum. He lives in Lexington, Kentucky, and first attended Bean Blossom in 1968.

The University of Illinois Press
is a founding member of the
Association of American University Presses.

---

Designed by Jim Proefrock
Composed in 11/14 Bulmer MT Std
with Avenir LT Std display
by Jim Proefrock
at the University of Illinois Press
Manufactured by Sheridan Books, Inc.

University of Illinois Press
1325 South Oak Street
Champaign, IL 61820-6903
www.press.uillinois.edu